The Criminalization
of a Woman's Body

The Criminalization
of a Woman's Body

Clarice Feinman
Editor

The Criminalization of a Woman's Body, edited by Clarice Feinman, was simultaneously issued by The Haworth Press, Inc., under the same title, as special issues of the journal Women & Criminal Justice, Volume 3, Numbers 1/2 1992.

Harrington Park Press
An Imprint of
The Haworth Press, Inc.
New York • London

ISBN 1-56023-009-6

Published by

Harrington Park Press, 10 Alice Street, Binghamton, NY 13904-1580

Harrington Park Press is an imprint of The Haworth Press, Inc., 10 Alice Street, Binghamton, NY 13904-1580.

The Criminalization of a Woman's Body was originally published as *Women & Criminal Justice*, Volume 3, Numbers 1/2 1992.

Library of Congress Cataloging-in-Publication Data

The Criminalization of a woman's body / Clarice Feinman, editor.
    p. cm.
    "Simultaneously issued by the Haworth Press, Inc., under the same title, as special issues of Women & criminal justice, volume 3, numbers 1/2 1992."
    ISBN 1-56023-009-6 (HPP : alk. paper)
    1. Abortion—Law and legislation. 2. Pregnant women—Legal status, laws, etc. 3. Abortion—Social aspects. 4. Pregnant women. 5. Motherhood. I. Feinman, Clarice.
    [DNLM: 1. Abortion, Induced—legislation. 2. Pregnancy, Unwanted. 3. Prenatal Care. 4. Public Policy. 5. Substance Abuse—in pregnancy. 6. Surrogate Mothers. 7. Women's Rights. HQ 1154 C929]
K5181.C75 1992b
363.4'6—dc20
DNLM/DLC
for Library of Congress
                                                91-20859
                                                CIP

CONTENTS

ABOUT THE EDITOR

Clarice Feinman, PhD in History, is Professor of Law and Justice at Trenton State College in New Jersey. She is author of the comprehensive text *Women in the Criminal Justice System* and co-editor of the text *Criminal Justice, Politics & Women: The Aftermath of Legally Mandated Change*. She is the author of numerous articles and reviews in criminal justice and history periodicals. She has lectured at the the Universities of Cambridge and Sydney and was the keynote speaker at the Australian Institute of Criminology Seminar on Women in Prison. She has worked as a project director of a rehabilitation program for women at the New York City Correctional Institution for Women and also as a consultant/lecturer for the New Jersey Department of Corrections Training Academy.

Introduction

Here is the truth, I tell you — see how right I am.
The woman you call the mother of the child
is not the parent, just a nurse to the seed,
the new-sown seed that grows and swells inside her.
The *man* is the source of life — the one who mounts.
She, like a stranger for a stranger, keeps
the shoot alive unless god hurts the roots.

(Aeschylus, *The Eumenides*.)

In *The Eumenides*, Apollo tells Athena and the Furies that
Orestes is not guilty of killing his mother, Clytemnestra, because
she is not his blood parent; his father, Agamemnon, is his blood
parent, the sole source of Orestes' life. Although *The Eumenides*
was written in the fifth century (before the common era), Apollo's
belief about the value and role of *woman* has persisted and can be
found in religious and secular literature, in laws and in court decisions. Those who hold these beliefs have little or no respect for
women: their autonomy, their privacy, their bodily integrity. They
would limit women's constitutional due process guarantees and formally and/or informally criminalize women's bodies to insure control over them, especially their reproductive capacities.

The laws and policies of our patriarchal legal, religious and secular institutions reaffirm Apollo's belief: women's value rests on
their fulfilling their expected roles as wives and mothers. Although
men are the dominant figures, both in numbers and power, in initi-
ating and enforcing these social values and in punishing transgres-
sors, many women agree with them. It appears that they fail to
realize that the consequences of this lack of respect for women also
affect them.

This special theme volume, *The Criminalization of a Woman's*

1

Body, addresses the concern many women have about the trend towards the criminalization of their bodies: the threat to their autonomy, their privacy, their bodily integrity and their constitutional guarantees. The contributors to this special theme volume bring international and interdisciplinary perspectives to this major problem facing all women.

The administrative implementing mechanisms of the abortion law in Israel are described by Delila Amir and Orly Biniamin. They explain that, although abortion is legal in Israel, the procedures required to obtain an abortion result in efforts to control women's sexual behavior by reinforcing normative attitudes toward women and especially toward motherhood. Tamar Pitch describes and discusses the current debate over the abortion law in Italy. The debate focuses on ethical terms rather than on social and political terms, and Pitch analyzes the implications of this ethical focus and the resultant divisions among the feminists.

United States Supreme Court Justice Byron White's antiabortion opinions, placing the right of the fetus over the right of the pregnant woman, are summarized by Sarah Slavin. She concludes that adoption of Justice White's position would curtail due process rights for pregnant women; such curtailment would tend to victimize women and also presume that they have committed a public offense, i.e., to criminalize their bodies.

Mary Gibson argues that contract motherhood must be seen not simply as a transaction among individual, but as a social practice arising in a particular social context. Consequently, she concludes that commercial contract motherhood should be prohibited and brokering criminalized. Michael Dahlem examines the judicial and legislative responses and the public policy implications of surrogate parenting contracts from the perspective of a morality of care. He presents arguments against the granting of specific performance of surrogate parenting contracts.

Joan Callahan and James Knight explore the moral and legal implications of interfering with the lives and bodies of pregnant women to protect the fetus. They believe that it is legally and morally unjustified and unacceptable to impose legal sanctions against pregnant women because these sanctions violate important moral values captured in our legal system and would contribute to the harm they would be instituted to prevent.

The power of administrative agencies to control and informally criminalize pregnant women and mothers, especially poor women who are drug users, is described by Lisa Maher. She concludes that the focus on informal criminalization and control of women who are "crack pregnant," deflects attention away from the fissure of gender, race and class that render these women's lives as publicly problematic.

Wendy Chavkin discusses the recent mother vs. fetus debate. She explains that policies meant to protect the fetus against harm from pregnant women who deviate from medically, socially and legally sanctioned behavior threaten the autonomy, bodily integrity and constitutional status of women, and may undermine fetal and maternal health by deterring women from involvement with medical care.

The consequences of criminalizing pregnant women who use drugs and placing their children in congregate or foster care are explored by Drew Humphries et al. They review the lack of drug treatment programs for these women and recommend community-based drug treatment that keeps families together.

Readers will find that the articles contain the language usage, spelling and manuscript style common to the nationality and discipline of the authors.

Clarice Feinman

Abortion Approval as a Ritual of Symbolic Control

Delila Amir
Orly Biniamin

SUMMARY. The variability of abortion laws and particularly, of the mechanisms employed to implement them attests to the socio-cultural specificity of the concrete solutions to the universal problem of reproductive control. The present study examines the implementing mechanisms of the abortion law in Israel, which is a medical committee. Based on interviews with 29 social workers (all women) who serve on the committees, this paper examines how the committees operate. At one and the same time it describes the "control culture" which emerges within the legal procedure; that is, the mechanism's structure, language, accepted discourses and rituals. Foucault's concepts of power/knowledge were found to be most enlightening in this context of regulating abortions.

The analysis of the abortion approval procedures portray characteristics of a ritual. A ritual that is analogous to a juvenile court on the one hand, threatening but not really punishing, and on the other hand, a confessional situation in which the woman has to confess her normative wayward behavior such as extra-marital relations, not using contraception, and enjoying sex with no reproductive intentions. The reinforcement of normative attitudes toward women and especially toward motherhood is manifested in the expressions used by the committee members referring to the pregnant woman's future behavior and the expectations from her to abide by them.

These two ritualistic facets are central components of symbolic control which the Israeli "reproductive deviant" woman is faced with.

Delila Amir, PhD in Sociology of Welfare and Health from the University of Pittsburgh, is Professor of Sociology and Coordinator of Women's Studies at Tel-Aviv University, Tel-Aviv. Orly Biniamin, is a PhD candidate at Wolfson College, Oxford and graduate student in sociology at Tel-Aviv University.

INTRODUCTION

The issue of reproductive control has been the focal point of the struggle of women to control their lives. One specific issue within the broader problem of reproductive control is that regarding a woman's right to abortion. Since the mid-1960s women's movements have centered around this issue, making it a major target of their struggle with political and religious establishments (Dhalerup, 1986; Lovendunski & Outshoorn, 1986). These movements have transformed the issue of abortion from the personal to a major political level, and as a consequence of their efforts, abortion legislation has been liberalized in most Western countries.

The variability of abortion laws and, particularly, of the mechanisms employed to implement them attests to the socio-cultural specificity of the concrete solutions to a universal problem. Research papers recently presented at conferences (Grela, 1990; Bortner, 1990; Germaine, 1990) have pointed not only to the specificity of these laws and their implementing mechanisms, but also to the subtleties of the control exerted by means of the regulations. Studies have also shown that the mechanisms regulating abortions reflect overt and covert social stances towards women's reproductive rights (Petchesky, 1984; Gordon, 1977; Kaufman, 1984). The present study examines the implementing mechanisms of abortion law in Israel in an attempt to reveal a process that contributes to the preservation of the structural position of women in Israeli society.

Israeli law defines four situations in which a pregnancy may be defined as socially "undesirable" and therefore can be legally terminated: (1) when the woman is under the legal age of consent (17) or is over forty years old; (2) when the pregnancy results from relations forbidden under criminal law, or from incestuous relations, or is out of wedlock; (3) when the newborn is liable to be handicapped in body or mind; and (4) when continuation of the pregnancy may endanger the woman's life or cause her physical or mental harm. The same law requires that a medical committee must decide upon the eligibility of each abortion candidate. This committee, which meets with the pregnant woman, is to be made up of two doctors and a social worker, one of whom must be a woman.[1] (In the large majority of cases, it is the social worker who fits this criterion.

Indeed, in the committees investigated in the present study, not one included a female doctor.) Women who seek an abortion and who can convince the committee that they fall into one of these four categories obtain approval for the abortion.

On the surface, this is a simple classification procedure and "a people processing setting" (Hasenfeld, 1974). In reality, it is a normalizing mechanism exerted over women and over issues of reproduction, to employ Foucault's terminology. In the present study, we examine how the committees operate and describe the "control culture" (Cohen, 1989) which emerges within the legal procedure, that is, the structure, language, accepted discourse and rituals of the regulating institution.

In examining the construction of this control culture, we raise two main questions. What is the normative sexual and reproductive behavior expected of women in contemporary Israeli society? And how is the woman who deviates from these expectations treated?

CONCEPTUAL FRAMEWORK: POWER/KNOWLEDGE AND SOCIAL CONTROL

In his analysis of power usage in modern society, Michel Foucault challenges the idea that power operates only by means of prohibitions, and draws attention to the complex network of disciplinary systems and technologies through which power is channelled. The power attached to these systems goes hand in hand with knowledge. In the words of Smart, who elaborated upon Foucault's analysis:

> Power produces knowledge; . . . power and knowledge directly imply one another; . . . there is no power relation without the correlative constitution of a field of knowledge, nor any knowledge that does not presuppose and constitute at the same time power relations. (Smart, 1985: 76)

Foucault's analysis of power in modern society is built upon two basic theoretical concepts which are pertinent to an understanding of social control over women: the discourse and absence of the subject.

Discourse

Foucault saw discourses as

> ways of constituting knowledge, together with the social prac-
> tices, forms of subjectivity and power relations which inhere
> in such knowledges and the relations between them. Dis-
> courses are more than ways of thinking and producing mean-
> ing. They constitute the "nature" of the body, unconscious
> and conscious mind and emotional life of the subjects which
> they seek to govern. Neither the body nor thoughts and feel-
> ings have meaning outside their discursive articulation, but the
> ways in which discourse constitutes the minds and bodies of
> individuals is always part of a wider network of power rela-
> tions, often with institutional bases. (Weedon, 1987:108)

While Foucault's concept of discourse is pertinent to the issue of
control over abortion, it is not wholly applicable to the case of the
pregnant woman. From her point of view, the unborn child is a
reality which has meaning beyond any discourse. Rather, we suggest that the institutional discourse reflects a power struggle over
the meanings of the body, thoughts, and emotions, and does not
actually produce these meanings.

Absence of the Subject

For Foucault, "there is no subject." The existence of the subject
is an illusion resulting from the practices of certain "normalizing"
disciplines and the modern world's discourses of rationalizations.
The problem with the concept of the "individual as a subject,"
according to Foucault, has become more significant in our time
(Diamond & Quinby, 1988). The assumption of the existence of
subjectivity legitimates a whole set of moral rules that dominate our
life. All "human sciences" have formed theories of the subject
which turn human beings into chronic foragers in the individual's
deepest hiding places, seeking his or her identity and the source of
his or her meaning. By turning the person into a subject, by controlling the discourse through which his or her physical and emotional
essence is sought, these disciplines have been able to accumulate

immense bodies of knowledge about human beings, which have become a means of control:

> . . . professional practices in modern society both create moral boundaries and serve gatekeeping functions, demarcating good and evil, deviance and normality, insiders and outsiders. Because professionals police the social margins, as it were, they often control values, beliefs, and their related social practices that are in turmoil. (Davis, 1985:14)

Social Control and Abortion

Several feminists have pointed to the relevance of the concept of social control to the issue of depriving women of the right to choose abortion (Hutter & Williams, 1981; Chilman, 1987; Figueria-McDonough & Sarri, 1987). In this vein, Schur claims that "restrictions on abortion epitomize the control of women through gender norms" and that "abortion forcefully poses for women the question of personal autonomy" (1984:98). Davis (1985) and Petchesky (1984) both consider the issue from the perspective of state mechanisms which negate or control the individual. Davis considers the institutions responsible for controlling birth rates as highly complex social institutions which exercise social control over reproduction according to ideologies and interests prevalent among public policy-makers (1985:19). Petchesky explains that public abortion policy is usually characterized by the denial of the woman's right to be the final authority on reproductive decisions (1984:89).

Notwithstanding the validity of these approaches, they fail to take into account the control mechanisms themselves and how these wield power over women (Cohen, 1989). The issue at hand requires a discussion of social control within a real anthropological context, that is, in term of the complexity of the control situation. Rather than considering control as a rational action, well-calculated and guided by the state's centralistic system, there is a need to examine the "control culture" that emerges out of the structure of the interaction and the concrete discourse (Cohen, 1989). In Cohen's words, "The project to elevate the sociology of social control into a subject with its own internal trajectory" can be achieved by "depicting the content of control cultures, doing ethnographies of control agencies or watching control agents at work'' (1989: 350).

Actually, Foucault and feminist writers alike have claimed that power and control over individuals (in our case over women) is exercised not only through the power of the state, but also in the intimacy of face-to-face formal encounters (Diamond & Quinby, 1988). Both approaches focus on the discourse and its potential to create and to maintain hegemonic power. In opposing the idea that power is exercised only through prohibitions and regulatory laws, Foucault turns our attention to the complex network of disciplines and technologies which, besides representing the state, exercise their localized power mainly through their discourse. Discourse is used as a technique of social control, especially owing to the institutionalization of such "normalizing" professions as medicine, psychology and education (in Diamond & Quinby, 1988). Foucault uses the term "normalizing disciplines" to emphasize their controlling functions, such as returning sinners and deviants to the fold, making them "normal" and insuring their normative behavior. This concept also encompasses the authority granted to such disciplines to define and classify individual behavior in "proper" or moral terms.

The Abortion-Approval Committee Meeting

The above conceptual framework serves as a point of departure in examining one means of social control over women in Israeli society. The situation that evolves in the committee meetings which decide on abortion approval or denial can thus be described in Foucault's terminology. The committee is a "micro mechanism of power" in which nurturance and care professionals participate, bringing with them their professional ethics and knowledge about the "subject" and hence of what is good or bad for her, and exerting power to rehabilitate her behavior.

METHODOLOGY

Data Source

The present paper is based on interviews with 29 social workers serving on 13 abortion approval committees out of the 19 committees active at the time the study was carried out (1986-1988). The six committees not included operated at the farthest northern and southern points of the country and were excluded due to budgetary limitations.

The reason for interviewing the social worker, rather than the doctors on the committees, was twofold. First, the social worker is the only committee member to accompany the women throughout the process. Second, the social worker is generally the more permanent figure in the committee, as the doctors frequently change. Some of the social workers interviewed have served on the committees for 10 years or more and took part in the institutionalization of the working procedures. The social worker thus seems to be a good source of information about the procedures which women seeking abortion go through and especially about the specific discourses that take place among committee members and between them and their clientele. Amir's (1989) report provided background data on Israeli abortion law and its operative instructions.

Procedure

Each interview lasted approximately two hours. Constructed interviews were conducted by the main researcher, together with several social work students, all females. The social workers were asked a large number of open-ended questions. Of relevance here are questions pertaining to three topics: (1) the abortion candidate's agenda on the day of the committee meeting (e.g., the sequence of events, the time span of each stage of the procedure); (2) the discourse at the committee meetings ("What do you speak about with the woman?"; "What does the doctor say during the meeting?"; "How do you make your decisions regarding the case?"); and (3) the social worker's attitudes ("Why is it important that the woman appear before the committee?"; "What should be discussed with the woman?"; "Who are the women that get to the committee?"; "How does the abortion influence the women?").

Data Analysis

In analyzing the data, we utilized Foucault's conceptual framework and Cohen's (1989) criteria for identifying and describing the "control culture." The analysis focused on the general features of procedures for approving or denying abortions and on the content and context of the discourse, particularly its major repetitive themes. It was assumed that common responses reflect events and attitudes that constitute the routinized procedures, as well as the reality that is created for the woman who requests the termination of her pregnancy.

In analyzing the interviews, we paid particular attention to spontaneous responses that were not necessarily directed at the specific questions which were asked. These offhand remarks clarified for us the essence of the situation that the pregnant woman goes through.

FINDINGS

Findings refer to three main areas: the work procedures characteristic of the medical committees; the discourse between the social workers and the abortion candidates; and the case of repeated applications to the committee.

The Committee's Working Procedures

Israeli law sets down three broad guidelines for the medical committee: its composition, the four situations in which abortion is permitted, and that "The committee shall not refuse to grant approval before offering the woman the opportunity to appear before it and present her reasons." These limited guidelines create a broad area of discretion. Yet, notwithstanding the broad realm of discretion and a lack of follow-up by state authorities, the 13 committees studied were found to have developed similar working procedures and similar task and role allocation.

In nine of the committees (69%), the woman is required to meet with the social worker prior to appearing before the committee. At that time she also has to complete a questionnaire on her social and medical history (in certain cases, the secretary fills out this questionnaire for her). The questionnaire inquires into the woman's ethnic background, education, occupation, marital status, and living conditions. It also asks about her past use of contraceptives and specifically for the pregnancy in question. Other questions address previous abortions and earlier applications to an abortion committee. The final question is: "Why do you wish to terminate this pregnancy?"

In 11 of the 13 committees (85%), the abortion candidate must appear before the committee, even though the law requires that the committee only meet with women for whom termination of pregnancy has not been approved. The gynecologist, who always serves as the chairman of the committee, is also the one to inform the woman of a negative decision. When abortion is approved, the social worker or secretary sometimes conveys the decision to the woman. Such role division is not required by law.

Twenty four social workers said that they do not keep in touch with the woman after the abortion. The other five said that they try to maintain contact in very exceptional cases.

The Content of the Encounter

Similarities between the committees were also revealed with respect to the discourse conducted both in the meeting with the social worker and in the encounter between the woman and the committee. Eighteen of the 29 social workers (62%) reported that they, or the whole committee, discuss contraceptives with the woman, inquiring into what she has used and what she intends to use. "The main part of the conversation," says one social worker, "is about contraceptives, about the fact that the woman must use them, and why." Another states:

> The women who come to the committee are given information about contraceptives. The doctor explains to them about the use of contraceptives . . . ; single women, if they have a serious relationship, are asked to bring their partner, and he receives an explanation about the dangers in terminating pregnancy with regard to their continued life together. The committee members are very much in favor of continuing pregnancies. One checks the situation as deeply as possible, and the women are told about the types of contraception that exist. We recommend not to have sexual relations unless the woman is protected.

This emphasis on contraception is prevalent even though the abortion law makes no reference to contraception and does not charge the committee with the responsibility of "educating" the pregnant woman.

The duration of the discussion between abortion candidates and committee members is brief. The meeting with the social worker usually takes 10-20 minutes at most (although in rare and exceptional cases it may last up to an hour), and the committee generally discusses the case for 10-15 minutes. Within these short periods of time, the topic of contraception is but one of the subjects on the agenda.

Nearly half the social workers reported that they found it important to examine the details of the abortion candidate's life, the circumstances of the specific pregnancy and the reasons that it is unwanted. However, in light of the time constraints, it is likely that this probing is not very comprehensive.

Slightly more than half the social workers said they perceive the abortion as a traumatic experience for the woman and discuss and present it in this vein to the abortion candidate. They also emphasized the abortion's potentially grave emotional consequences.

In those cases in which the abortion candidate must appear before the committee (11 out of the 13 committees studied), she goes through a second stage. The woman, who has already told the secretary and/or the social worker about the circumstances of her pregnancy and why it is unwanted, and who has already been "reprimanded" for the failure to use contraceptives, now reaches the committee forum. In this forum, intimate details of her life are again exposed and she has to repeat her description of the circumstances of the pregnancy and the reasons for its being defined as "unwanted."

The Social Worker's Discourse with the Researchers

When asked why they think the pregnant woman should have to appear before the committee, many of the social workers indicated that they considered the meeting an educational opportunity. First, it is a means of convincing the women to use contraceptives regularly. In the words of one social worker, "We try to give her habits that she won't forget." Second, appearance before the committee teaches the woman a lesson with regard to taking responsibility for her body and her actions. As one social worker explains it, "[The woman] must appear in person so that all members of the committee can talk to her and hear from her why she wants to have an abortion. She must also undergo a gynecological examination because it is her pregnancy, and she must be responsible for it and for her body." Another states, "The first thing from the educational aspect is her responsibility. She is the one who has to take responsibility for the case and not the social worker."

The emphasis on the need to educate the women to "take responsibility" is joined by covert reproof: "Even if I had a large amount of money, I would not 'wrap them in cotton wool,' I would not give the woman the feeling that what she is doing is of no consequence." Another social worker states: "If she gets to the committee more than once or twice, she shouldn't be approved. She should learn to use contraceptives, they are less painful and less dangerous." On the other hand, "In the case of an unwanted pregnancy that happened to a woman with an IUD, I fight like a lion to get her the approval." Another social worker expressed similar feelings: "I think that termination of pregnancy should be approved automatically for a woman who took steps for contraception, but became pregnant because of some medical 'screw-up.'"

Many of the social workers perceive their role mainly in terms of collecting information from the abortion candidate. This information serves two purposes. Firstly, the social worker examines the extent of the woman's determination to forgo the pregnancy. Where determination is lacking, she is likely to encourage the woman to continue the pregnancy. That kind of ambivalence is the declared justification of the committee mechanism itself: the prevention of "unnecessary abortions," as defined by policy makers (Amir, 1989:44). Secondly, she examines the candidate's eligibility on the basis of the criteria which permit the committee to approve termination of pregnancy.

This probing for information usually focuses on the circumstances under which the pregnancy developed. Even young, unmarried women, who are clearly eligible for the abortion (because they fit the age criteria) are required to describe the nature of the relationship within which the sexual event happened and to explain why they cannot build a family together with the man who is a partner to the pregnancy. The social workers explain that, in order "to understand the case," or in order to represent the woman before the committee, "it is important to understand the pregnancy itself, and its consequences for the woman and for the family." One social worker said that she brings "details beyond those in the questionnaire" to the committee. That is, the social workers ask about many additional details that have to do with the woman's sexual behavior. "If the woman doesn't cooperate," says one social worker, "I explain to her that for her own good, it is best that she tell of the whole picture so that I can best explain her motives to the committee." Another social worker has not encountered such difficulties in persuasion and says: "It is a good diagnostic tool, we don't have to ask a lot, they tell everything in order to get the approval."

Many social workers expressed negative character judgements of the women that appeal to the committee. Such labels as "irresponsible," "impulsive" and "ignorant about contraception" were often attached to the abortion candidates.

Repeated Application to the Committee

There is general consensus among the social workers that a woman who makes repeated applications to the medical committee should not be granted an abortion again: "If she gets to the committee more than once or twice, she shouldn't be approved." Another social worker reported, "There is a question about a woman who gets to the committee for the second or third time; should her abortion be approved or refused, since she did not use contraceptives?" Yet another social worker emphasizes the educational aspect: "We note on her report that such a conversation [about contraceptives] was held, so that if she comes back to the committee, pregnant again, she will not have the abortion approved, because that means that she just disregards both the committee and herself."

DISCUSSION

The findings reveal a complex mechanism of social control wielded by the Israeli medical committee for the approval or denial of abortions to women with unwanted pregnancies. The abortion candidate is covertly scolded for her actions, labelled as a deviant, warned not to repeat the behavior, and "educated" in the usage of contraceptives. This scenario is common to the vast majority of the committees operating in Israel, despite the lack of specific guidelines dictated by Israeli law.

The strong resemblance between committees points to a powerful mechanism of social control which may best be understood in terms of the "normalizing" professional ethics of committee members, the structural characteristics of the situation (participants and their role division) and the discourse conducted therein. The observed structure and discourse suggest a similarity between the control mechanism operating in the medical committee and two well-researched control mechanisms for treating deviance: the confession and juvenile court.

The Confession

Because the social worker considers it her responsibility to uncover as much as possible about the abortion candidate, she makes a continual effort to broaden the boundaries of the information she seeks. The abortion candidate is subjected to intimate personal exposure in the context of a threat that the abortion will be denied if she holds back information. This is a clear case of "discourses concerning sex . . . as the exercise of power itself . . . " (Foucault, 1981:18). Even women whose eligibility for an abortion is certain, such as adolescent girls or unmarried women, are required to expose their innermost lives, as if approval of the abortion is contingent on this.

The interview with the social worker is similar to confession to a priest on three different levels. On the structural level, it is a conversation between the individual and a figure of authority who dictates, evaluates and becomes involved in the confession in order to judge, punish, forgive and console. This moral authority defines the boundaries of normative behavior for the individual making the confession, in our case, sexual relations only with contraceptives.

On the level of discourse, the talk with the social worker is in the realm of intimate behavior, an area that is not normally discussed, especially with strangers. The resemblance to the confession in this respect is striking. According to Foucault, "The confession is a ritual of discourse in which the speaking subject is also the subject of the statement" (1981:61). The conversation about herself within a context of threat exposes the pregnant woman to control on the most intrusive level.

Finally, like the confession, the interview with the social worker is characterized by absolution, offered in a supportive context after the sin has been confessed. The social worker's willingness to forgive the woman, to represent her before the committee and to make an effort to get the abortion approved represents the absolution which is contingent on her commitment not to repeat the sin. The social workers stress their willingness to approve an abortion for the woman only under the condition that the "woman does not disregard the committee," and that she is not applying for a third or fourth time. In the talk with the social worker, as is often true of the confession, sin is related to sexual behavior, to lack of control over sexual urges. But whereas confession to the priest refers to the sin of forbidden lust or adultery; "confession" to the social worker refers to the sin of "irresponsible sexuality," i.e., surrendering to the spontaneity that underlies the failure to use contraceptives.

The Juvenile Court

The abortion candidate's appearance before the full medical committee is very much a repetition of the confession process. This time, however, confession is made before the representatives of the collective, to whom the pregnant woman has to admit that she has deviated from normative behavior. The repeated discussion of her marital status, her relationship with her partner and her use of contraceptives is now conducted within a structural context characterized by a ritualistic division of roles, reminiscent of the juvenile court.

There are several points of similarity between the juvenile court and the committee proceedings.[2] First, both are held behind closed doors for the sake of discretion and to protect the "transgressor" (the youth or the pregnant woman) from stigmatization.

Second, role division is similar. The social worker plays a role resembling that of the probation officer; both represent the interests of their "clients" before a judge and can only make recommendations. Along the same lines, the role of the gynecologist who functions as the committee chairman is parallel to that of the judge. It is he who notifies the woman of the "verdict": the committee's decision. Moreover, in both cases the distinction between roles is not sharp. Like the juvenile judge, the doctors do not only make the final decision, but also take an active part in questioning, guiding and educating the abortion candidate.

Third, in both cases the "offense" itself is not central to the discussion. While the offense is the formal reason for holding the discussion, which is usually conducted on the basis of the "defendant's" admission of guilt, the discussion itself emphasizes the circumstances in which the offense was committed and ways to prevent its recurrence. Thus, the committee discussion focuses on the circumstances in which the woman became pregnant and on the use of contraceptives to prevent future unwanted pregnancies.

Finally, just as juveniles are not punished for first offenses, so too is the first-time abortion candidate treated.

> The juvenile court's role is to educate the delinquent, to complete what he was deprived of at home. It is supposed to deter, to act as a psychological counselor, taking advantage of the possibility for rehabilitation which arises from the shock which the minor experiences. It is supposed to punish and teach, assist, deter and guide, all at the same time. (Cohen, 1975)

The situation seems to be similar for the pregnant woman. The low refusal rate which the social workers report resembles the low rate of jail sentences for juvenile delinquents. Moreover, just as juveniles with repeated offenses are often subject to punishment, women who apply for an abortion more than once or twice are likely to be "punished" for their repeated offense; several of the social workers expressed their belief that abortion should not be approved in these cases. This perception of denial of the abortion as a punishment for "disregarding the committee" and not using contraceptives is supported by the empathy expressed by the social workers towards those pregnant women who had used contraception. In essence, the social workers seem to suggest that such a woman has not committed an offense, and therefore should not be punished.

The emphasis on the educational aspect of the situation at the juvenile court (as opposed to the adult court) reinforces hidden meanings which also exist in the committee situation. Youth are not responsible for their actions; they lack sufficient wisdom to be responsible. Like the offending minor, the pregnant woman is perceived as incapable of understanding the significance of her offense. Her "delinquent" behavior proves that she is unable to uphold the rules of normative behavior. Indeed, the fact that it is the medical committee which must decide whether or not the woman should have an abortion points to such a conception of women in general. Oakley (1981) reports a similar patronizing attitude on the part of the care establishment toward women. These attitudes, anchored in the described institutional context, create and preserve women's place in society.

Symbolic Control

The social control wielded by the medical committee over the abortion candidate is characterized by the manipulation of the woman as subject and as object. When it comes to taking responsibility for her body and using contraceptives, she is a subject with an independent entity, able to make important decisions about her life without any institutional interference. However, when her behavior is perceived as irresponsible, because she has neglected to obey the order to use contraceptives, she is deprived of the right to be a subject, i.e., to make decisions which are extremely significant for her life. The very fact that she is applying to the committee attests to her lack of responsibility. Consequently, she is regarded as an object lacking basic rights, such as the right to make decisions and choices about her life. The structure of the committee and the threatening power of the professionals that compose it are part of the social regard toward her as such an object. Society punishes what it defines as lack of sexual control or irresponsible sexual behavior by true lack of control, where the responsibility and the ability to choose are taken from the woman and transferred to the committee. The low rate of refusals underscores this situation. It is the right to choose, and not the right to an abortion, which is taken away from the Israeli woman.

The institution of the medical committee for the approval of abortions resembles other control mechanisms, but with one important difference: the deviant behavior itself is not controlled. Women apply to the committee and are granted an abortion, sometimes more than once. Rather, the control wielded by the committee lies in its labelling of the woman as a deviant, which emerges from the procedure as a whole. That is, by resembling other situations of deviant behavior, the meanings of deviant behavior are transferred, without the need for overt repressive control. We call this treatment *symbolic control*.

A salient example of such symbolic control revolves around the issue of contraception. Our findings have shown that the discussion of contraceptives is a major part of the committee's discourse and control culture. The committee members perceive the situation as an opportunity to discuss the subject, which actually bears the character of a reprimand for not having used contraceptives. The pregnant woman, anxious about the committee's decision, undertakes to obey the guidelines set by the social worker regarding the assumption of responsibility for her own sexual behavior. That is, she is coerced, by her fear of the committee's refusal, to declare her intentions to use contraceptives in the future.

Ostensibly, the discussion of contraceptives is directly related to the prevention of future unwanted pregnancies. However, the situation is such that there is no follow-up of the woman's behavior. Except in the few cases in which an IUD is inserted immediately after the abortion, none of the committee members knows if the recommendation about contraceptives has been implemented and whether the woman has encountered difficulties in using them. Moreover, the discussion about contraceptives takes place within the context of a threat, and it is constrained by time limits. In order for such a discussion to be significant, i.e., for the social worker to decide upon the type of information and support she should give, she would have to learn about the woman's experience with contraceptives and about how she regards her sexuality in general. Petchesky (1984:209) claims that most women have no problem regarding information on contraceptives and where to obtain them;

rather, the difficulty lies in defining themselves as sexually active. Thus, the introduction to contraceptives given by the social worker does not constitute effective encouragement to use them. She is certainly unable to learn of the woman's misgivings about using contraceptives in the short time allotted to the interview, particularly since the abortion candidate is led to believe that her stated acceptance of contraceptives will ensure approval of the abortion.

The discussion of contraception is also problematic because of its disregard for the limited options available to most women. Some contraceptives are not 100% safe, and those that are have dangerous side effects which, as Pollock (1984) claims, constitutes a problem that receives too little attention from doctors. Under these conditions, failure to use contraceptives may actually reflect the assumption of responsibility for one's body.

It therefore seems that the discussion of contraception is not actually aimed at preventing future unwanted pregnancies. Rather, we contend that it is used by committee members to underscore the boundary of normative sexual behavior expected of women in Israeli society. The committee's discourse seems to suggest that the only legitimate sexual behavior for women is "responsible" behavior aimed at preventing unwanted pregnancies.

Why are the doctors and social workers interested in reducing the number of pregnancies defined as unwanted? Our findings suggest that this control mechanism is a response to the threat that abortion poses to normative reproductive behavior. The abortion, and especially defining a pregnancy as unwanted, contradict the social ethos that perceives pregnancy and its outcome as unconditionally welcomed by the mother. The idea that women only choose motherhood under certain conditions does not fit in with the social expectation of women as mothers first and foremost (Hutter & Williams, 1981; Oakley, 1981; Fisher, 1987). Indeed, Luker (1985) and Figueria-McDonough (1987) claim that the controversy about abortions in the United States is actually about the place and the significance of motherhood, a controversy about the meaning of women's lives. One cannot fail to see such a link between sexual and reproductive behavior in the case before us as well. In Israel, notwithstanding certain accepted limitations on motherhood owing to religious and welfare considerations (Amir, 1989), women are still expected to perceive their maternal potential as a primary, binding imperative. Women who challenge this imperative by defining their pregnancy as unwanted are treated symbolically as sinners and delinquents. In cases where the abortion is not approved, the women are forced to become real delinquents and break the law, performing abortions in unsupervised frameworks and endangering their fertility.

The doctors and social workers on the committee for the approval or denial of abortion can be considered mediators between the social morality and the individual. In this sense, they wield what Foucault called "pastoral power;" the same kind of power that characterizes the priest in the confessional endows the professional of the human sciences with the power of moral guidance. By means of the discourse and control culture of the committee, they serve the normalizing function that Foucault attributes to professionals. Their professional ethos and their place within the social structure call on them to teach the woman how to behave, thereby helping to preserve the existing balance of power in society.

NOTES

1. Section 315 of the abortion law states:
   The committee shall be composed as follows:
   (1) A certified doctor who possesses the title of specialist according to the Ordinance in delivery and gynecology;
   (2) An additional certified doctor whose occupation is in one of the following professions: obstetrics/gynecology, internal medicine, psychiatry, family medicine, public health;
   (3) A registered social worker, according to the Welfare Law, 5718/1958.
   At least one of the members of the committee must be a woman.
2. The discussion of the juvenile court is based on the work of the criminologist Yona Cohen (1975).

REFERENCES

Amir, Delila, 1989, The Politics of Abortion in Israel. Discussion paper series, discussion paper No. 13-89. The Pinhas Sapir Center for Development, Tel-Aviv University, Tel-Aviv, Israel (Hebrew).

Bortner, Peggy, 1990, "Public Policy and Reproduction," paper presented at the 4th IICW, Hunter College, New York.

Chilman, Catherine S., 1987, "Reproduction Norms and Social Control of Women." In: Figueira-McDonough, J., and Sarri, R.C. (Eds.), *The Trapped Woman: Catch-22 in Deviance and Control.* Beverly Hills, Calif.: Sage, pp. 34-52.

Cohen, Stanley, 1989, "The Critical Discourse on 'Social Control': Notes on the Concept as Hammer." *International Journal of the Sociology of Law,* 17: 347-357.

Cohen, Yona, 1975, *Juvenile Delinquency in Israel.* Tel-Aviv, Israel: Cherickover (Hebrew).

Davis, Nanette, 1985, *From Crime to Choice: The Transformation of Abortion in America.* Westport, Connecticut: Greenwood Press.

Diamond, Irene, and Quinby, Lee, 1988, *Feminism and Foucault: Reflections on Resistance* (Introduction). Boston: Northeastern University Press.

Dahlerup, Drude, 1986, *The New Women's Movement.* London: Sage.

Figueira-McDonough, Josefina, 1987, "To Protect or to Control: An Inquiry into the Correlates of Opinions on Abortion." In: Figueira-McDonough, J., and Sarri, R.C. (Eds.), *The Trapped Woman: Catch-22 in Deviance and Control.* Beverly Hills, Calif.: Sage, pp. 53-80.

Figueira-McDonough, Josefina, and Sarri, R.C., 1987, "Catch-22 Strategies of Control and the Deprivation of Women's Rights." In: Figueira-McDonough, J., and Sarri, R.C. (Eds.), *The Trapped Woman: Catch-22 in Deviance and Control.* Beverly Hills, Calif.: Sage, pp. 11-33.

Fisher, Sue, 1987, "Good Women After All: Cultural Definitions and Social Control." In: Figueira-McDonough, J., and Sarri, R.C. (Eds.), *The Trapped Woman: Catch-22 in Deviance and Control.* Beverly Hills, Calif.: Sage, pp. 318-347.

Foucault, Michel, 1981, *The History of Sexuality* (Volume 1, An Introduction). New York: Vintage Books.

Germaine, Adrienne, 1990, "Reproductive Rights as International Human Rights: Towards Concepts and Strategies for Implementation," paper presented at the 4th IICW, Hunter College, New York.

Gordon, Linda, 1976, *Woman's Body, Woman's Right: A Social History of Birth Control in America.* New York: Grossman.

Grela, Christina, 1990, "International Population and Family Planning from a Feminist Perspective," paper presented at the 4th IICW, Hunter College, New York.

Hasenfeld, Yeheskel, 1974, "People Processing Organizations." In: Hasenfeld, T. and English, B. (Eds.), *Human Service Organization.* Ann Arbor, Michigan: University of Michigan Press, pp. 60-72.

Hutter, Bridget, and Williams, Gillian, 1981, "Controlling Women: The Normal and the Deviant." In: Hutter, B., and Williams, G. (Eds.), *Controlling Women.* Oxford Women's Series. London: Croom Helm, pp. 9-39.

Kaufman, K., 1984, "Abortion, A Woman's Matter: An Explanation of Who Controls Abortion and How and Why They Do It." In: Arditti, Rita, Duelli

Klein, Renate, and Minden, Shelley (Eds.), *Test-Tube Women: What Future For Motherhood?* London: Pandora, pp. 213-234.

Lovendunski, John and Outshoorn, Joyce, 1986, *The New Politics of Abortion,* London: Sage Publication.

Luker, Kristin, 1985, *Abortion and the Politics of Motherhood.* Beverly Hills and Los Angeles: University of California Press.

Oakley, Ann, 1981, "Normal Motherhood: An Exercise in Self-control?" In: Hutter, B. and Williams, G. (Eds.), *Controlling Women.* Oxford Women's Series. London: Croom Helm, pp. 70-107.

Petchesky, Rosalind Pollack, 1984, *Abortion and Woman's Choice: The State, Sexuality, and Reproductive Freedom.* The Northeastern Series in Feminist Theory. Boston: Northeastern University Press.

Pollock, Scarlet, 1984, "Refusing to Take Women Seriously: 'Side Effects' and the Politics of Contraception." In: Arditti, Rita, Duelli Klein, Renate, and Minden, Shelley (Eds.), *Test-Tube Women: What Future For Motherhood?* London: Pandora, pp. 138-152.

Schur, Edwin M., 1984, *Labelling Women Deviant: Gender Stigma and Social Control.* New York: Random House.

Shapiro-Libai, Nitza, 1975, "The Right to Abortion." *Israel Yearbook on Human Rights,* No. 5, pp. 120-140.

Smart, Barry, 1985, *Michel Foucault.* New York: Tavistock.

Weedon, Chris, 1987, *Feminist Practice and Post-Structuralist Theory.* New York: Basil Blackwell.

Decriminalization or Legalization?
The Abortion Debate in Italy

Tamar Pitch

SUMMARY. The debate over the abortion law resurfaced in Italy in 1988 after seven years of silence. Unlike the debate in 1981, in 1988 the feminist front was more diversified and abortion was discussed in ethical terms rather than in social and political terms. This paper describes and discusses the current debate on abortion by making reference mainly to the feminists' positions.

Abortion returned as an issue of public and political debate in Italy in 1988 after seven years of silence. The last discussion had taken place in 1981 when a referendum to abolish the 1978 abortion law had been launched by the pro-life movement, and another referendum proposing decriminalization had been launched by the Radical party. Both referendums were defeated: the recent law was upheld by a large majority of the Italian population, feminists included.

The contemporary scenario is very different. Attacks on the abortion law have been launched not only by pro-life "extremists", but also by the (Christian Democrat) minister of health, and even by some Socialist ministers. The feminist front, on the other hand, is today more diversified than before, and in general less inclined to wholeheartedly support the present law. But the main difference lies in the way the question of abortion is approached today. What was discussed mainly, even by Catholics, in social and political terms, is now discussed in ethical terms. This is of course not true of abortion only: indeed, an increasing number of "problems" tend

---

Tamar Pitch, PhD, is a researcher at the Institute of Cultural Anthropology, University of Perugia, Perugia.

to lose their social status and acquire an ethical one. It would be too long to try and ascertain why this is so. I suppose some of the reasons reside with the deep crisis of left-wing ideologies and policies. Other reasons have probably to do with the decline of "modern" culture, the crisis of the notion of progress, the increasing sensitivity to ecological questions, and in general the new consciousness of the "limits" to human interventions and manipulations. "Lay" culture (whether liberal or radical) has proved itself lacking in the elaboration of values able to compete with religious ones. Thus, this new interest in ethics, the rephrasing of questions in ethical terms, is in many respects an extremely serious and important way to come to terms with some fundamental problems in today's society. It is also, sometimes, an evasion, a way not to confront social and political questions as such.

I shall describe and discuss the current Italian debate on abortion by making reference mainly to the feminist positions. In order to do that, I shall have to tell the story of the abortion debate in Italy since the early seventies and describe the law that regulates this matter. I choose to almost exclusively concern myself with the feminist debate, not only because it is, obviously, the richer, nor because it has been, and still is, influential on legislative decisions and political party positions, but also because I believe that it is with women that knowledge about abortion mainly, if not exclusively, resides, and it is women who will have to take moral, legislative and practical decisions about it. Besides, the feminist debate often echoes other debates, if only for refuting many of the things that are asserted there.

THE HISTORY

Abortion appeared on the public agenda in the early seventies. The law introducing divorce had just been passed (1970) in Parliament, signalling an important victory for the so-called "lay" parties against the Christian Democrats, and the time seemed mature to approach the question of abortion. I shall not go into the details of bills presented to Parliament. Rather, I shall try to outline which kind of political cultures confronted themselves on the issue, and by doing so I shall collapse together positions which were expressed during various years (roughly from 1971 to 1978).

The first proponents were the Socialists, at the time promoters of a civil rights culture (always very minoritarian in Italy) as an instrument of modernization. Legal norms had to be brought up to date in order to meet the transformations of Italian society, especially in the areas of family, sexual mores, and interpersonal conflicts. Thus, Socialists were supporters and promoters of an extension of civil rights, but through the instrument of law: *more* law, not less, was deemed necessary towards "modernization." The Communists (the second largest party after the Christian Democracy), on the other hand, shared with the Catholics a distrust of the culture of civil liberties: society must be transformed, not modernized. The extension of civil liberties was seen at best as an illusion, at worst as an evasion of the real task which was the eradication of the *causes* of problems. Also, they shared with the Catholics the idea of the ethical State, a State which should not merely bring legislation up to date with changed mores, but actively promote values. Their first reaction to the Socialist bill on the legalization of abortion was then typical: the problem was not so much *illegal* abortion, but abortion per se. It was the conditions which compelled women to search an abortion which had to be changed, whereby a law permitting women to have an abortion was a false solution. Undoubtedly, more strictly political considerations, e.g., the fear to alienate many Catholic votes on the one hand, and on the other to embark on a battle which they thought could not be won in Catholic Italy, had also a big influence on the Communists' stance (as it did in the case of divorce). A small but influential voice was also that of the so-called Radical party, the first real attempt at a purely civil libertarian force in Italy. They defined abortion purely as a civil right and consistently asked only for its decriminalization, opposing any new legislation *permitting* abortion (*less* law, a restriction of State intervention in the areas of "private" life being their goal).

The Catholic camp was not so consistently against legal abortion as might be thought. Of course, the Church, the Christian Democratic party, and a sizable majority of Catholic voters were against it. But it must be remembered not only that many Catholics voted for parties other than the Christian Democrats (the Communist party first and foremost), but also that at the time Catholic dissent was flourishing, both among intellectuals and the "popular masses". Also, ironically, in a country where Church and State had banned information on contraceptives, and the Church did (does) not accept any other form of contraception but the "natural" methods, abortion was not only widespread, but somehow perceived and accepted by (Catholic) women as a "natural" form of birth control.

But a new voice was making itself heard in those years, that of the women's movement. Decentered, based on small collectives, most of them based on the practice of consciousness raising, but many also involved in self-help health practices and soon in dispensing illegal abortions, neo-feminism had grown within the left-wing and marxist culture of the late 60s and early 70s. Though it immediately started a critique of the forms of organization and the male supremacist ideology of the new left, the culture that it expressed was still somewhat influenced by not just marxism, but the prevailing left-wing culture which in Italy had its reference points in the Communist party and in the big unions. Yet, the issue of abortion showed, more than the question of divorce had, the great and ever growing differences between feminist cultures and all the others. The plural is important, as on this issue feminist internal differences clearly showed themselves.

Simplifying, three main feminist positions may be identified in the 70s. The first one was articulated by one of the oldest and more radical groups, Rivolta Femminile: the legalization of abortion was but another violence against women as it was the outcome of a project of modernization and rationalization devised by men. In a patriarchal culture, women's sexual and reproductive freedom cannot be sanctioned by a law which in fact supports and legitimizes precisely the conditions of their oppression, e.g., a sexual culture that promotes male sexual pleasure (penetration) and denies as nonexistent or immature female sexual pleasure, which in fact has nothing to do with penetration. The legalization of abortion risks silencing women, denies their right to free sexual expression, and emphasizes their capacity to make themselves receptive to the sexual needs of men who want contraceptives and legal abortions in order that their pleasure may not be threatened by overpopulation. Legalized abortion denies not only men's responsibility but it is an act of distrust towards women because it compels them to accept society as judge of their choices and relegates them to the role of mere "reproducers": "A reproducer must be examined by a committee of reproduction experts. Her case of conscience becomes a bureaucratic act" (Rivolta femminile, 1975, reprinted in *Archivio della Libreria delle donne*, 1990). This position remained a minoritarian one within the movement in the 70s, but it is gaining new prestige today, and I shall return to it more fully later on.

A second position was that taken by a group of Milan women (Libreria delle donne di Milano, 1987) who, through various elaborations, decided they also would not be active in a battle for an abortion law. They shared many of the assumptions of Rivolta, plus a notion of women's politics which denied any gain for women's freedom from "mass" mobilizations as they, among other things, implied negotiations with other political forces which could not but entail a reduction of women's requests and their redefinition in terms of "needs."

The majority position shared with the two just mentioned the refusal to separate the question of abortion from all the other, more fundamental, questions: sexuality, motherhood, patriarchal culture. It also, with the others, refused to consider legal abortion a "civil right." While it fought against the prevailing left-wing position which considered (illegal) abortion as a "social problem" and a "tragedy," concerning especially poorer women, it supported the struggle for legalization. Yet, even this part of the women's movement refused to get involved in the actual writing of a bill or to work with other political formations to write it. It mobilized to obtain "on demand, free and medically assisted abortion": it preferred this to simple decriminalization for three reasons. The first reason was the same as that advanced by left-wing parties (and shared their preference for public versus private, market solutions): only through a law could abortion become accessible to all women, whereby decriminalization would have opened the door to an abortion "market." But the second and main reason was more complex and went well beyond what traditional political parties were disposed to concede: a law that stated the legality of abortion on demand would symbolically sanction women's self-determination. The principle of women's autonomy would thus find a symbolic recognition. The third reason was also important (and it is the reason most forgotten today): legalization would give the "State" responsibility in securing adequate health care, thus, on the one hand liberating women from having themselves to secure abortion services, and on the other hand constituting a new terrain of conflict, an open tension between the women's movement and state institutions.

The law that finally passed in 1978 was of course a very unsatisfactory compromise. First of all, it was passed thanks to the victory of the "social problem" approach to abortion, which was shared by Communists and many Catholics. This view was not only reductive and in many ways offensive for women, it was also ambiguous (similar, in this, to other questions, prostitution and drug use, for example), because it purposely confused two issues: the problem of *illegal* abortion and that of abortion. To legalize abortion, then, came to be justified not so much in terms of reducing the victims of *illegal* abortion, but in terms of abolishing *abortion*. For example, the law's success would be measured by the decrease of the recourse to abortion, rather than from the decrease of deaths and injuries due to illegal abortion. By separating abortion from women's ongoing reflection on sexuality, motherhood, the family, and power, it was reduced to a problem of misinformation, lack of access to contraception, and ignorance. However, the law did accept the principle of women's self-determination (thanks, also, to the radicalization and mobilization of Communist women who obliged the party not to make concessions on this point). Women must consult with doctors and obtain certificates from them, but, in the first three months, their choice is what counts. On a symbolic level, one main drawback was that abortion was defined as "therapeutic," that is women, to obtain it, had to say they needed it for the sake of their physical or psychological health. A fiction, of course, since it was well known, and experience proved it, that no such reasons would be requested from women asking for abortions. Yet, an important fiction on the symbolic level, as it on principle denies women's full responsibility and subordinates their moral choice to a number of external factors, only the existence of which justifies abortion in front of "society." Practically (but they also have a symbolic impact) two other norms made legal abortion difficult for many women: the norm that states that minors can have abortions only with the consent of their parents or their guardians, and the one that allows medical personnel to abstain from performing abortions pleading conscientious objection (it must be remembered that the law states that abortion is legal only if performed in public hospitals).

The passing of the law signalled the decline of the abortion question and its virtual disappearance from the public scene.

THE CONTEMPORARY DEBATE

The two referendums I mentioned above did not incite a new debate. The positions remained unchanged, save for a few more women's voices in favor of simple decriminalization. And, as I said, both referendums were defeated, showing a large popular support for the law, but also a certain tiredness on the part of feminists to continue to discuss abortion.

During the years, a number of researches on the implementation of the law showed that it worked mostly in the northern and central regions, whereas the south was characterized by a larger quota of conscientious objectors, and women had more difficulty in getting abortions (see, for example, Spinelli et al., 1987; Quintavalla and Raimondi, 1989). Yet, the question of conscientious objection on the part of medical personnel (doctors, nurses, anesthetists) became more of a problem as years passed. Especially doctors increasingly refused to continue to perform abortions: many said that, given so many had already pleaded conscientious objection, those who did not were in practice relegated to be full time abortionists, to the detriment of both their careers and their morale. Pro-life Catholic activists gained more voice, and started denouncing the ease with which abortions were granted: abortion, they said, had become a mere form of birth control (against, supposedly, the tragedy it had been when abortion was illegal). Their strategy was now directed towards asking for more rigid controls, rather than merely agitating to repeal the law.

In 1988, the Christian Democratic minister of health launched a campaign of inspection, sending police to investigate some major hospitals. This campaign, together with the proposed introduction in Italy of the French "abortive pill," contributed to launch a new public debate on abortion; but now, the "social problem" approach was abandoned by all. The Socialist vice-premier, speaking, he said, as a private citizen, felt that the law did not take into account a number of moral questions, prominent among them the right of the potential father to have a say in the decision. Women who decided to have abortions were declared, not only by pro-life activists, to be selfish, to choose an abortion (again, in the words of the Socialist vice-premier) in order to be able to "write a book" and have a career.

Two new facts had intervened during these years. The first was the "discovery," through researches, of something women had always known: women who chose to have an abortion were not, in the majority, poor and ignorant women. By and large, they were adult, educated, working, but also housewives, women who had access to contraception, and in fact used it. Many had one or more children. These data were interpreted as signalling a diffuse "selfishness" on the part of women, and in general of the dominance of a sterile, consumeristic culture.

The second, more important, fact was the proliferation of and discussion over reproductive technologies, which not only changed the terrain of reproduction, increasing and multiplying the possibilities of conceiving and bringing to life a fetus, but brought to the fore critical ethical questions. Also, it contributed to the construction of the image of an increasing desire of parenthood in general, and motherhood in particular. To give birth was again "fashionable." Paradoxically, the debate over technologically assisted versus "natural" maternity gave an impulse to this new, widespread, "pro-reproduction" climate. How ambiguous and anti-women this debate, from both fronts, could be, was shown by the anti-abortion stance of many ecologists, led to this position by their "pro-nature" and "pro-life" ideology. One of the results of this new development could be reconceiving abortion again as a crime: where before it was substantially a crime against the rights of fathers, it could now become a crime against the rights of fetuses.

Feminists, while firmly separating the abortion question from that of reproductive technologies, at least from the point of view of policies, did not refuse the ethical approach. They, by and large, felt that although the political climate was very unfavourable to an ameliorative change of the law, they would not simply stand in its defence, not only because it had not given such a good proof of itself, but especially because feminist analysis had gone well beyond it.

Abortion is today more firmly situated, by feminists, within the whole, complex, female experience. While not denying that abortion may entail psychological agony and often is a difficult choice, feminists refuse its interpretation as always a "defeat" for women, as a sign and symptom of women's social weakness of which women are "victims" and from which women must be "saved." With different nuances, the abortion experience is by most feminists seen as related to female sexuality, rather than read wholly in terms of affirmed or denied motherhood. Abortion does not necessarily signal either the mechanical failure of contraception or the unconscious capitulation to an unrecognized desire of motherhood. Pregnancy, giving birth, having and raising children are different experiences, the desire of one might not imply the desire (or the ability and possibility) of the others. It may not be a child that is ambivalently desired, when we, unwillingly and unknowingly, become pregnant, but the experience of the power of the female body to be fertile, full (see, in particular, Boccia, 1990, but also Fattorini, 1990, and Molfino, 1990). Thus, the possibility of abortion is constantly inscribed in all women's lives, and cannot be approached merely in terms of "necessity," "defeat," "drama," "problem," "exception" (though, of course, a concrete abortion might imply all these). A very provocative, and in many ways scandalous approach which has the merit of recognizing the complexity of the question, and of doubting any merely "social" or "technical" solution: abortion is here to stay, it is not born only of ignorance, carelessness, poverty, lack of "perfect" contraception (which, in any case, cannot but be a myth).

Women's total self-determination on this matter (in the first three months: the question of a time limit different from this one has not yet been discussed, see Mancina, 1989) derives not from biological facts. Rather it derives from the way these biological facts are morally interpreted. Let us go back to Rivolta Femminile's old position. They said: "We know that within us life and death coincide: if we give life we can give that arrest of development that is a form of death, just as the fetus can kill us. But it is meaningless to call this homicide. Men kill, are killed. They are obsessed by the need to exorcize their fear of denying life, they need principles that affirm their respect for life. They need to convince themselves that in their civilization life is sacred: because it is not, and they know it. When the fetus swims within its mother it is still the mother and like her it lives in that reality where death and life coincide. When men criminalize or want to regulate abortion, they show their inability to accept the deep meaning of motherhood . . . '' (Rivolta femminile, 1975). I gave this long quote because I think it says a number of things which have important moral consequences. It says that abortion cannot be separated from what makes women women, that is human beings different from men. It says that this difference is not merely biological, nor only existential, but also has moral implications. This line of reasoning leads to this conclusion: what women have always been obliged to do, e.g., to take sole responsibility for their decision to have an abortion, must become an explicit choice and gain general recognition. The assumption of full responsibility is at the same time an act of freedom and the discharge of a moral obligation. Here abortion regains its tragic character. This character, then, is intrinsic to abortion: it derives neither from its being illegal (though of course illegality has more tragic consequences), nor, in a way, from its being a result of patriarchal heterosexuality. On this second point, Rivolta's contention that abortion is uniquely related to the suppression of female pleasure is reductive and somewhat inconsistent with the rest of their analysis because it is part of the female identity the potential to be fertile and also the desire of experiencing this fertility, including lesbian women or women who do not wish to actually have children. Illegality or regulation, on the other hand, are directly related to men's domination.

To affirm women's self determination on the question of abortion means to recognize freedom as responsibility towards ourselves and the fetus, first of all, but also towards men and the species in general. Self determination implies a power over others, a power that must be recognized and affirmed as responsibility. Women's experience of the "other" within ourselves could and should be elaborated towards the production of a new ethics of reproduction, valid for both women and men (see Boccia, 1990) (on the ethical status of the fetus, see Mancina, 1989; Zuffa, 1989).

These analyses have given rise to two policy positions. The first, simple decriminalization, is gaining strength. The existing law is declared as indefensible for its many inadequacies, but it is the principle of a juridical regulation of abortion that is more fundamentally refused. The arguments are many: the invasion of privacy, the obligation to translate and reduce one's choice in terms acceptable to "society," the power given to doctors, the pathologization and atomization of female experience, and more fundamentally, the symbolic recognition of the State (men's) authority over women's bodies and the entire sphere of sexuality and reproduction, and therefore the denial of women's competence, knowledge, responsibility. Whereas, it is said, even (in fact, especially) when abortion was illegal, it was subject only to other women's authority, competence, and knowledge and needed and produced female community and solidarity (albeit clandestine and, though "tolerated," kept under surveillance: Chabrol's movie *Une Affaire des Femmes* is a brilliant and moving reconstruction of that climate) (see *Testo per ragionare insieme sulla possibile depenalizzazione dell'aborto*, 1990). Also, from a moral point of view, the principle of self determination appears more consistent with simple decriminalization as it means that it is only and always women who may decide (Fattorini, 1990; Tatafiore, 1990).

While few feminists defend the existing law, there are at least two arguments advanced in preference of a law versus simple decriminalization. The first is a traditional one: decriminalization would amount to deregulation, thus leaving "disadvantaged" women to cope with an abortion market (Rossanda, 1989). The second is more complex. It recognizes the authoritarian and manipulative aspects of legalization, but wonders whether the choice to go back to a classic notion of negative freedom, of freedom as a limit to regulation (as simple decriminalization implies) may not merely be a defensive move. Women would be freer as to the how, when, and where to have an abortion. But this freedom would not be formalized, and the principle of women's self determination, which is also a principle that regulates reproduction by recognizing and sanctioning the sexes' asymmetry on this matter, would lose its symbolic legitimation.

CONCLUSIONS

I did not touch on many other questions debated by Italian feminists (for example, how to analyze the question of women choosing abortions because their partners do not want to have (more) children (see Serra, 1990); and I chose not to address the feminist psychoanalytic debate (see, instead, Vegetti Finzi, 1989; Minetti 1990). Echoes of this last, anyway, are contained in the discussion I did relate.

To conclude, I shall skip the debate's ethical dimensions, to briefly comment on the two policy proposals (without taking into consideration their relative potential to be actually adopted, which is extremely low in both cases, at least at present). Certainly, the pro-law position expresses the current approach to law by movements which exploit the law's symbolic potential. Elsewhere I pointed out the risks of this approach (Pitch, 1989), especially in the case of criminal laws. The abortion law, however, is not a criminal law. It could be argued that, if properly amended especially by eliminating the obligatory (though in fact perfunctory) acquisition of a doctor's certificate, extending to minors the rights of adult women, and making more stringent the obligations of medical personnel to provide abortions, a law would not only give symbolic recognition to the principle of women's self determination over procreation matters, it would also establish a complementary *duty* on the part of public institutions to provide resources and adequate care which would make defaults and non performance actionable by women. It would establish another principle, also important on the symbolic level: women's right to make use of public resources, in all matters regarding procreation in particular and their health in general. Yet, of course, abortion would remain a crime, if not performed according to the law.

Simple decriminalization would probably go in the same direction, as in Italy any medical intervention may be obtained free in public hospitals within the National Health Service: the argument that decriminalization would be to the detriment of more disadvantaged women by opening an abortion market is, per se, not valid. What decriminalization would do would be to make abortion legal also if obtained privately (like any other medical intervention). There would be practical as well as "symbolic" gains: women would have more choice, and they would not have to subject themselves to the scrutiny of the "State." Yet, public non performance would be more widespread and more difficult to act against politically.

Paradoxically, to gain from an amended law, women should be much stronger, politically and symbolically, than they should be to gain from decriminalization: they should be strong enough to impose the recognition that such a law regulates the conflict between the sexes establishing the principle that there are *two* sexes, and that on matters of procreation it is the female sex which has full responsibility (rights *and* duties). It could mark the beginning of what some call gendered law (on this, see Irigaray, 1985; Campari and Cigarini, 1989; Pitch, 1989), that is a law that embodies the principle of the existence of two sexes.

This strength, however, can derive only from the production of a women's "community": e.g., from the construction of a culture whereby women gather strength and authority from other women, and they make of each other the main reference point to interact with the world. The supporters of decriminalization argue that legalization has the effect of keeping women divided by undermining women's solidarity and competence and by making them individually accountable to the State. In support of the law it could be said, on the other hand, that it requires women's constant mobilization.

In order to decide over the two options, one cannot refer to their relative probability to become policies, since, as I said, this probability is low in both cases. Thus we shall have to see which of the two is more productive in terms of the (symbolic) creation of that community I mentioned above: which also means which of the two might be more innovative in cultural and political terms. I tend to believe the law option might prove to be so.

REFERENCES

Boccia, M.L., 1990, "Aborto, pensando l'esperienza," in Coordinamento Nazionale Donne per i Consultori, *Storie, menti e sentimenti di donne di fronte all' aborto*, Roma, Eliograf.

Campari, M.G., Cigarini L., 1989, "Fonti e principi di un nuovo diritto," in Libreria delle donne di Milano, (ed) *Un filo di felicita', Sottosopra*, gennaio.

Fattorini, E., 1990, "Forza e debolezza della soggettivita' femminile. Consapevolezza psicologica e scelta morale di fronte all' aborto," in Coordinamento Nazionale, cit.

Irigaray, L., 1985, *Etica della differenza sessuale*, Milano, Feltrinelli.

Libreria delle Donne di Milano, 1987, *Non credere di avere dei diritti*, Torino, Rosenberg e Sellier.

Mancina, C., 1989, "Le donne, la morale, l'aborto," *L'Unita'*, 17 July.

Minetti, M.G., 1990, "Dalla parte dell'inconscio: non definire, ma comprendere l'aborto," in Coordinamento Nazionale, cit.

Molfino, F., 1990, "L'aborto come sintomo della femminilita," in Coordinamento Nazionale, cit.

Pitch, T., 1989, *Responsabilita' limitate*, Milano, Feltrinelli.

Quintavalla, E., Raimondi, E. (eds.), 1989, *Aborto, perche'?* Milano, Feltrinelli.

Rivolta Femminile, 1975, no title, in *Archivio della Libreria delle Donne*, 1990, Rassegna Stampa.

Rossanda, R., 1989, "Di aborto non si parla cosi," *Noidonne*, luglio-agosto.

Serra, P., 1990, "Una violazione taciuta del corpo femminile," *Reti*, 4.

Spinelli et al., 1987, "L'interruzione volontaria di gravidanza in Italia," *Istisan*, 2.

Tatafiore, R., 1990, "Perche' non richiediamo la depenalizzazione?" in Coordinamento Nazionale, cit.

Vegetti, Finzi S., 1989, "L'aborto, uno scacco del pensiero," in Quintavalla E., Raimondi, E., cit.

Zuffa, G., 1989, "Ripensare l'aborto," *Reti*, 5.

Unwanted Pregnancy,
Due Process of Law
and Justice White

Sarah Slavin

SUMMARY. In *Thornburgh et al. v. American College of Obstetricians and Gynecologists, et al.* (dissenting opinion), 476 U.S. 809 (1986), United States Supreme Court Justice Byron White argued that a state's interest in the life of a fetus justifies "the infliction of some degree of risk of physical harm" on the pregnant woman exercising her constitutionally-based liberty to abort. The position of this article is that the adoption of Justice White's premises would curtail extensively due process rights for this woman. Such curtailment would tend to victimize her and also presume that she has committed a public offense, i.e., to criminalize her body. There is reason to believe Justice White's position may become the law of the land. The author concludes that differentiation in constitutional law of a woman's body by pregnant and not pregnant will be costly.

INTRODUCTION

For 20 years, United States Supreme Court Associate Justice Byron White has held that the state has a compelling interest in preserving the life of the fetus. It follows that he also wants to set aside the Court's 1972 decision, *Roe* v. *Wade*, 410 U.S. 113. Justice White's position appears further to point toward a legal frame-

Sarah Slavin, PhD in Political Science from The George Washington University, is Associate Professor at Buffalo State College. She is the former Editor of *Women & Politics: A Quarterly Journal of Research and Policy Studies* and a member of the Editorial Board of *The Journal of Homosexuality*.

This article is a revised version of a paper presented to the International Symposium on Public Policies Towards Unwanted Pregnancies, University of Pittsburgh, 1990.

41

work in which a pregnant woman lacks the autonomy necessary to justify legal protection of her physical self. In the Justice's opinion, the Court in *Roe* "rejected a rule based on her interest in controlling her own body during pregnancy" (*Planned Parenthood* v. *Danforth*, 428 U.S. 94 (1975)). More tellingly, in *Thornburgh et al.* v. *American College of Obstetricians and Gynecologists (ACOG) et al.*, 476 U.S. 809 (1986), Justice White argued a state's interest in the life of a fetus justifies even "the infliction of some degree of risk of physical harm" on the pregnant woman. This article focuses specifically on Justice White's *Thornburgh* dissent and its implications for women, pregnant or not pregnant.

THE THORNBURGH CASE

The parties on appeal in *Thornburgh* were the Governor of Pennsylvania, the District Attorney from Montgomery County and other administrative officials. (Then Governor, later United States Attorney General Thornburgh had some years previous vetoed an early version of the Pennsylvania abortion regulation statute. This version was struck down later by the United States District Court for the Eastern District of Pennsylvania.) The appellees were comprised of the Pennsylvania section of ACOG, certain doctors licensed to practice in the state, members of the clergy, a person who had bought insurance with abortion coverage from a Pennsylvania insurer, and a group of abortion counselors and providers.

At the trial court level, ACOG challenged the State Abortion Control Act of 1982. The 1982 statute was a rider on a bill to regulate paramilitary training. It was modelled on a prototype recommended by a non-profit antiabortion organization. Plaintiffs asked the district court for a preliminary injunction against the statute to preserve the relative positions of the parties until the commencement of trial. The district court granted a preliminary injunction against one provision of the statute but declined to do so for other provisions central to plaintiffs' case. The injunction required that the State of Pennsylvania refrain from enforcing the one provision. Plaintiffs appealed the denial of an injunction against the other provisions, and defendants cross-appealed against the preliminary injunction that was granted. After a delay, a United States Court of

Appeals (3d Cir.) panel of judges found all provisions of the statute unconstitutional and denied a petition for rehearing by the entire bench.

No formal hearing on the facts had yet occurred at the trial court level, and so the appeals court finding was not final. The United States Supreme Court majority exercised its discretion in sending for the records of the case in order that it might judge the merits of the case. It grounded its assertion of authority on the unconstitutional character of the Pennsylvania statute.

The appeals court panel had found invalid on their face six statutory provisions dealing with informed consent, printed information, reporting requirements, determination of viability, degree of care required in postviability abortions, and requirement of a second doctor in a postviability abortion. The Supreme Court majority upheld this finding, saying "the States are not free . . . to intimidate women into continuing pregnancies. . . . [The statutory provisions] wholly subordinate constitutional privacy interests and concern with maternal health in an effort to deter a woman from making a decision that, with her physician, is hers to make" (476 U.S. 760-761).

JUSTICE WHITE'S THORNBURGH DISSENT

Dissenting in *Thornburgh* and joined by Chief Justice William Rehnquist, Justice White argued that the Supreme Court is bound to correct plain errors in its prior reviews. Justice White contended that *Roe* v. *Wade* is in error for three reasons. (1) While a kind of liberty, a pregnant woman's choice to abort is not a fundamental freedom that demands a high degree of judicial scrutiny to ascertain any diminishment "of constitutional value that reflects . . . basic choices made by the people themselves in constituting their system of government" (476 U.S. 791-792). These basic choices are referred to as the exercise of popular sovereignty. (2) It is arbitrary to define the boundaries of a state's compelling interest in protecting "'potential human life'" as fetal viability alone (476 U.S. 794-795). (3) Without a fundamental freedom and a narrow state interest such as viability, state regulation of abortion would not be a problem and could be held compelling.

In *Thornburgh*, Justice White argued that deference by the Supreme Court to the Pennsylvania state legislature was warranted because, first, the informed consent provisions in state law maximized choice by offering accurate information, were a reasonable, fair way to stimulate women to give birth instead of to abort, and did not overextend a legislature's ability to regulate the medical profession (see Nelson 1987). Second, Justice White believed the statute's reporting requirements should have been upheld because not only did they satisfactorily assure confidentiality but also because to find otherwise was to bypass [informal] factual findings by the trial court in disregard of the Federal Rules of Civil Procedure. Further, according to Justice White, not to uphold the reporting requirements was to judge inappropriately on incomplete evidence taken informally on a motion for preliminary injunction. Third, Justice White argued that *Roe* permitted Pennsylvania to require the performance of a postviability abortion by means protective of a fetus even if it posed a physical risk to the pregnant woman. The Justice found this to be so even though the Pennsylvania statute actually forbade methods posing real identifiable risk to the pregnant woman. Fourth, Pennsylvania's second physician requirement for postviability abortions, with its defense for noncompliance of medical necessity, could have been construed by the Court to include a medical-emergency exception as part of medical necessity. Such a construal would have avoided finding the requirement unconstitutional. Finally, according to Justice White, state parental notice and consent procedures ought not to have been enjoined. Instead, White found that the Court's previous decisions required an assumption that the state Supreme Court's new rules would expedite adequately a minor's application for a court order approving her decision to abort or a court's decision that a minor could herself give informed consent.

DUE PROCESS OF LAW
IN JUSTICE WHITE'S DISSENT

In arguing to overrule *Roe* v. *Wade*, Justice White identified two tests as to whether increased judicial scrutiny should apply to regulation of a pregnant woman's unenumerated liberty to choose an abortion. (An unenumerated liberty is not specified in the Constitution; it is instead implied from the Constitution's language.) The first may be called the "ordered liberty" test, the second, the "historical-traditional roots" test. For White, the usefulness of either test lies in trying to show that "some source of constitutional value" mirrors decisions essential to exercise of popular sovereignty. White found that regulation of a pregnant woman's unenumerated freedom to choose an abortion did not meet either test and hence, excited no more than "the most minimal judicial scrutiny" *(Thornburgh* v. *ACOG*, 476 U.S. 790).

A "source of constitutional value" may be either a logical implication or matter of concord and doctrine handed down across time. The former emerged in treatment by the Supreme Court of claims that procedural guarantees in the Bill of Rights applied to defendants in criminal cases at the state as well as federal level. A fundamental freedom was defined as an interest so "implicit in the concept of ordered liberty" that "neither liberty nor justice would exist if [it] were sacrificed" *(Palko* v. *Connecticut*, 302 U.S. 319 (1937); overruled in 1969). The idea here is not that liberty protected by the fourteenth amendment's due process clause incorporates, e.g., the first amendment 'right of association'; it is that a right such as association is essential or indispensable to a "principle of justice" righteously and traditionally established. Such principle is rationalized by its systematic and established succession; it has "proper order and coherence" *(Palko* v. *Connecticut*, 302 U.S. 325). Regulation of a pregnant woman's unenumerated liberty to choose an abortion is not subject to increased judicial scrutiny because, according to Justice White, "a free, egalitarian, and democratic society does not presuppose any particular rule or set of rules" that would apply here, as it would in the case of a fundamental freedom *(Thornburgh* v. *ACOG*, 476 U.S. 788-789). By extension, to regulate a pregnant woman's unenumerated liberty to choose an abortion supposedly will not create the unendurably severe and horrifying suffering that *Palko* v. *Connecticut,* 302 U.S. 328 required for a fundamental freedom. Nothing is due such an unenumerated interest, according to Justice White ((dissenting opinion), *Moore* v. *East Cleveland*, 431 U.S. 546 (1977)).

The historical-traditional roots test dates back to an 1865 decision about the protection of the property of certain United States government employees against seizure and sale to satisfy outstanding taxes. In 1884 a test from that decision was narrowed by the United States Supreme Court in a state case about criminal procedure to focus on settled practice in England and the United States. By 1908 this settled practice was treated as having become fundamental, inherent to free government, and inalienable from its citizens. In discussing the historical-traditional roots test, Justice White's choice of a specific precedent lay with the 1977 decision, *Moore* v. *East Cleveland*, from which he dissented. *Moore* concerned a housing ordinance that would have prohibited two grandchildren who were not siblings from living with their grandmother. The *Moore* decision characterized the fundamental freedom which is the family institution as "deeply rooted in this Nation's history and tradition" (431 U.S. 504). For Justice White, in that case, "what the deeply rooted traditions of the country are is arguable; which of them deserves the protection of the Due Process Clause is even more debatable" ((dissenting opinion), 431 U.S. 549-551). According to the Justice in *Thornburgh*, regulation of a pregnant woman's unenumerated liberty to choose an abortion is not subject to increased scrutiny under the historical-traditional roots test because the liberty at stake is not that deeply rooted. Both this test and the ordered liberty test for fundamental freedoms were inapplicable for Justice White for the additional reason that there is controversy over abortion in the history of privacy, the 'hue and cry' implicating public grievance and invocation of public authority.

Implications of Justice White's Dissent

It seems clear that a legitimate end for state regulation in exercising its police power is to offer incentives to women to give birth, i.e., to encourage normal childbirth. Minimal judicial scrutiny of a challenged regulation would begin by assuming the regulation's constitutionality, and would require a showing by the challenger that the means of accomplishing this legitimate end are not rationally related to it. A minimal level of scrutiny basically assures that a constitutionally based challenge will not succeed. That is, a state could limit with impunity a pregnant woman's unenumerated liberty to choose an abortion by claiming in doing so that its aim is to encourage normal childbirth, *and* when the level of judicial scrutiny of the challenged restrictions is minimal. If the liberty to choose abortion is not a fundamental freedom, as White argues, then judicial scrutiny will be minimal. Women incur penalties by virtue of the continuance of such limitations on their body. One significant penalty may be weak due process guarantees for pregnant women.

Pregnant women are obligated to society to bear a child even if, historically, to fulfill the obligation unwillingly has tended to diminish women's exercise of personal sovereignty and brought about conditions of powerlessness or victimization in their lives (Copelon 1989, 299). Choosing to abort rather than to fulfill this obligation is argued by pro-fetal-life advocates to be murder. Murder is unlawful killing. The idea is that the offense is so serious an affront to society's health, safety and welfare that government must be implicated in the prosecution and punishment and/or rehabilitation of the offenders. However, many pro-life supporters have stated that this killing should not be made punishable by the state in a criminal procedure against the woman who aborts.

But disinterest in prosecution of supposedly abnormal behavior by women, which for some may amount to criminality, leaves women subject to an implied criminal status and also without the strong procedural due process rights that actual criminal defendants possess. (Procedural due process rights refer to the incorporation against the state by the fourteenth amendment's due process clause of guarantees in the form of criminal procedure found in the Bill of Rights.) Without procedural due process, women subject to an implied criminal status are in a poor position to defend themselves against the treatment prescribed. For example, a woman terminally ill with cancer and in the third trimester of pregnancy may choose not to undergo a caesarean section recommended by her physician to simplify the baby's delivery (Gallagher 1985, 94). Some might argue this is criminal behavior because deliveries of dead pregnant women are difficult. Physicians may avail themselves of court orders through a civil, not criminal process, where the burden of proof greatly is reduced. The woman may forfeit with her life when she wanted to live out what was left of it.

Justice White observed in his *Thornburgh* dissent that "the termination of a pregnancy typically involves the destruction of another entity: the fetus" (476 U. S. 793). For Justice White, the state has a compelling interest in preserving the life of a viable fetus. Compelling interests "are so weighty as to justify substantial and ordinarily impermissible impositions on the individual, impositions that, I had thought, could include the infliction of some degree of risk of physical harm" (476 U.S. 809), i.e., danger to a pregnant woman exercising her liberty to choose to abort. In a clinical setting, this infliction of danger would occur on an individual basis rather than involve the generalized treatment of similarly situated persons that ordinarily is strongly required by due process in criminal proceedings.

In his dissent Justice White quoted paradoxically but approvingly from *Roe*, the precedent he wants set aside: "The pregnant woman cannot be isolated in her privacy" (476 U.S. 791-792). According to Justice White, because the pregnant woman cannot be isolated, she lacks the autonomy necessary to participate in the Court's substantive due process findings of privacy as a source of constitutional value. (Here, the due process clause of the fourteenth amendment, which protects us from arbitrary deprivations by the state of our life, liberty or property, is read as also protecting us from the substance of legislation depriving us, e. g., of the right to privacy.) The *"life"* of a fetus demands that review of restrictions on a pregnant woman's unenumerated liberty to choose to abort be "sui generis," different from review of other claims of deprivations of liberty in family life (476 U.S. 793). (According to *Black's Law Dictionary*, 'sui generis' means the *only one* of its own kind; peculiar.) It will be remembered that biosocial theories of crime include the notion that females are capable of sexual aberration; 'aberration' means differing from a common type. Justice White may not have had these theories in mind when he separated a pregnant woman's claims to privacy in deciding to abort from other claims to privacy; he nonetheless has acted as if "putative mothers," as he calls these pregnant women in *Doe* v. *Bolton*, 410 U.S. 221, are not to be trusted.

In summary, in his *Thornburgh* dissent, Justice White advocated curtailing both the procedural due process and substantive due process rights of pregnant women seeking to exercise their constitutionally unenumerated liberty to choose to abort. This is another way of saying that a pregnant woman lacks necessary autonomy to claim privacy as a source of constitutional protection because she may be deprived procedurally of the liberty necessary to exercise autonomy.

Nor is this the end of it. In a footnote in *Thornburgh*, Justice White argued that the state's interest in "protecting 'potential life'" is not finally dependent on viability or, apparently, on whether life or potential life is under discussion (476 U.S. 796). As a result, "the legitimate goals that may be served by state coercion" (476 U.S. 797-798) as recognized in *Roe*, are not outweighed for Justice White by any due process guarantees procedural or substantive belonging to pregnant women. He points the way beyond what Rhonda Copelon already calls "a highly truncated and socially regressive concept of autonomy" (Copelon 1989, 288). Or, to give Justice White the last word:

> Even if the Pennsylvania statute is properly constructed as requiring a pregnant woman seeking abortion of a viable fetus to endure a method of abortion chosen to protect the health of the fetus despite the existence of an alternative that in some substantial degree is more protective of her own health, I am not convinced that the statute is unconstitutional. (*Thornburgh* v. *ACOG*, 476 U.S. 809)

DISCUSSION

Justice White's *Thornburgh* dissent suggests that sharp differentiation of a women's body, by pregnant and not pregnant, could occur as the state reacquires leeway to restrict a pregnant woman's unenumerated liberty to choose an abortion. According to Justice White, a pregnant woman has reduced procedural and substantive due process guarantees. The argument is contemptuous of those women he calls "putative mothers" (*Doe* v. *Bolton*, 410 U.S. 221). In *Doe* he weighed the life of the fetus against "the convenience, whim, or caprice" of a pregnant woman and found her interests to be lacking in substance (*ibid.*, 221-222). It is hard for this author, at least, to find his appraisal other than insensitive to the conditions faced by a pregnant woman who does not want to be pregnant. According to the Justice, the Constitution does not warrant investing in her a "right to exterminate" human life *(Doe* v. *Bolton*, 410 U.S. 222).

It is important to recognize that Justice White's use of the label, "sui generis," emphasizes but is not confined to reduced access to substantive due process for a pregnant woman who does not want to be pregnant. By arguing *this* woman's differentiation from a common type, those women entitled to privacy guarantees in a family setting and presumably those men, the Justice suggests the extent to which her exercise of her unenumerated liberty to choose an abortion may offend the state. He seems not to be interested in prosecuting this offense. He would leave it to impositions by the state, which conceivably could be dangerous to the 'offender.' Such impositions would be inflicted in a clinical setting instead of as a result of proceedings imbued with strong procedural due process guarantees for individuals accused of an offense against the state and presumed innocent until proved beyond a reasonable doubt not to be. From Justice White's perspective, a pregnant woman who chooses to end an unwanted pregnancy is presumed, rather than accused of being offensive; i.e., her choice about the use to which her body will be put is criminalized without benefit at a minimum of notice and hearing. He would consign her to a sphere obscured from public view; and yet, who could doubt that her choice to end or even not to end her pregnancy would be publicly structured? The majority opinion in *Thornburgh* referred to this process as intimidation.

Criminalization of a pregnant woman's choice not to be pregnant anymore is insidious and for more than the obvious reason that there is no crime to commit. Copelon calls the controversy over *Roe* v. *Wade* "and its power to recognize unenumerated rights" an issue of "critical value choices" about, among other things, sexuality and gender (Copelon 1989, 288). Eisenstein emphasizes the degree to which "pregnancy is a value-laden construct mediated through a culture that is defined by gender" (Eisenstein 1988, 197). Justice White in his *Thornburgh* dissent would open the door wide to such impositions without benefit of public hearing of pregnant women who do not want to be pregnant.

Viewed through Justice White's *Thornburgh* dissent, a pregnant woman who does not want to be pregnant would be subject both to victimization and criminalization. One consequence of classifying non-pregnant women's bodies with men's bodies, to emphasize to the greatest possible extent sexual equality, is going to be a more definitive and different pregnant body than at present. More than one commentator in the eighties has argued in favor of differentiating women's bodies by pregnant and not pregnant. Nor are these commentators all of Justice White's ideological bent. In a chapter entitled "Beyond the Phallus and the Mother's Body," Eisenstein states: "The importance of differentiating the female body from the mother's body is a key point in this book" (*ibid.*, 192). Eisenstein goes on to cite well known feminist attorneys Sylvia Law and Herma Hill Kay as advocates of such differentiation. However, she cautions readers to be sensitive to the political context of differentiation, in that women's experiences with pregnancy are many and various, but their context is a product of rule by the father (*ibid.*, 288).

From the standpoint of women with unwanted pregnancies, the socioeconomic costs alone of this outcome will be high, and their sexual inequality is a foregone conclusion. Feminist attorneys bent on equality need to address this outcome as a matter of law rather than in effect to encourage it. It would be a serious error to contribute to the scapegoating of pregnant women who do not want to be pregnant by those who fear women's equality with men.

As feminist attorneys turn ever more from an increasingly limited right to privacy to equal protection arguments, they need to be alert to the hazards of trading off any of pregnant women's interests. Trade offs come readily in public arenas accustomed to dealing with relative questions; feminist attorneys, though, by inclination should be sensitive to the more fundamental classification process. The question is, who is to be classified here, and where? This author contends that supporting the differentiation of a woman's body by pregnant and not pregnant, at the least when a pregnant woman does not want to be pregnant, leaves her exposed to potentially invidious treatment. In Justice White's view, she is equal, but to others similarly situated. Consequently she belongs in a classification of 'her own,' and judicial review of state restrictions levied on her uneumerated liberty to choose an abortion is different, i.e., "sui generis," from review of other privacy claims. A woman's unenumerated liberty to choose an abortion in consultation with her physician during the first and second trimesters of pregnancy is part of the independent right of privacy that has been implied by the United States Supreme Court from clauses in amendments one, three, four and five in the Bill of Rights. The independent right of privacy in turn is part of substantive due process.

Worth remembering is that most women still become pregnant during their lifetime, and their interests extend not only to terminating a pregnancy but also to bringing it to term, having access to parental leave policies and so on. Further, there are today more single mothers than in the past, and many of these women are affected by the feminization of poverty. Their households are essentially unprotected and always ripe for public intervention. Pregnant female intravenous drug users and women with Acquired Immunodeficiency Syndrome have legitimate concerns, too. Practically speaking, abortion seems not much to have been considered an option for them, and yet there appear to be suggestions on the horizon that perhaps it should be made mandatory. The risk of having a baby with AIDS is alarming, and simultaneously, for some women the possibility that the fetus they carry may not be infected is compelling. Also of concern to these women are issues such as reporting and contact tracing.

Pregnant and potentially pregnant women have reason to be concerned in other arenas. Able bodied women who could become pregnant even though they are not currently are challenging employment practices that limit their opportunities in some segments of the paid work force in accordance with their fertility. Concern about the effects of certain working conditions on the fetus is real enough; so is access to the higher paying jobs that may present these conditions. In Buffalo, N. Y., a woman with a broken leg was told that if she were pregnant, she could not be given an anesthetic; she waited in pain for 36 hours until the hospital had determined to its satisfaction she was not pregnant. And women who see their obstetricians/gynecologists regularly, and women who need but do not seek prenatal care, may be affected by a tendency at law to resist finding "constitutional warrant" for giving their interests high priority. (See Justice White (dissenting opinion), *Doe* v. *Bolton*, 410 U.S. 333.) Who is a putative mother? Only time will tell as the courts decide on the Pennsylvania, Guam and Utah strict abortion regulations cases.

This author contends that problems such as these will be exacerbated by adoption of the premises of Justice White (dissenting opinion) in *Thornburgh*. Justice White is an important and central member of the United States Supreme Court's Reagan majority. He also now is voting in the majority on abortion related decisions (*Webster* v. *Reproductive Health Services*, 75 U.S.L.W. 5023 (1989); *Ohio* v. *Akron Center for Reproductive Health et al.*, 58 U.S.L.W. 4979 (1990)). Further, during the Supreme Court's 1989-1990 term, he wrote more majority opinions than anyone else on the Court (*Wall Street Journal*, June 28, 1990, B1). The task of writing an opinion is assigned by the Chief Justice when he votes with the majority. William Rehnquist is the Chief Justice of the United States Supreme Court. Not only is he voting along with Justice White in the majority on abortion related decisions at this time, but he also joined Justice White in his *Thornburgh* dissent in 1986 and dissented himself in *Roe* in 1972. What is more, in 1989, in the *Webster* decision, with Justices White and Kennedy, Chief Justice Rehnquist quoted from Justice White's *Thornburgh* dissent: " 'The State's interest, if compelling after viability, is equally compelling before viability' " (476 U.S. 763). Justice White may in the near future prove influential in restructuring pregnant women's private choices about their unwanted pregnancies in a manner that reinforces victimization/criminalization and sets pregnant women further apart than they are from men and non-pregnant women, in private and public spheres alike.

REFERENCES

Bullough, Vern L., Brenda Shelton and Sarah Slavin. 1988. *The Subordinated Sex: A History of Attitudes Toward Women*. Athens: University of Georgia Press.

Copelon, Rhonda. 1989. Beyond the Liberal Idea of Privacy: Toward a Positive Right of Autonomy. In *Judging the Constitution: Critical Essays on Judicial Lawmaking*, ed. Michael W. McCann and Gerald L. Houseman. Glenview: Scott Foresman.

Eisenstein, Zillah. 1988. *The Female Body and the Law*. Berkeley: University of California Press.

Gallagher, Janet. 1985. Fetal Personhood and Women's Policy. In *Women, Biology, and Public Policy*, ed. Virginia Sapiro. Beverly Hills: Sage.
Nelson, William E. 1987. Deference and the Limits to Deference in the Constitutional Jurisprudence of Justice Byron R. White. *University of Colorado Law Review* 58:347.
Rulings Ranged from Criminal Law to Taxes. June 28, 1990. *Wall Street Journal* B1.
Talarico, Susette M. 1985. An Analysis of Biosocial Theories of Crime. In *Women, Biology, and Public Policy*, ed. Virginia Sapiro. Beverly Hills: Sage.

Contract Motherhood:
Social Practice in Social Context

Mary Gibson

SUMMARY. This paper begins with an account of, and location of the author's (socialist feminist) approach within, the feminist debate about contract or "surrogate" motherhood. Contract motherhood must be seen not simply as a transaction among individuals, but as a social practice arising in a particular social context. After exploring

Mary Gibson, PhD in Philosophy from Princeton University, is Associate Professor at Rutgers, the State University of New Jersey. She is the author of *Workers' Rights* and a member of the Task Force on Reproductive Practices of the New Jersey Commission on Legal and Ethical Issues in the Delivery of Health Care.

An earlier version of this paper was presented at the American Philosophical Association Eastern Division meetings, Washington, DC, December 1988. I am deeply indebted to the commentator, Iris Young, for her patience and encouragement as well as her constructive and insightful comments. I also want to thank the participants in the discussion at that session. I have benefitted from discussions with and comments by many people, including the participants in a faculty/guest discussion group that met regularly during the Spring 1988 semester at Rutgers, New Brunswick; participants in a graduate seminar on Feminist Ethics and Reproductive Practices I conducted at Rutgers in the Fall 1988 semester; the members and staff of the Task Force on Reproductive Practices of the New Jersey Commission on Legal and Ethical Issues in the Delivery of Health Care (the Task Force met approximately once a month from Spring 1988 through November 1990); participants in the Center for the Critical Analysis of Contemporary Culture, Rutgers University, 1988-89; and the participants in a presentation/discussion October 1990 in the Rutgers Philosophy Department's Colloquium series. The Rutgers University Research Council provided a grant that covered some photocopying and telephone costs associated with this project. Individuals (some in the above-mentioned groups and some not) I especially want to thank are Barbara Andolsen, Adrienne Asche, Sarah Boone, Martin Bunzl, Mary Sue Henifin, Nancy Holmstrom, Helen Holmes, Alison Jaggar, Howard McGary, Anne Reichman, Fadlou Shehadi, Lee Silver, Nadine Taub, Alan Weisbard, Bruce Wilshire, and Linda Zerilli.

55

the social context, objections to the practice on grounds of exploitation, commodification, alienation, and autonomy are discussed and defended. The author concludes that commercial contract motherhood should be prohibited and brokering criminalized, and that all motherhood contracts, paid or unpaid, should be void and unenforceable.

INTRODUCTION

There is very broad consensus among feminists concerning the need to protect women's access to safe, legal abortions, and more generally to protect women from governmental interference in our reproductive lives. Yet, there have emerged deep and difficult divisions concerning the appropriate stance with respect to contract motherhood.[1] These difficulties arise, at least in part, from the fact that the issues it raises intersect two more general ongoing debates among feminists that are seen, correctly in my view, as having enormous theoretical and practical/strategic import. These two larger debates may be termed (1) the debate over the priority of the individual or the social, and (2) the debate over the meanings and relative importance of equality and difference both between and among women and men (the equality vs difference debate). Both debates involve metaphysical/ontological, methodological, and political/strategic dimensions. The theoretical and the practical/strategic aspects are, of course, closely but complexly related.

The contract motherhood debate illustrates the significance of the difference between focussing on individual choices and acts on one hand and on social practices in social context on the other. It shows how one's choice of individual or social focus is likely to influence one's stand on the equality vs difference debate. At the same time, it challenges us to make clear the implications of divergent interpretations of difference.

Many liberal feminists, who see the ultimate defense of women's reproductive freedom in terms of individual rights to privacy and personal choice, respect for the autonomy of each woman as an individual and related notions, tend to see these same considerations as providing, indeed entailing, a defense of women's right to engage in contract motherhood. In their view, to deny women this right is not only to violate their privacy (as well as that of the person(s) who might wish to engage their services); it is to treat gestation and birth, capacities unique to women, as fundamentally different from other human capacities that are routinely contracted and paid for in our society, and to treat women, in their exercise of this capacity, as less than fully rational or responsible, that is, as less than equal. If women may be denied this reproductive choice on such grounds, what is to prevent their being denied all reproductive freedom on the same grounds? Thus liberal feminists tend to come down on the individual side of the individual vs social focus debate and on the equality side of the equality vs difference debate.

Others, socialist feminists for example, while recognizing both the importance of these considerations and the strategic necessity often to press the case for reproductive freedom in terms of rights to privacy and choice (individual rights being the "coin of the realm"), have been concerned to recognize and articulate the limitations of this approach. As socialist feminists see it, the tendency of most contemporary liberal Western moral theory to concentrate primarily on individual acts, and the attendant tendency to separate ethics (conceived of as concerned with the behavior, intentions, and motives of individuals) from social/political theory[2] severely limit the capacity of these theoretical approaches adequately to deal with issues that have profound socio-political as well as personal implications. Thus socialist feminists have been working to develop less individualistic approaches more attuned to the interaction and interdependence of the personal and political.[3] In these approaches, the actual existing social, historical circumstances, including the potential for development or change in various directions, assume a degree of primacy, in that specific conceptions of rights, privacy, and autonomy are seen as shaped and conditioned by them. There is no given, historical realm of privacy, for example, that can fix appropriate limits of governmental/societal concern and intervention. For socialist feminists, the actual and potential impacts of existing and proposed social practices and policies on various social groups, particularly oppressed or subordinated groups, play a fundamental role in determining theoretical and practical principles and priorities.

Socialist feminism, then, denies the inherent priority of either the individual or the social, regarding them as inextricably interdependent, and insisting that individual acts and relationships be considered in their social context.

In this paper, I employ such an approach in examining and assessing the practice of contract motherhood. For, in my view, it is crucial to a theoretically adequate understanding of contract motherhood, and hence to morally and politically acceptable resolutions of the issues it raises, that it be viewed, not simply or even primarily, as an interpersonal transaction among individuals, but as a social practice arising from particular institutional, structural, and ideological conditions within a particular social context and having particular meanings and implications constructed and conferred by that social context. A social practice may be constituted by constellations of individual acts, but the practice is not reducible to the acts that constitute it. For the acts are the particular acts they are, incorporating the intentions and beliefs and eliciting the understandings and responses they do, largely in virtue of the social context in which they occur, including the existence of the practices they help constitute.[4]

This is not, of course, to suggest that all socialist feminists would agree with all aspects of either the discussion or the policy proposals presented here. One place we often diverge is at the strategic or policy level of the equality vs difference debate. Socialist feminists hold that, while differences are real, their significance is socially constructed and conferred. Thus, disputes arise about whether and in what ways feminists should insist that women be treated the same as men, even where the significance of difference is great (in an attempt to deconstruct, or at least not reinforce its significance), and when we should insist that we be treated differently in recognition of the real disadvantages we otherwise suffer given the pervasiveness and persistence of societal practices, institutions and attitudes that constitute the impacts of gender on every aspect of our lives. Thus some socialist feminists are persuaded that the consequences for women in our society of prohibiting or severely restricting the practice of contract motherhood would be worse than the consequences of permitting and regulating it.

For better or worse, the approach is sufficiently open-ended, the issues raised by contract motherhood sufficiently complex and multi-faceted, and the empirical judgments concerning the likely effects of various policies sufficiently speculative as to leave room for some variation in conclusions, even among persons who share the basic approach and assumptions. At the same time, for those of us who favor prohibiting at least commercial contract motherhood, there is the uncomfortable fact that our policy proposals on this matter are substantially in line with those of some feminists and many non-feminists or even anti-feminists with whom we profoundly disagree on some (in the latter cases, virtually all) basic assumptions.

In the first category are essentialist and some cultural feminists[5] with whom we agree that the severing of the relationship between birthmother and child is one of the worst aspects of contract motherhood and that there should be a strong presumption in favor of the birthmother in the event of a custody dispute arising out of a contracted birth. We are in agreement on both the urgent need to protect and expand reproductive freedom for women and the danger that societal developments that appear to enhance such freedom in individual cases may in fact diminish it by increasing medical, technological, judicial, and other forms of societal control over reproductive options, choices, and experiences.

We do not, however, agree with what we see as a tendency on the part of these feminists to romanticize and mystify the mother-child connection, based on gestation and birth, and to privilege this over all other relationships.[6] Such an essentialist view of the meaning of motherhood, and hence of the significance of the difference in reproductive roles of women and men, strikes us as dangerously close to the views of those who, on religious or other grounds, regard women's nature and purpose as bound up with our presumed reproductive capacity in such a way as to justify restricting or eliminating entirely our reproductive choices, as well as prohibiting or controlling other activities that might interfere with our "natural" reproductive function. These, then are the strategic stakes in the equality vs. difference debate.

For these reasons, one of the most difficult aspects of this topic, for me and for many other feminists struggling with it,[7] is to find an appropriate and tenable ground between treating gestation and birth as nothing (merely a reproductive service, incubation) and treating it as everything (the most profound and creative human act, giving rise to the deepest and most valuable of human relationships). Indeed, many discussions of the topic seem to presuppose that one must choose between glorification and nullification of pregnancy and childbirth. Glorification stresses the uniqueness and importance of gestation at the risk of reducing women to our (presumed) reproductive role and hence encouraging compulsory motherhood. Nullification minimizes gestation, refusing to privilege it over the male contribution to reproduction, in order to stress that, like men, women are more than our (presumed) reproductive capacities. It risks denying the substantial difference between the involvement of women and men in the process of reproduction and hence ignoring the potential impact of this difference on relative advantage and disadvantage in other pursuits. Nullification also encourages dismissing the uniqueness and the profound importance to many women and children of the relationship that often does develop between woman and fetus/infant during the processes of gestation, birth, and nursing.

We cannot afford to choose between the options so conceived, for the dangers perceived in each are very real, and they do not function as counterweights, but rather as complements to one another: on one hand, women are equated with our presumed role in reproduction, and on the other, women's role in reproduction is equated with men's. Women are thus reduced to reproducers and diminished as reproducers. Feeding either head nourishes the same beast. We must insist *both* on the importance and uniqueness[9] of gestation *and* on the fact that women are more than their (presumed) gestational capacity and can be whole persons without having or expressing that capacity.

SOCIAL CONTEXT

As the practice of contract motherhood has emerged in our society, the most typical situation giving rise to it is that of a traditional, heterosexual married couple (the intended receiving parents) who want to have one or more children but are unable to because the wife is infertile, that is, unable to conceive and/or to sustain a pregnancy. In the "standard" case, the contract mother is artificially inseminated with the sperm of the intended receiving father, conceives, gestates, gives birth to an infant, delivers the infant into the custody of the receiving couple, and renounces all rights to a parental relationship with the child.

Although infertility is by no means a necessary condition for contract motherhood,[10] many people regard the pain experienced by infertile couples as a compelling reason to welcome, or at least permit, contract motherhood as a procreative option. Indeed, there are some who would restrict it to such couples.[11] In this context, it is relevant to consider the incidence and the causes of infertility in the United States.

The most recent data available on the national incidence of infertility are from 1982.[12] At that time, an estimated 2.4 million married couples (8.5%) were infertile.[13] The causes of infertility are not fully known, and several factors may be involved in a given case. Among the currently known causal factors are the following: *pelvic inflammatory disease*, often resulting from sexually transmitted diseases such as gonorrhea and chlamydia; *iatrogenic causes*, including drugs such as DES, devices such as IUDs, and infections resulting from operations such as D and Cs and appendectomies; *surgical sterilization*, whether fully voluntary or not; *environmental and workplace toxins*, such as ionizing radiation, lead, and dibromochlorpropane (DBCP); and *postponed childbearing*, largely in response to the difficulty of combining paid employment and family responsibilities in a society without adequate childcare, family leaves, and so on.[14] Thus many of the physical causes of infertility are directly or indirectly generated by social conditions, practices, and institutions, all of which can and should be seriously addressed.

Prevention of infertility wherever possible is surely preferable to any after-the-fact response, and the measures needed to address the causes mentioned would serve other socially desirable purposes as well: improving health education including sex education, providing access to health care, holding manufacturers of drugs and devices liable for the harm they cause, strictly enforcing informed consent procedures to prevent sterilization abuse, cleaning up the

environment and workplaces, and carrying out the social reorgani-
zation needed to eliminate the barriers to combining paid work and
family are all measures that warrant the allocation of substantial
societal resources. That they would also help to prevent the pain of
infertility is one important reason among many. At the same time, it
must be noted that "Pain is not an inevitable response to the fact of
infertility . . . a physical reality takes on significance in a particular
social context."[15]

In this light, it is ironic that many of the features of our society
that make contract motherhood so very attractive to many people
are the same features that make it so morally and politically troubling. The features of our society that I have in mind are (1) the
subordination of women, (2) class inequalities, (3) pronatalism, (4)
a narrow, mystified conception of the family, (5) racism, (6) our
market-oriented, contractarian conception of public personhood,
and the relations and interactions among all of these. If these features were absent, contract motherhood might not be morally objectionable, but much if not all of its attractions would also be absent.
This suggests that if there were a society in which contract motherhood would not be morally objectionable, the practice probably
would not exist.

Subordination of Women and Class Inequalities. The subordination of women both within the family and outside of it means,
among other things, that severely limited roles, opportunities, and
resources are available to most women. The most meaningful and
fulfilling activities available to many women are those involved in
bearing and rearing children. For working class women, fewer avenues are open to other fulfilling endeavors than for "middle" or
"upper" class women, who are likely to have access to challenging
career (or volunteer) opportunities.[16]

Thus, when women's subordination and class inequalities are
combined, it is not surprising that some working class women welcome the chance to be contract mothers. They can get paid for engaging in one of the most meaningful activities available to them.
They can do it while staying home and caring for their other children (the ultimate "home work" or cottage industry). They can do
it while working at another paid job, assuming that they don't lose
the other job as a result of the pregnancy. They can, indeed must,

do it even while reading, sleeping, eating, bathing, and making love. Thus it can be an attractive prospect for a woman who has few options and opportunities.

But these same factors, the subordination of women and class inequalities, are among those that make contract motherhood so morally and politically troubling. As the terms "surrogate mother" and "surrogate uterus" make clear, the practice reflects and reinforces a view of women as primarily suited for reproduction and of our role in reproduction as that of a vessel carrying a man's child.[17] Women are doubly demeaned by this view: first, we are reduced to our reproductive role, and second, the uniqueness and importance of that role are denied. This attitude not only demeans women, it also implicitly justifies and hence contributes to the restriction of roles and opportunities for women. In addition, it supports direct interference with the activities, and violation of the bodily integrity of women who are engaged in reproduction. Here I have in mind actions that have recently been taken against women who were not contract mothers: prohibition or restriction of abortions (including recent attempts by potential fathers to prevent pregnant women from obtaining abortions), forced fetal surgery, forced caesareans, and the arrest of a woman on charges of fetal abuse for disobeying her doctor's advice.[18]

There is a strong and arguably growing tendency for physicians and judges to regard a pregnant woman as simply "the fetal environment," and sometimes a hostile environment from which the fetus must be protected. Her interests in self-determination and bodily integrity may, on this view, be overridden by the interests of the fetus in life and wellbeing.[19] This tendency would be even stronger in cases of contract motherhood, and stronger still for purely gestational contracts. (According to some proponents of contract motherhood, one of its advantages over adoption is the ability of the intended receiving parent(s) to "monitor the pregnancy.")[20]

The chance to bear children for others for a fee does nothing to break down the gender stereotyped roles and attitudes that so limit the options, opportunities and aspirations of women, especially working class women, in our society. If it had any effect at all, contract motherhood would tend to *reduce* pressures to open other avenues for working class women. If poor and working class women are to be paid for pregnancy, let it be for bearing and rearing *their* children, as in family allowances, not just for bearing children for the more affluent.[21]

Thus class inequalities raise serious concerns about exploitation of the economic situation of poor women.[22] These concerns will be examined in more detail in the discussion of exploitation, below. Let us now turn to explore some features of our society that make contract motherhood attractive to the intended receiving parents.

Pronatalism, Narrow Conception of Family, and Racism. Our pronatalist ideology combines with a narrow, rigid, mystified conception of the family and with the pervasive racism of our society to make contract motherhood[23] more attractive to many would-be parents than alternatives, whether alternative routes to parenthood or alternatives to parenthood. In our pronatalist society, the desire for children is presumed to be universal, and parenthood is regarded as a normal and necessary developmental task. Those who do not conform are stigmatized, regarded as deviant, selfish, emotionally immature, psychologically maladjusted, sexually inadequate, and unhappy. Parenthood is considered not just a requirement for personal development and fulfillment, but also a religious, moral, and civic responsibility. The infertile not only face these attitudes in others, but, sharing this ideology, are subject to severe loss of self-esteem and potential psychopathology as a consequence of their inability to satisfy societal and personal expectations. The damage to self-esteem and risk of psychopathology are greatest for individuals whose self-identity is closer to the feminine stereotype than to androgeny or to the masculine stereotype. Although parenthood is considered normative for both men and women, it is considered more important for women.[24]

Thus pronatalism helps to explain not only why many people will go to great lengths to become parents, but also why infertile wives may feel especially inadequate and even guilty. As one woman put it:

> I felt guilty, lots of guilt. I felt that I had stuck my husband with this woman that would never give him the children that we had wanted. I felt asexual, I felt very neutered . . . I felt I had lost my womanness.[25]

Contract motherhood gives these wives the opportunity to allow their husbands to fulfill their biological and developmental "destinies" and to themselves become the social and in some cases the genetic mothers of their husbands' children. Pronatalism also seems to play a role in the motivation of contract mothers themselves. While most say they would not do it if they were not paid, many are moved by the real pain and the perceived emptiness of the lives of the infertile and feel good about being able to help fill that "void."[26]

When the social imperative of parenthood is combined with our society's narrow, mystified conception of the family, we can see why, despite the supposed universality of the desire or drive to procreate, pronatalism is actually restricted to married or stable heterosexual couples. Given the strength of pronatalist ideology, it is remarkable that, not only are single persons and those in homosexual or non-couple relationships, the different, the disabled, and the very poor not socially required to have children, *they* are regarded as selfish, immature, maladjusted, and irresponsible if they *do* have children. Those who don't fit the "normal, healthy" family picture are expected to suppress their desire to procreate for the sake of the (preferably nonexistent) children.[27]

Some feminists and others have welcomed alternative modes of reproduction as offering expanded procreative choices for persons not in so-called "traditional" families, and perhaps helping in the long run to broaden the societal definition of the family. I have serious reservations. First, although informal arrangements are carried out employing reproductive practices that do not require special equipment or expertise,[28] current professional practice is highly discriminatory. The fact that these restrictive views and attitudes appear to be widely shared by relevant professionals (reflected also in adoption policy) suggests that any regularizing of these practices would, in our current social climate, almost certainly reflect and reinforce rather than revise the rigid, narrow definition of the family.

My other reservations about welcoming alternative reproductive modes as enhancing the options of "nontraditional" families arise from concerns about contract motherhood (and also, to some extent, about AID (artificial insemination by donor)) whether commercial or unpaid, and whether the families are "traditional" or not. People tend to want a child of their *own*, with "own" having many different, if overlapping, meanings that are of differing importance to different people. One of the things it seems to mean is that they want any "extra" parents (sperm donor, egg donor, gestating mother) excluded from involvement in the life of the child. But I am not sure that anyone should be expected to renounce all knowledge of and contact with a child that is his or hers though not, in the exclusive sense, his or her *own*, or that a child should be denied knowledge of and contact with any of her or his parents. I recognize that some people may prefer anonymity and no contact, but I question, first, whether such a preference at a particular time can or should be binding for all time, and second, whether a child's right, need, or wish to know (or know about) his or her parent should be denied because of the parent's preference.

The reasons for the social parents wanting to exclude the "extras" are, no doubt many and varied. But, in the case of otherwise "traditional" families, a major factor seems to me to be a desire to make the family structure as much as possible like the mythical "normal" family consisting of breadwinning father, nurturing mother (now possibly also a career woman/super-mom), and their genetic offspring (preferably, first a boy, then a girl) conceived, carried, and born the old-fashioned way. Contract motherhood, if the contract mother is excluded, allows infertile couples to come as close as possible to the "norm."[29] The exclusive, possessive quality of family relationships involved in this conception of the family also contributes to a view of children as the *property* of their parents. And this view of children is conducive to the commodification of the child that is inherent in contract motherhood so long as the contract includes the alienation of the child from the birth mother. In a society with a broader, more open (and more realistic) conception of the family or of famil*ies* there might be far more openness about the use of alternative modes of reproduction and far less urgency to exclude anyone. The term "collaborative reproduction," which I find misleadingly euphemistic when applied to contract motherhood in our society, might more accurately describe the practice that might exist in that sort of social context. To the extent that it might exist, I am suggesting, it would not be the same practice.[30] On the other hand, in such a society, other ways of becoming parents or of being significantly involved with children, or *not* being significantly involved with children might be far more attractive, so that such a practice might not exist at all. Thus pronatalism and our narrow conception of the family contribute both to the attraction of contract motherhood and to some of its morally troubling features. In addition, I would argue, although I don't have time to do so here, that both pronatalism and the "traditional" conception of the family reinforce and are reinforced by the subordination of women.[31]

The attempt to make one's family conform to the "traditional" family picture has racial implications as well. First, despite the Cosby show and the Jeffersons, the family in this picture is, unless otherwise specified, white; that is the "norm." Just as only women are thought of as being of a particular gender (men are just regular persons) so only people of color are thought to have race. But to think that white people's identities are not fundamentally shaped by race in a pervasively racist society is a serious mistake. No one can completely escape internalizing the racism as well as the sexism of our society. Hence, the desire to conform to the traditional family picture combined with the importance of race in all of our identities result in a very restricted view of "adoptable" children. At the same time, one does not have to be a bigot to regard transracial adoption in a racist society as problematic.[32] Thus I am not placing responsibility for all the children of color who need homes on the doorsteps of infertile white couples. I believe we, as a society, all share that responsibility, and in many cases the best way to carry it out may not be to take the children out of their communities but to provide the communities with the requisite resources (child-care, medical care, programs for those with physical or psychological disabilities, jobs, housing, and so on) to give them homes.[33]

What I am saying is that racism in our society undeniably contributes to the fact that there are, on one hand many people who want desperately to be parents and on the other many children who need homes; yet it is difficult or impossible for them to fulfill each others' desires and needs. And this fact contributes to the pressure to create children by contract while other, existing, children languish in institutions or foster care, surely a morally troubling situation, even if one resists pointing fingers of blame. In a nonracist society with a more open conception of the family it is plausible to suppose that this situation would not exist.

Further, the desire for white infants plus the economic disparities associated with racial difference in our country and around the world, together with the feasibility of embryo transfer, make it all too likely that women of color will be hired to bear white babies.[34] Again, in a non-racist society, this prospect might not be alarming, but in our society it is. And again, the same features that make it so likely are those that make it alarming.[35]

Market-Oriented, Contractarian Conception of the Public Person. There is a sharp contrast between our societal conception of the family and its members and the relations among them on one hand and our conception of individuals and the relations among them in the larger world outside the family. We have inherited from liberal political philosophy the notion that there is a clear distinction between the "private sphere" of the family and the "public sphere" of the marketplace and political life. The family is a "haven in a heartless world" and although in it "each man is king," it is the domain of women who provide nurture and sustenance to weary breadwinners and prepare the next generation for their appointed roles. The wife/mother is thought of as emotional, physical, dependent, and essentially self-less. She lives for and through her husband and children.[36] By contrast, the public individual, the "normal healthy adult" is thought to be essentially rational (not physical and emotional) and *in*dependent. Free, equal, rational, autonomous individuals are thought to have no essential connections to one another. Each seeks to promote his or her own interests or conception of the good, and relations among these agents are voluntary, contractual ones.

Now a simple and inadequate feminist view (made even more simplistic here, with apologies) is that, if women are subordinated and stunted in their wife/mother role in the family, what they have to do is get out into the "public" world and learn to be more like men: independent, competitive, assertive, self-confident, and so on.[37] But neither of these conceptions, the dependent, emotional, nurturant, self-less wife/mother nor the independent, rational, competitive, market individual is either an attractive or a realistic conception of a person, whether man or woman. Yet contract mother-hood, paradoxically and incoherently, combines the worst aspects of each. The disembodied, rationalistic, market-oriented conception of persons encourages us to think of our bodies and our physical capacities as property, appropriate for sale or rental in the market. Thus, women are seen as more autonomous if they recognize and exploit their marketable capacities that were hitherto exercised for free. They can rationally decide not to become emotionally involved, and even if they do, they should be able to honor a commitment made in a cooler moment. (Like much of traditional Western moral theory, this view denies the moral significance of the emotions and of embodiment.) On the other hand, the contract mother is often seen (and often sees herself) as making the ultimate sacrifice: she is self-less; she erases herself. In the words of one contract mother, "I'm only an incubator."[38] The rational, independent, self-interested market individual dissolves into the nurturant, subordinate, self-effacing, invisible woman. Does contract motherhood offer women increased self-determination and economic opportunity or increased subordination and exploitation? Let us examine the issue of exploitation.

EXPLOITATION

There is one sense of the verb "exploit" that means simply "to make use of; utilize; turn to account."[39] We shall not be concerned with this first sense. There is a second sense: "to make *unethical* use of for one's own advantage or profit; turn selfishly or unfairly to one's own account." This is the sense intended in the charge that contract motherhood is exploitative.[40] A plausible candidate for at least a partial account of unethical use of *persons* is, of course, Kant's second formulation of the Categorical Imperative: it is morally inappropriate ever to treat persons merely as means and not also as ends in themselves. I take it that many, like me, who do not accept, or even understand, much else of Kantian ethics find this principle compelling. Still, among people who subscribe to the principle, there can be disagreement as to whether specific actions, attitudes, or practices conform to or violate it. But perhaps we can identify some fairly common features of exploitation of persons, in the hope that they will be at least widely agreed to.

Exploiting other persons often involves turning to one's own advantage the situations of persons who are vulnerable in one or more respects, whether economically, socially, or psychologically. Thus, although various forms of economic exploitation, such as usury, underpayment of workers by employers,[41] and overcharging unwary customers, are prominent instances of exploitation, morally inappropriate use of persons can take noneconomic forms as well.[42]

Thus exploitation may take place along several different dimensions (economic, social, psychological) either alone or in combination. There can be various degrees or levels of vulnerability along each of these dimensions, and various degrees or levels of advantage taken along each. The severity of exploitation depends on all of these factors.[43] A person or group may be exploited simultaneously by one or more other persons and/or groups in the same or different ways. Further, although it may be more reprehensible if done deliberately, exploitation need not be consciously intended by the exploiter. By the same token, the exploited need not necessarily *feel* exploited.

Let us now distinguish two forms of commercial contract motherhood arrangements, *brokered* and *paid private* forms, and ask, for whom do issues of exploitation arise under each of these forms, and how?

I propose that, in brokered contract motherhood, the broker exploits the contract mother at least economically (by taking advantage of the vulnerability resulting from her limited financial resources and security), but often also socially (by taking advantage of the vulnerability resulting from the restricted social roles and resources available to one in her combined gender and economic status),[44] and psychologically. The psychological exploitation can involve taking advantage of one or more of several possible vulnerabilities, for example, those resulting from the impacts on self-esteem of societal attitudes toward women and the economically insecure. As mentioned in the previous section, internalized ideologies of pronatalism and feminine altruism can constitute additional aspects of psychological vulnerability, especially for women whose other avenues to social recognition and achievement are extremely restricted. Further, significant percentages of women who apply to be contract mothers report feeling the need to "work through" previous experiences of loss through abortion, miscarriage, or relinquishment of a child for adoption. (I have seen nothing to indicate that the experience of losing yet another child through contract motherhood would be likely to help such a woman come to terms with her previous loss.) Finally, some interviews with contract mothers indicate that the attention they receive during the pregnancy from the intended receiving parents is a major motivating factor.[45] This suggests that a need for familial connections moves some women to engage in contract motherhood. These women are then subjected to a double loss upon the birth of the child, being cut off from both the child and the receiving parents.[46]

In addition, I contend that, in brokered contract motherhood, the broker exploits the intended receiving parent(s) economically and psychologically by taking advantage of the vulnerability resulting from the pain and impact on self-esteem of the experience of infertility in a pronatalist society with a narrow conception of the family. Further, in both brokered and paid private forms, the receiving parent(s) exploit the contract mother economically, and often in some or all of the additional social and psychological ways outlined above in connection with commercial brokers.

Finally, I suggest that all the adults involved (broker, if any, receiving parent(s) and contract mother) exploit the contracted-for infant by treating her or him as a mere means to their own ends.[47] The purposes of the parties may be legitimate: for example, on the part of the broker, to make a good living; on the part of the receiving parent(s) to have an infant to raise; on the part of the contract mother, to pay college tuition for herself or her other children, to work through feelings of loss, to experience familial connections, to "give the gift of experience life." But legitimate purposes do not justify the use of another person solely as a means to achieve those purposes.[48]

Let us now consider some likely objections to the case outlined so far against contract motherhood on grounds of exploitation.[49] One common objection points to the fact that there are many dull, demeaning, risky, low-paid jobs in our society, many of them more obviously exploitative than contract motherhood, so why single out and ban the latter? But the fact that there exist in our society many exploitative relationships, including many jobs that ought not to exist in anything like their current form, is no reason to welcome, or even permit, the introduction of a new highly exploitative practice if we can prevent it.

Another objection denies that the practice is really exploitative. There are those who argue that, not only is it a boon to the infertile and others who might choose this reproductive option,[50] it opens up potentially beneficial, even liberating, opportunities for women.[51] They argue that it is inconsistent, even hypocritical, to favor denying this option as long as there are women who would prefer it to the other options available to them. Some suspect that it is only because women have the market for this opportunity cornered that there is so much sentiment for restricting or banning it.[52]

I agree that it would be hypocritical to oppose contract motherhood on grounds of exploitation if one were not at the same time actively committed to improving the circumstances of those for whom it would currently be a relatively attractive alternative.[53] Further, as I have acknowledged above, it is a judgment call as to whether contract motherhood does, or would if widely practiced, open new opportunities for women and new possibilities for family structures or, on the contrary, serve to reinforce existing roles for and attitudes toward women and the existing narrow conception of the family. In my judgment, the latter is far more likely.[54] I am acutely aware that people on both sides of the issue readily dismiss optimistic or pessimistic speculation by their opponents, while invariably engaging in it themselves. I see no alternative. We must concern ourselves with what kind of a society we are and would become if different policies were adopted, and there is some irreducible uncertainty involved.

Some proponents deny that even current commercially brokered contracts exploit contract mothers.[55] This position is indefensible. Under the terms of Mary Beth Whitehead's (standard) contract drawn up by the Infertility Center of New York, she was to receive $10,000 upon delivery of a live child. That is less than half the minimum hourly wage for the time involved in a normal full-term pregnancy. She received no compensation for unsuccessful inseminations; she would receive no compensation if she miscarried in the first four months, and $1000 after four months in the event of miscarriage, stillbirth, or abortion mandated by William Stern.[56]

Other proponents grant that currently the practice often is highly exploitative, but they argue that appropriate regulation could make it morally acceptable.[57] They propose requiring adequate compensation for all of the time involved and risks incurred. This requirement would more than double the minimum amount payable to contract mothers, raising once again the issue of access: the more expensive the practice for the receiving parent(s), the smaller the privileged group who will be able to avail themselves of this choice. That one class will provide women to bear children exclusively for members of another class is ensured.[58]

Another issue raised by the job-upgrade approach is the concern that much higher pay would constitute an undue inducement for women of limited means thus rendering their consent less than fully voluntary.[59] It might be asked why this worry arises in this case and not, e.g., in those of domestic work, poultry work, retail sales, clerical work? I believe it clearly signals the recognition that to become a contract mother is an especially profound decision.[60] If decent pay would constitute an undue inducement, it appears that the job of contract mother cannot be offered on morally acceptable terms: it will involve either direct economic exploitation or undue inducement. Moreover, might not the going $10,000 be a large enough sum to someone in financially difficult or insecure circumstances to constitute an undue inducement?

There seems to me to be at least two additional problems with this approach. One involves the question whether any monetary fee can fairly compensate not only for the process of becoming pregnant, carrying, sustaining and nurturing life that is thus enabled to develop, and laboring and giving birth to a child, but also for relinquishing that child for life. Some kinds of jobs cannot be made good jobs, and a decent society won't countenance them even if there are people willing to do them. I suggest that contract motherhood is such a job.[61]

The second problem arises from the fact, as I see it, that part of what a contract mother does is sell her child. That poor women or families in our society should find themselves faced with the option of selling a child in order to provide food, shelter, or education to other family members is both morally and legally repugnant. This aspect of contract motherhood raises most emphatically the issues of class division and exploitation. It also raises the closely related issue of commodification, to which we now turn.

COMMODIFICATION

One way of treating people as mere means, and not as ends in themselves, is by treating them as commodities, things, property. Thus commodification of persons is, on the present account, a species of exploitation of persons.[62] I regard all commodification of persons, their capacities, and relationships as morally inappropriate. Commodities are things that are appropriately owned, exchanged, and consumed, used and used up, by persons.[63] Persons are not property; we are not the sorts of entities that can, morally speaking, be owned, even by ourselves. We *are* ourselves; we don't *own* ourselves. Thus, in some respects, contract motherhood is not, to my mind, different in kind, as regards the commodification of human capacities and activities, from other low-paid, highly exploitative forms of wage labor.[64]

How, then, would I respond to the following challenge: "All of us who have jobs commodify our physical, intellectual, nurturant, and/or other capacities and skills. What is so different about commodifying women's reproductive capacity?" My answer has four parts: (a) the difference is one of degree, not of kind;[65] (b) that people are inappropriately treated as commodities in some respects does not justify inappropriately treating them as commodities in other respects; (c) the commodification of women in our society goes far beyond that inherent in wage labor and both reflects and contributes to women's subordinate status, in particular, to the fact that women are not regarded and treated as whole persons; hence further commodification of women particularly should be resisted; and (d) women are not the only persons commodified by contract motherhood. Even if commodification of women's reproductive capacities is, or could be, morally and legally on a par with other forms of wage labor, commodification of contracted-for children is not. Here we have commodification of whole persons.

Commodification of the child in contract motherhood exacerbates commodification of the contract mother. For potential receiving parents will assess the suitability of applicants in terms of physical and other traits they hope will be passed on to the child.[66] Thus, not only are the woman's reproductive capacities on the market, her appearance (hair, eyes, nose, lips, skin tone, bone structure, height, weight, and so on), her eyesight, intelligence, talents, sense of humor and so forth are all actually or potentially on the market, valued not for the contribution they make to the person she is, but for their possible incorporation into the product of her reproductive activity.

With regard to that product, the child, most proponents of contract motherhood deny that the practice involves baby-selling.[67] These denials employ a variety of arguments and strategies, none of which seem to me successful. One approach is definitional. Here is one version: Argument (1) "We don't regard persons as property; As we cannot sell what we do not own, we cannot be selling babies."[68] But from the fact that X cannot morally and/or legally sell Y, it doesn't follow that X does not in fact sell Y. If it did, no one could be convicted of selling stolen property.[69] A second version of the definitional approach is this: Argument(2) "The receiving father (typically, so far anyway) is the genetic father of the child, and he cannot buy what is already his."[70] But this argument either equivocates between genetic relationship and ownership or illicitly infers the latter from the former.[71] Perhaps not surprisingly, these two definitional arguments taken together assert that mothers cannot, while fathers can and do own their children, an accurate description of the legal situation in the not very distant past.

There are many other arguments. Space permits only the briefest runthrough. Argument (3) "Children aren't treated as property or slaves in contract motherhood arrangements because, once the child is turned over, there are restrictions on treatment of children that apply to receiving parents as to all other parents."[72] But there were restrictions on the treatment of slaves, and there are restrictions on the treatment of pets and laboratory animals. Such restrictions do indicate that these creatures are regarded somewhat differently from other commodities, but not that they are not property, not bought and sold.

Argument (4) "If there is commodification of children, it is at most 'incomplete commodification,' for the receiving parents cannot sell the child in turn.'"[73] But if there is nothing wrong with the first sale, what would be wrong with the next?[74] If the answer is that second sales must be blocked in order to avoid opening up a general market in children, we need to ask, if a market in contract children is ok, what would be wrong with a general market in children? If the difference is that the contract children are sold as newborns, so are not bonded to the seller and won't suffer insecurity about being sold in the future, then if the turn-around is quick enough, the same could apply to sale by the receiving parent(s). And it would apply to infants who are relinquished for adoption, whose birthparents are not now legally permitted to be paid for relinquishing them. Argument (5) "Contract motherhood is different from commissioned adoption (where a woman contracts for a fee to conceive and bear a child for adoption by person(s) not genetically related to the child).[75] The latter is producing a baby for sale; the former is not." But would we then permit contract motherhood for couples where the woman is infertile (or chooses not to bear a child for medical, genetic, or other reasons) but not where the man is also sterile (or chooses not to genetically father a child, whether for genetic reasons or, say, because he does not want to have a genetic relationship to the child that his partner cannot share) and not for single persons who cannot (or choose not to) be genetic parents? This seems arbitrary and discriminatory, and ensures that the practice would reinforce, rather than open up our restricted conception of the family. Further, it seems to rely on the second definitional argument, above, that a genetically related father does not buy what is already his.[76]

Argument (6) "The 'commodification' of children involved in contract motherhood is not actual, but symbolic. Dislike of a practice on symbolic grounds is not sufficiently weighty to justify restricting the choices of those who would engage in the practice."[77] But the commodification involved in most actual contract motherhood cases seems to me to be entirely literal. All or a major portion of the fee is paid only when the child is actually turned over and a waiver of parental rights signed. There *is* potential *symbolic* commodification of children (and women) associated with contract motherhood, in addition to the actual commodification, in that a socially accepted, widespread practice that actually commodifies some children (and women) symbolically commodifies all children (and women).[78]

Argument (7) "The practice *could be* structured so that it involves payment only for insemination, conception (or embryo implantation), gestation, and birth. Payments would not be contingent on the birthmother relinquishing the child, and there would be no additional payment if and when she did so."[79] But now suppose the birthmother decides to keep the child (and the money, as she is entitled to do). The intended receiving parent(s) may remind themselves that she did, after all, perform the service contracted for, so they have no complaint. Will she get good recommendations for future employment in this line of work, or will she be discriminated against for something that purportedly had nothing to do with the job? Perhaps careful psychological screening could minimize such occurrences, but what is the justification for screening a potential employee for a characteristic (namely, being likely to turn over the child) that is purportedly not job related? In truth, the restructuring of the payments changes the form, but not the basic nature and purpose of the transaction.

Also, in the case just considered, what service has the birthmother performed and for whom? She has gestated and given birth to a child, whom she will now raise. No doubt that involves work. But if it is a service, it is the same service every "natural" mother performs, and if it is *for* anyone, it appears to be for the future child (and/or the community, perhaps). To treat gestation and childbirth as a service that individual women provide to individual men (ordinarily for free or in exchange for full or partial economic support) is to perpetuate a patriarchal conception of the relationships among men, women, and children according to which women bear and raise children *for* men. Rather, I believe we should be promoting a conception of motherhood as something that women who do it do on their *own account* (though not necessarily on their own) because they find it fulfilling and worthwhile.

Argument (8) "Contract motherhood involves the sale, not of babies, but of the parental rights of the birthmother." But the concept of parental rights reflects recognition of and respect for a fundamental human relationship. To commodify parental rights is, in effect to commodify the parent-child relationship. In my view, that, too, is morally inappropriate. Morally, and I believe, as a matter of law, parental rights are not transferrable, either as gift or as sale.[80] Moreover, it is not clear that a meaningful distinction can be made between sale of a child and sale of parental rights in relation to the child. If I sell you my car, I sell you my property rights in that car. And part of what makes them property rights is that I *can* sell them. Hence, viewing parental rights as saleable assimilates them to property rights and children to property. Further, if parental rights are saleable, why not at any time?

I do not believe commercial contract motherhood can avoid commodification of women, children, and the parent-child relationship. Some proponents of the practice would reply, "Whether you call it commodification or not, you haven't shown what is wrong with it. Don't give us rhetoric about respect for persons as ends in themselves; show us the harm involved."[81]

First, individuals can be wronged without being harmed.[82] I believe that buying and selling persons wrongs them even if it does not demonstrably harm them. There are other ways in which individuals can be wronged without being harmed, for example, by being placed at substantial and unnecessary risk of harm. Whether or not a potentially harmful practice is wrong depends in part on the nature of the harms involved, of the benefits involved, and on the distribution of harms and benefits. All benefits of contract motherhood accrue to adult participants in the practice, whereas the contracted-for children bear perhaps the greatest risk of harm. The adult in the most vulnerable and exploitable situation, the contract mother, and her family also bear a substantial risk of harm. The kinds of harm I have in mind can be grouped under the general heading of alienation.

ALIENATION

When a whole person is treated by others as a commodity, to be owned, used, bought, and sold by them, not a party to the transaction, with no choice or voice in the decision, her or his personhood is denied and undermined. The person is, of course, still a person, but it must be extraordinarily difficult to develop and maintain a sense of oneself as a full person. I don't think we have any adequate understanding of the implications of this kind of commodification for self-concept, self-respect, and ability to connect with others. I know I don't. One way to gain insight here would be to study the lives, experiences, self-concepts and relationships of slaves and former slaves. I do not mean to suggest that the lives of contract children are or will be like the lives of slaves. Such a suggestion would be doubly outrageous: it would both belittle the many evils of slavery and malign receiving parents of contract babies. But when we consider the potential risks to contract children (and mothers) of the fact of commodification, I do not believe that the slave experience can be dismissed as entirely irrelevant.[83]

In addition, of course, the experience of adopted children must be taken into account. The feelings of abandonment, insecurity, and incomplete identity some adopted children experience are forms of alienation that must inform our assessment of the risks of harm imposed on contract children.[84] (Some AID children have also experienced difficulty dealing with their origins.)[85]

Some proponents of contract motherhood urge that surely these children will feel especially loved and wanted, knowing that their receiving parents went to such lengths to get them. This confidence is not borne out in the adoption case. The knowledge that one was planned and conceived to be relinquished by one's birthmother, does not seem likely to be more welcome or less apt to give rise to feelings of abandonment, insecurity, and incomplete identity than the thought that one's birthmother relinquished one reluctantly, as in the usual adoption case. Thus, in my view, commodification of children is wrong not only because it fails to respect them as ends in themselves but also because it imposes on them, unnecessarily and without their consent, significant risk of harm.[86]

We must also consider the potential alienating affects on other members of a contract mother's family in their relationship to her and the process of her pregnancy and childbirth, in their relationship to the fetus she carries and the baby to which she gives birth, and in their conceptions of themselves, their sense of wholeness, security, and connectedness within the family.[87] There are risks of harm here as well. And we must consider the potential alienation of the contract mother herself.

When we commodify aspects of ourselves, renting out or selling our human capacities, our bodies or portions thereof, we are said to fragment ourselves. We temporarily or permanently alienate aspects or portions of our persons. So it is when a worker sells her capacity to work, her labor power; so it is when a woman rents out her womb or her reproductive capacity.

This fragmentation is necessary if there is to be a self remaining to collect the rent or enjoy the proceeds of the sale. Otherwise, our whole self, our personhood, would be alienated in the transaction, as in indentured servitude or selling oneself into slavery. But the person or person-fragment that remains is diminished, and is further undermined when aspects of her self now in the domain of another are used to gain further control over her person.[88] So it is and will be when commercial brokers and receiving parents seek to monitor and control every aspect of the lives and medical care of contract mothers to get full benefit of the reproductive services they have bought and to ensure an undamaged, quality product, at the same time disempowering the woman, demeaning her personhood, her dignity, self-determination, and bodily integrity.

In fact, the fragmentation that permits a substantial self to remain sovereign, so to speak, while aspects of the person are commodified is largely illusory.[89] A contract mother rents her womb or her reproductive capacity or sells her reproductive services. But a woman is pregnant with her whole self: physical, mental, and emotional. Her entire body is involved: nausea, swollen ankles, aching back, compressed organs, enlarged breasts, shortness of breath, and so on. If the fetus needs more calcium than her diet provides, the calcium comes from her teeth and bones. She is consciously aware of the progress of her pregnancy. She feels the fetus move inside her. But, as a contract mother, she is not to become emotionally involved with the life that is developing within her, not just contained by her, but an integral part of her. She contracts not to form a relationship with her fetus, and for her own good she had better not form one. Yet, as a conscientious contract mother, she is expected and expects herself to take every care for the wellbeing of the fetus, to be mindful of its needs and vulnerabilities just as she would a future child she intended to raise herself.

The separateness or separability of body, mind, and emotions presupposed by these contractual terms and expectations reflects the fundamentally fragmented nature of the conception of persons prevalent in our culture. The combination of attitudes toward herself, her pregnancy and her fetus that contract motherhood requires of a woman impresses me as perhaps the profoundest possible form of self-alienation. These attitudes are called for because, upon the birth of her child, she is expected to alienate that baby from herself completely and irrevocably.[90] These forms of alienation, I contend, are not only potentially harmful to contract mothers, but also pose significant threats to their autonomy, and ultimately to the autonomy of all women in our society.

AUTONOMY

The conceptions of autonomy most prevalent in our culture presuppose the separation of mind, body, and emotions, the fragmentation of personhood, remarked just above. The autonomous self is conceived either as a purely rational self, with body and emotions irrelevant to its nature and to its autonomous decisions, or as divided against itself, with rationality winning out over base physicality and unruly emotion. In addition, autonomy so conceived presupposes separation from other persons, independence, unless a relationship is voluntarily entered into by mutual consent.[91]

Such conceptions of autonomy seem to figure in the arguments of those proponents of contract motherhood who contend that prohibition or serious restriction of the practice would violate the autonomy of women. But these conceptions of autonomy are inadequate. Many feminists (and others) criticize such conceptions, and the liberal, contractarian moral theories in which they prominently figure, on grounds that can be labeled individualism, rationalism, voluntarism, and egalitarianism. The charge of individualism points to the realities of human interdependence and socialization as incompatible with the received conceptions of autonomy. The charge of rationalism questions the separation and privileging of the " purely" rational or intellectual over the emotional and embodied. The charge of voluntariness points to the pervasiveness and moral significance of relationships that are not chosen. And the charge of egalitarianism notes the pervasiveness and moral significance of relationships that are essentially unequal.

These criticisms must be taken seriously. We cannot, I think, deny that there can be nonintellectual springs of autonomous insight and action; we often do and should rely on feelings or gut reactions that we cannot even articulate, much less justify. We do not (or should not) want to say that the only autonomous response to non-voluntary relationships is to avoid or extricate ourselves from them. Nor can we pretend that all relationships in which autonomous persons engage are or ought to be among adult peers who are equal in all relevant respects. I am one among many feminists and others currently working to develop a more adequate notion of autonomy, one that would not be subject to these criticisms. Since the job is far from done, if it can be done at all, its full implications for the contract motherhood debate cannot yet be drawn. But a few already seem clear.

For example, some feminists believe that respect for women's autonomy requires that women be able to make, in advance, a valid, enforceable contract to relinquish a child that is not yet conceived. Any other policy, they fear, would reinforce the notion that women are incapable of responsible decisionmaking.[92] One feminist ethicist responds, writing of Mary Beth Whitehead's change of mind:

> She decided not to surrender her baby in part because of bodily experiences. She gave birth; she saw her newborn baby; she breast fed the infant. These physical experiences were among the factors that led Whitehead to conclude that she would not give her baby up. . . . Whitehead's behavior seems to confirm misogynist western cultural traditions. Women's perceived deeper ties to their bodies have been used as the rationale for disqualifying women as moral agents. . . . However, the solution to this threat to women's standing as moral agents is not to insist that birth mothers be compelled to honor the contractual promises they made prior to birth. . . . Rather, feminists and others need to challenge the view that disembodied, rational judgment is the moral ideal.[93]

I would add that the emotional response to physically seeing, holding, and nursing the infant, resulting in the realization that "I cannot sell my baby!'' constitutes a moral insight and a moral imperative. To hold a woman to a decision made prior to this experience would be to deny, not uphold, her moral autonomy.

Other proponents of contract motherhood agree that any decision as profound as this one must be revocable up until the time of actual performance.[94] They advocate a waiting period after the birth of the child during which the birthmother may change her mind. They maintain that respect for the autonomy of potential contract mothers and for the procreative choice of potential receiving parents requires that we permit the practice with this proviso.

I doubt that an adequate conception of autonomy will support this position, but I cannot demonstrate that here. However, if I am correct about the commodification of contract children, I don't have to. Neither respect for autonomy nor respect for procreative choice can require that we permit the buying and selling of nonconsenting persons.

Earlier, I alluded to another threat to the autonomy of contract mothers. Presumably, self-determination in one's daily activities and in decisions concerning one's medical care and bodily integrity will be central features in any acceptable account of autonomy. Contractual provisions or judicial decisions that allow receiving parents and/or brokers to monitor and control the daily lives and medical decisions of contract mothers for the protection of the fetus would seriously undermine their autonomy. Some proponents of the practice actually advocate that such provisions be required. Others, however, recognize both direct violation of the autonomy of contract mothers and by extension of the policies, an increased threat to the autonomy of all pregnant women and even all fertile women.[95] They suggest that contractual clauses of the sort in question be explicitly prohibited by statute. So motherhood contracts would be legal, but they could not contain any restrictions on the contract mother's activities or medical care nor any provisions for mandatory testing, monitoring, or treatment of the fetus during the pregnancy.[96] I do not think this approach is viable for a couple of reasons.

First, other employees are often required not to smoke or drink, for example, while on the job. What could justify prohibiting such restrictions in the case of the job of contract mother? If, as proponents assert, it would be paternalistic of government to prohibit contracts for motherhood, would it not be paternalistic to prohibit contractual provisions concerning the employee's behavior? (Of course, there is the difference that there are no rest breaks or off periods during pregnancy, so one cannot go out for a smoke. But the woman knows that when she signs the contract, so why shouldn't she and the other parties be free to include any terms allowable under existing labor law?) I don't see how statutory prohibition of such restrictive clauses would hold up.

Second, it might be that courts would not, in the end, uphold contract provisions or judicial orders requiring invasive medical procedures without the actual current consent of the contract mother. However, recent decisions in cases not involving contract motherhood are not reassuring, and as I suggested above, such decisions would be far more likely in cases where intended receiving parent(s) were seeking such orders for the protection of "their" future baby. Here again, the unequal social and economic resources available to the parties would be an important factor.

Thus, respect for women's autonomy does not entail permitting the practice of contract motherhood. Indeed, the practice poses several serious threats to women's autonomy.

CONCLUSION

Taken together, the considerations, concerns and arguments offered above persuade me that, in our existing and foreseeable social context, the practice of commercial contract motherhood is morally and politically unacceptable. Moreover, no system of regulation can adequately address all of the compelling objections to the practice. For if my view of commercial contract motherhood as baby selling is correct, no statute or regulation can change the nature of the transaction or make it morally acceptable. That objection aside, we saw repeatedly above that attempts to address one sort of objection by regulatory means inevitably exacerbated other concerns. For example, to address the exploitation objection by mandating higher pay for contract mothers would increase concerns both about the money constituting an undue inducement and about the high cost limiting access to the most affluent in a class stratified society. Addressing the exploitation and undue inducement objections by rejecting poor women as contract mothers discriminates against them, violates their autonomy, and denies what proponents insist is a relatively attractive occupational option to those in greatest need. Attempts to reduce the risks to all parties of the pains and possible lasting harms of broken or regretted agreements by mandating screening and counseling of potential contract mothers and intended receiving parents raise concerns about violation of autonomy and reproductive freedom and about discrimination against potential receiving parents not in traditional heterosexual couples. Attempting to prevent contract mothers from losing autonomy by restricting or prohibiting contractual provisions concerning their behavior while pregnant are themselves subject to the charge of paternalism and are unlikely to be legally sustainable. Further, administering any regulatory scheme would entail substantial expense, and it is difficult to see how government could justify expenditures to facilitate or regulate the creation of genetically related infants for those who want them, while existing children in need of homes might be placed if the resources were used to make it economically feasible for willing persons to take them in. In addition, if such resources were spent on the measures needed for *prevention* of infertility, they would more equitably benefit all who want to be parents, not just those who can afford the commercial fees (and, as we saw above, would serve other pressing social needs, as well.)

I conclude that commercial contract motherhood should be expressly prohibited. Commercial brokering should be a criminal offense. Paid private contracts should be void and unenforceable, and the parties subject to civil penalties.[97] Unpaid private agreements can be carried out legally under existing adoption law, but government should avoid promoting or endorsing the practice. (If it is carried out among strangers, the complete alienation of birthmother from child is still likely to be a common feature of the practice. Without governmental facilitation, it is more likely to be carried out among family and friends with some ongoing relationship possible.)[98] Based on the degree of actual involvement with the fetus during pregnancy, there should be a strong presumption at the time of birth and for at least the first three months in favor of birthmother's custody in case of dispute, whether or not the birthmother is also the genetic mother. Finally, the measures outlined above for prevention of infertility should receive high social priority.

ENDNOTES

1. I avoid the terms "surrogacy" and "surrogate motherhood" because I hold that a woman who bears a child is a mother, not a surrogate or substitute anything. (Note, though, that I use the indefinite article: I am not contending that she is *the only* or *the real* mother, to the exclusion of possibly different genetic and/or social mothers.) I shall use the term "contract motherhood" and understand it broadly enough to cover all arrangements, whether formal or informal, paid or not, in which a woman agrees to become pregnant, bear a child and relinquish the child to another person or persons. That other person or persons will be called the "receiving parent(s)," leaving it open how many they are, whether they are of the same or different sex, and whether one, two, or none of them is a genetic parent of the contracted-for baby.

2. Or, in the case of libertarianism, to reduce the latter to the former (see, e.g., Robert Nozick, *Anarchy, State and Utopia* (New York: Basic Books, 1974)).

3. e.g., Rosalind P. Petchesky, *Abortion and Woman's Choice: The State, Sexuality, and Reproductive Freedom*, (Boston: Northeastern University Press) 1984, especially Chapters 8 and 9; Alison M. Jaggar, *Feminist Politics and Human Nature*, (Totowa, NJ: Rowman & Allanheld) 1983, especially pp. 39-48, 123-163, 185-203, 303-346. As Jaggar notes, socialist feminism draws upon both Marxist and radical feminist critiques of liberalism as well as upon radical feminism's critique of traditional Marxism.

4. Similarly, societies, social groups and subgroups, are constituted by, but not reducible to, their individual members. For the individuals are who and what they are largely in virtue of the natures and structures of, and relations among, the social groups to which they belong. (cf. Marx, *Theses on Feurbach # VI: the human essence as the ensemble of social relations*.) None of this is to say that individuals and their actions are mere passive results of their contexts.

5. There are overlaps here, but I do not want to conflate the two categories, nor do I want here to get into trying to sort out and characterize all the varieties of feminism.

6. See, for example, Phyllis Chessler, *Sacred Bond: The Legacy of Baby M*, (New York: Random House) 1988.

7. cf. Nadine Taub "Feminist Tensions & the Concept of Motherhood" in Joan Offerman-Zuckerberg, ed., *Gender in Transition* (New York: Plenum Medical, 1989); and "Surrogacy: Sorting Through the Alternatives" *Berkeley Women's Law Journal* 4, No. 2 (1989-90) pp. 285-299.

8. Compare the other untenable pairs of alternatives (double binds) women

confront in our society, for example, virgin or whore; frigid or insatiable; clinging vine or castrating bitch.

9. To say that gestation is unique is not to privilege it relative to other endeavors. It is a fact that this is something that, so far, only women can do; in that way, it is unique. It is different from, but not necessarily more or less valuable, creative, spiritual, natural, human, animal, transcendent or immanent than any other activity for which women (or men) may have the capacity and in which they may choose to engage.

10. Indeed, in the first case to receive widespread public attention, that of "Baby M", Elizabeth Stern, the intended receiving mother, was presumably not infertile, but had decided not to bear a child because she believed that she had multiple sclerosis and that pregnancy and childbirth would likely exacerbate her condition.

11. Others argue that there should be no restrictions on who can be a party to such a contract, just as there are no controls on who can become a parent by means of sexual intercourse.

12. U. S. Congress, Office of Technology Assessment, *Infertility: Medical and Social Choices*, OTA-BA-358 (Washington, DC: U.S. Government Printing Office, May 1988). (Hereafter, OTA Rpt.) The Report cites 3 national demographic surveys: the 1965 National Fertility Study, the 1976 National Survey of Family Growth (NSFG) Cycle II; and the 1982 NSFG Cycle III. In addition, NSFG Cycle IV was conducted between January and July 1988, but the results are not yet available (OTA Rpt. pp. 50-51).

13. This figure is based on a definition of infertility as inability to conceive after one year of sexual intercourse without contraception (OTA Rpt. p. 35). Many couples who satisfy this definition will conceive later without medical intervention (OTA Rpt. p. 52).

14. Nadine Taub, "Surrogacy: A Preferred Treatment for Infertility?" *Law, Medicine & Health Care* 16 (Spring 1988) pp. 89-95 (Causes of Infertility, pp. 90-93.) In addition to inability to conceive and carry a pregnancy to term, we must be concerned with infant mortality and morbidity resulting from lack of prenatal and neonatal care. U.S. rates of maternal and infant mortality are far higher than other industrialized nations. One half million (15%) US women who give birth each year have no health insurance, private or public. Taub, "Surrogacy: Preferred Treatment?" pp. 92-93.

15. Taub, "Surrogacy, Preferred Treatment?" p. 90.

16. In all classes, domestic work and childrearing are regarded as primarily women's responsibilities (though more affluent women can often hire other women to do some of it). Some proponents and most opponents of contract motherhood see it as yet another way in which more privileged women can relegate some of "their" responsibilities to other women who have fewer options and opportunities.

17. Note, by the way, that if a fetus is deemed a person from the moment of conception (or at any time during pregnancy), the role of the gestating mother in

the creation/development of the person it may become is completely denied (or correspondingly diminished).

18. See Eleanor J. Bader, " 'Father's Rights' — What's Next?," *Guardian: Independent Radical Newsweekly*, June 1, 1988; Linda Kahn, "Fetus Died; Mother Prosecuted," *New Directions for Women*, 16 (January-February 1987); Jennifer Terry, "The Body Invaded: Medical Surveillance of Women as Reproducers," *Socialist Review*, 19 (July-September 1989) pp. 13-43.

19. In addition to articles cited in the preceding note, see Christine Overall, *Ethics and Human Reproduction: A Feminist Analysis* (Boston: Allen & Unwin, 1987) and Emily Martin, *The Woman in the Body: A Cultural Analysis of Reproduction* (Boston: Beacon Press, 1987). This tendency is displayed in the New Jersey Supreme Court's ruling *In the Matter of Baby M*, (A-39-87), note 13, pp. 63-4, in which the Court mentions with apparent approval decisions requiring a nonconsenting pregnant woman to undergo a blood transfusion and another to undergo a caesarean section "because unborn child's interests outweighed mother's right against bodily intrusion."

20. Peter H. Schuck, "Some Reflections on the *Baby M* Case," *The Georgetown Law Journal*, 76:1793-1810, p. 1802.

21. One woman, who later fought for custody of the twins she bore on contract, reported that she decided to agree to the arrangement in order to earn enough money so that she and her husband could afford to have a child themselves by donor artificial insemination because her husband was sterile. (This case raises issues of exploitation of poor and working class women and issues of such women's access to reproductive alternatives available to the more affluent, to be discussed below.) Laurie Yates (as told to Jean Libman Block), "Don't Take My Babies from Me!" *Good Housekeeping*, March 1988.

22. Proponents suggest that an appropriate response to these concerns might be, not to eliminate the job, but to regulate and upgrade it: require that payments be more generous and that all of the time put in be compensated. This proposal will be discussed below.

23. And artificial insemination by donor (AID). Many proponents of contract motherhood point to AID as a widely accepted practice and argue that contract motherhood should be seen as analogous. Aside from the important disanalogies, in that sperm "donation" requires far less involvement of the "donor" even than egg "donation" (which requires an invasive procedure) and nothing comparable to gestation and childbirth, contract motherhood has prompted me to rethink the easy acceptance of these practices involving the sale of genetic material for the creation of a child who will be irrevocably cut off from at least one of her or his genetic parents.

24. Steven E. Perkel, "Infertility, Self-Esteem, Sex-Role Identity, Psychopathology, and the Social Meaning of Parenthood," Presentation to Task Force of Reproductive Practices of the New Jersey Commission on Ethical and Legal Problems in the Delivery of Health Care (hereafter, NJ Bioethics Comm TF), June 1, 1988. See also Deborah Gerson, "Infertility and the Construction of Desperation," *Socialist Review*, 19 (July-September 1989) pp. 45-64.

25. Christine Overall, *Ethics and Human Reproduction*, p. 142.

26. Adrienne Asche and Anne Reichman, NJ Bioethics Commission staff report to Task Force.

27. cf. Michelle Stanworth, "Reproductive Technologies and the Deconstruction of Motherhood," in *Reproductive Technologies: Gender, Motherhood and Medicine*, ed. Michelle Stanworth (Minneapolis: University of Minnesota Press, 1987).

28. Insemination can be accomplished, for example, by means of a turkey baster or, of course, sexual intercourse.

29. Often the rationale for this quest on the part of receiving parents, adoptive parents, and parents of children conceived by AID is (a) that having "extra" parents in the picture would make childrearing decisions hopelessly complicated because of potential disagreements among the several parents, and (b) that it would introduce potential rivals for a child's affections. This rationale seems to ignore the fact that, even in the mythical "normal" family, there is more than one parent (both of whom have legal standing to make decisions on the child's behalf, which would not necessarily be the case for the "extra" parent). These two parents may disagree about important childrearing decisions and/or compete for a child's affections. In addition, there are generally an assortment of grandparents, aunts and uncles, child-care workers, teachers, close friends and neighbors any of whom may seek to participate in childrearing decisions and/or become (or be viewed) as rivals for a child's affections. When we consider as well the variety of blended families, joint custody arrangements, single parent families, gay and lesbian parent families, and so on, the notion of a "normal" family in which childrearing decisions are uncomplicated and affections unrivaled appears both unrealistic and an inadequate basis for severing all contact. (The threat to lesbian mothers of losing custody to an AID father is, however, very real in our heterosexist, patriarchal society.) There is an encouraging trend toward more openness in adoption; see Jeanne Warren Lindsay, *Open Adoption: A Caring Option* (Buena Park, CA: Morning Glory Press, 1987).

30. According to anthropologist Catherine A. Lutz in *Unnatural Emotions* (Chicago: University of Chicago Press, 1988), on the Micronesian atoll of Ifaluk and neighboring islands, there is a practice that somewhat resembles, but is importantly different from each of the U.S. practices of adoption, (non-commercial) contract motherhood, and the informal extended family system in the African American community described by Carol Stack in *All Our Kin* (New York: Harper & Row, 1975). Nearly every household on Ifaluk has "adopted" children (Lutz, p. 132) and 40% of all children over five years of age are "adopted" (Lutz, p. 161). Children are offered for "adoption" by families with both parents living, for it is considered an act of generosity and caring to offer a child to a couple who "needs" one. Common reasons for "adoption" include " barren" marriages, the death of a child, and the desire to have children of both genders (important because of the complementarity of gender roles between brothers and sisters) (Lutz, pp. 132-3). It is a matter of course that contact and caring continue between adopted children and their biological parents.

31. cf. Martha E. Gimenez, "Feminism, Pronatalism, and Motherhood," in Joyce Trebilcot, ed., *Mothering: Essays in Feminist Theory* (Totowa, NJ: Rowman & Allanheld, 1984) pp. 287-314.

32. Adoption of Black children by white families is strongly opposed by the National Association of Black Social Workers (Statement by President William T. Merritt at Hearings of Senate Committee on Labor and Human Resources, June 25, 1985. National Association of Black Social Workers, 271 West 125th Street, New York, NY 10027).

33. In the constant competition for societal resources, it is difficult to see how government could justify expenditures to facilitate or regulate contract motherhood in order to create genetically related infants for those who want them, while existing children in need of homes might be placed if the resources were used to make it economically feasible for otherwise willing persons to take them in.

34. Indeed, there is now a case in California of a black woman, Anna Johnson, who has born the genetic child of Mark and Crispina Calvert (he is white and she is Filipino) and is seeking visitation rights. Temporary custody has been awarded to the Calverts. (*Courier News*, 9/21/90, reprinted from *The Los Angeles Times*.) As in the Baby M case, the temporary award of custody makes it highly likely that permanent custody will go to the contracting couple because the infant will have lived and bonded with them. Moreover, the facts that the child is not genetically related to her and that he is considered not of her race, are almost certain to count against her attempts to maintain a parental relationship with him.

35. It has been argued, in defense of contract motherhood, that racism itself would preclude this: "racially or ethnically privileged groups will not rush to have their children borne by members of despised minorities" (Christine T. Sistare, "Reproductive Freedom and Women's Freedom: Surrogacy and Autonomy," *The Philosophical Forum*, 14 [Summer 1988]: 227-240, p. 234). But, in addition to the advantage in potential custody disputes, note that slave owners and others had no objections to having their infants cared for and breast fed by members of despised minorities. Given the attitude, inherent in contract motherhood, that gestation is merely a service, any healthy woman should do just fine. (In considering the importance attributed to the genetic connection as a motivation for engaging a contract mother, it is worth reflecting upon another aspect of the slave experience: white slaveowners impregnating slave women, producing lighter skinned slave children who would fetch a higher price at market.)

36. If this picture seems somewhat outmoded from a perspective within academia, it is nonetheless still very prevalent, as ideal even if not as reality, in much of our society.

37. cf. Virginia Held criticizes such a view in "Non-contractual Society: A Feminist View" in Marsha Hanen and Kai Nielsen, eds. *Science, Morality & Feminist Theory* (*Canadian Journal of Philosophy* Supplementary Volume 13, 1987) p. 122.

38. Philip J. Parker, "Motivation of Surrogate Mothers: Initial Findings," *American Journal of Psychiatry* 140 (January 1983), 118. Quoted in Christine

Overall, "Surrogate Motherhood," *Science, Morality & Feminist Theory*, Hanen and Nielsen, eds., p. 303.

39. *Webster's New World Dictionary*, College Edition, 1967.

40. *id*. Many kinds of behavior might come under this definition. For example, certain ways of treating nonhuman animals and/or the environment could constitute exploitation in this sense.

41. It is a matter of dispute between Marxists and others whether all wage labor is exploitative; it is a matter of dispute among Marxists and Marx scholars whether exploitation of wage labor is (or was held by Marx to be) exploitation in the sense under consideration here, i.e., unethical because unjust or unfair. See, e.g., Marx, Justice, and History, Nancy Holmstrom "Exploitation," *Canadian Journal of Philosophy* VII (June 1977) pp. 353-369; Allen Buchanan, *Marx & Justice* (Totowa, NJ: Rowman and Littlefield, 1982), Chapter 3; Ziyad I. Husami, "Marx on Distributive Justice" in Marshall Cohen, Thomas Nagel, and Thomas Scanlon, eds., *Marx, Justice, and History* (Princeton: Princeton University Press, 1980). I tend to side with the Marxists on the first question and with those who interpret Marx as regarding wage labor as unjust on the second. (Closest to my views are Holmstrom and Husami.) For a somewhat broader account of exploitation as it relates to oppression, see Iris M. Young, "Five Faces of oppression," *The Philosophical Forum* Vol. XIX, no 4, (Summer 1988) pp. 276-280. The account I attempt to develop here is broader still.

42. For example, for an adult physically to use a young child for his or her own sexual gratification is, among other things, for the adult to exploit the child, regardless of whether the adult persuaded, bribed, or coerced the child to be used in this way. For another example, when a teacher improperly benefits from the vulnerability of a student in the teacher-student relationship, the teacher exploits the student. Because this relationship frequently overlaps with other relationships, such as those within a social circle or among casual or even close friends, as well as those of supervisor or employer to employee, it can often be difficult (for either party, or anyone else) to determine precisely where the line is beyond which treatment is improper in this way, and hence exploitative. Thus on this account, a person need not feel exploited to be exploited. (Compare: the Task Force on New Reproductive Practices of the New Jersey Bioethics Commission termed contract motherhood "degrading" rather than exploitative on the grounds that degradation is objective in this way while exploitation may not be.)

43. I do not mean to suggest that levels, degrees, or severity of exploitation can, in general, be measured or even compared with precision. If Marx is right, the rate of exploitation of wage labor by capital can be precisely stated as the ratio of surplus value to variable capital (*Capital*, Vol. I [New York: International Publishers, Inc.] p. 218). Whether or not he is right, there may be other dimensions of exploitation operating simultaneously (for example, taking advantage of a worker's social, psychological, or economic vulnerability to get him or her to report on other workers, to extract personal services or favors from the worker over and above his or her wage labor, to require the worker to rent company housing or shop in a company store). In such a situation, some workers may be

more exploited than others overall, even if the rate of surplus value is the same. These other dimensions and hence the overall level of exploitation cannot be precisely measured.

44. Consider that Mary Beth Whitehead asked William Stern to recommend an attorney to represent her in the case that Stern had brought against her for custody of their child. For an incisive and insightful analysis of the class and gender biases at work in the testimony of the expert witnesses in the trial, see Michelle Harrison, "Social Construction of Mary Beth Whitehead," *Gender & Society* 1 (September 1987) pp. 300-311.

45. Adrienne Asche and Anne Reichman, "Surrogacy Matching Services: Field Trips," Staff Report to New Jersey Bioethics Commission New Reproductive Practices Task Force, December 7, 1988. The report also indicated that the directors of the three centers visited all appeared to have a real sense of mission to help the infertile to have desperately desired children. Although all three of the centers are for-profit businesses, two of the three reported not having shown a profit yet (they did not report having lost money either, and the salaries of directors and staff were not reported).

46. Unless they are permitted a continuing role in the life of the family. I have heard of one case in which a paid contract mother has a continuing relationship with the child and the receiving parents (conversation with Nadine Taub 12/88). It will become evident below, if it has not already, that I take the alienation of the birthmother from the contracted child as a central feature of contract motherhood in our society. Several, though not all, of my objections would be eliminated or mitigated if this feature were absent.

47. Since the infant does not yet exist, indeed, has not yet been conceived, at the time of the original contract, it is the *attitude* of the adults toward a possible child-to-be that is exploitative at that time. Actual exploitation awaits the birth of an actual child.

48. Would Kant agree that one can violate the Categorical Imperative without intending to? I think he'd have to: suppose one didn't even apply it? But what if one just didn't formulate the maxim "correctly"?

49. In the most general terms, it might be objected that the account of exploitation is so broad that, at least in a capitalist or profit-driven market society such as ours, virtually everyone exploits and is exploited by others most of the time. When people transact business in the marketplace, each is out simply to maximize his or her own returns and regards others merely as competitors or as means. It would seem to follow that either all of market society, not just contract motherhood, should be condemned or my account of exploitation is seriously flawed by being overly broad. Either way, the case against contract motherhood as exploitative fails to distinguish it from other practices widely regarded in our society as perfectly legitimate. But I do not agree that market relations are, in themselves, incompatible with treating others as ends in themselves (as well as means to one's own ends). That we officially recognize rules against fraud, coercion, misrepresentation, price-fixing, gouging, etc., is evidence that we regard respect for the personhood of others as constraining acceptable market behavior. At the same

time, the degree, and it is substantial, to which participants in our society violate (often with impunity) standards of treatment required by full respect for personhood does constitute grounds for serious criticism of many aspects of our society.

50. Some who favor contract motherhood argue that there should be no screening or restrictions on those who would engage contract mothers (except, presumably, as needed for the protection of the health of contract mother and child). Whether they are infertile or choose this option for other medical or non-medical reasons is no one's business but their own, any more than the motives, medical conditions, and marital status of those who procreate by means of unaided sexual intercourse. (Sistare, p. 232).

51. e.g., Lori Andrews, "Alternative Modes of Reproduction," *Reproductive Laws for the 1990s: A Briefing Handbook,* ed. by Sherrill Cohen and Nadine Taub, (New Brunswick, NJ: Rutgers University, 1989) (Available for purchase from Humana Press, Clifton, NJ. See also the response by Wendy Chavkin, Barbara Katz Rothman and Rayna Rapp, "Alternative Modes of Reproduction: Other Views and Questions, same volume, pp. 299-303); Laura Purdy, "Surrogate Mothering: Exploitation or Empowerment?" *Bioethics* 3 (January 1989) pp. 18-34; Sistare.

52. e.g., Sistare, pp. 230, 237.

53. cf. Sara Ann Ketchum, "Selling Babies and Selling Bodies: Surrogate Motherhood and the Problem of Commodification," presented at Eastern Division American Philosophical Association, December 1987, New York City.

54. The only way to find out for sure would be to adopt a welcoming or permissive approach to the practice and carefully observe the resulting social patterns. Even then, social developments would be difficult or impossible to attribute with any certainty to this rather than myriad other possible factors. On balance, I do not consider the experiment even remotely worth the risk.

55. e.g., Skoloff, Keane. Lori Andrews, arguing that the practice is not, or need not be exploitative, argues that many contract mothers are not in desperate straits. She says that she is not aware that private education is considered a basic need in this society. But consider that Mary Beth Whitehead intended to put her other two children through college with the $10,000 she was to make as a contract mother. Yet the American Council on Education estimates that the average cost *per year* in 1990-91 of all *public* higher education institutions, for students who reside on campus, will be $6,950. One student for one year at a *private* institution will cost $15,060. After taxes and inflation, it is unlikely that Whitehead's fee would pay for one year of college for one of her children at a public institution, even assuming that a family as economically insecure as theirs could actually have kept it from being eaten away by major or minor financial crises along the way.

56. *Baby M, II,* 109 N.J. appendix A. Stern was entitled to all interest on the $10,000 escrow account, a test of the fetus before the twentieth week, and abortion on demand if it was genetically or congenitally abnormal. He was obligated to pay all Whitehead's medical expenses not covered by her insurance, and to pay to the Infertility Center $7,500 in advance, not refundable whether or not Whitehead

became pregnant and whether or not she relinquished the child. (*Baby M II*, appendix B) (Presumably, the Center had already collected $7,500 from the man with whom Whitehead had previously worked unsuccessfully for several months before entering the arrangement with Stern.)

57. Proposed regulatory schemes are enormously varied and often mutually contradictory. Some, e.g., would provide a waiting period after birth when the contract mother could change her mind about relinquishing the child; others would require specific enforcement of the agreement to turn over the child so that the parties would know exactly what they were getting into. Some would prohibit any attempts to control the contract mother's behavior during pregnancy and childbirth; others would strictly regulate her behavior and give control over her medical care to the intended receiving parent(s) or the broker. Some would require careful psychological screening and counseling. It would be a long and tedious job to consider and respond to all the possible permutations of these proposals. Some will be taken up in later sections.

58. Proponents of the practice who favor a free-market rather than regulatory approach respond to this concern with the assurance that, as the practice becomes more widespread and availability increases, the price will come down. This, of course, just intensifies the exploitative potential and raises again the prospect of super-exploitation of women of color and an international traffic in contract mothers (or their babies, if gametes, embryos and infants are transported instead of women).

Another, very different, response to the concern about access would be to propose subsidies so that all who would choose this option would have access to it. But frankly, it strikes me as ludicrous to suppose that our society would consider paying women to bear children for poor, economically marginal, and working class families or individuals. It is more likely, in a classist society, to be seen as a virtue of contract motherhood that those who cannot afford (more) children can enjoy pregnancy and childbirth and some extra cash and turn the babies over to people who can give them the advantages their birth mothers lack (cf. Sistare, p. 237).

59. Sistare is not exactly concerned: "The prospect that the lure of payment will keep poor women too busy incubating babies for the rich to reproduce for themselves is implausible and easily debarred by maximum fees or other regulations" (Sistare, p. 235).

60. Compare organ sales/donations.

61. Others would be gladiator, live organ and body-part source, and contract slave or indentured servant. (I would include on this list many jobs that currently exist in our society as well.)

62. For an interesting account of changes in the economic and sentimental value placed on children in the U.S. between the 1870s and the 1930s, see *Pricing the Priceless Child: The Changing Social Value of Children* (New York: Basic Books, 1985).

63. I am not what Margaret Radin calls a "universal noncommodifier." Margaret Radin, "Market-Inalienability," *Harvard Law Review* 100 (June 1987)

pp. 1849-1937 (Universal Noncommodification, pp. 1871-1877). On her account, a universal noncommodifier opposes all markets on the grounds that once they exist they inexorably invade all aspects of a society, transforming all human relationships into either market relationships (e.g., owner, buyer, seller, renter, competitor, etc.) or commodities (as in the sale of friendship, loyalty, love, etc.). Contra Radin, I don't think Marx opposed the existence of commodities, markets, or money either. I take it that the problem arises with the transformation of money into capital. Marx distinguishes the simple circulation of commodities with money as medium of exchange (represented by the formula C-M-C) from the circulation of capital (represented by the formula M-C-M). He says:

> The circuit C-M-C starts with one commodity, and finishes with another, which falls out of circulation and into consumption. Consumption, the satisfaction of wants . . . use value, is its end and aim. The circuit M-C-M, on the contrary, commences with money and ends with money. Its leading motive, and the goal that attracts it, is therefore mere exchange-value.
>
> In the simple circulation of commodities, the two extremes of the circuit have the same economic form. They are both commodities, and commodities of equal value. But they are also use-values differing in their qualities, as, for example, corn and clothes. The exchange of products . . . forms here the basis of the movement. It is otherwise in the circulation M-C-M, which at first sight appears purposeless. . . . Both extremes have the same economic form. They are both money, and therefore are not qualitatively different use-values. . . . The character and tendency of the process M-C-M, is therefore not due to any qualitative difference between its extremes . . . but solely to their quantitative difference. More money is withdrawn from circulation at the finish than was thrown into it at the start. (*Capital* I [New York: International Publishers, 1967] pp. 149-150)

He goes on to say:

> The repetition or renewal of the act of selling in order to buy, is kept within bounds by the very object it aims at, namely, consumption or the satisfaction of definite wants, an aim that lies altogether outside the sphere of circulation. But when we buy in order to sell, we, on the contrary, begin and end with the same thing, money, exchange-value; and thereby the movement becomes interminable. (*Capital* I, p. 151)

When the purpose of market transactions is the exchange of commodities for the satisfaction of human wants and needs, the existence of commodities, markets, and money poses no automatic threat to human persons and relationships. It is when the point of the transactions is the expansion of capital, realizing a profit, that the pressure is on to commodify everything, including persons, their capacities, and interpersonal relationships. One would have no reason to treat one's own person or the persons of loved ones as commodities if one had alternative ways to meet one's needs and the needs of those one feels responsible for.

On the other hand, it must be recognized that people have been treated as commodities in noncapitalist societies, most notably slaves and (non-slave) women and sometimes children So the absence of capitalism does not *ensure* that persons are not treated as commodities (or in other morally inappropriate ways). Still, the presence of capitalism does ensure the commodification of human capacities, in particular, all those capacities that constitute the ability of persons to work: labor power. And pursuit of capital expansion exerts constant pressure to commodify ever-increasing aspects of persons and our lives.

64. There are differences: 24 hours a day, no breaks, etc., that make it hard to take it seriously as a job that can be appropriately regulated in terms of existing labor law.

65. I don't think one has to agree with me about wage labor in general, though, to agree with my views on the unacceptability of the forms of commodification involved in contract motherhood. Presumably, one who regards at least some forms of wage labor as unobjectionable will want to say either that wage labor does not involve commodification, or that commodification of some kinds of capacities and skills is ok, but reproduction and family relationships ought not to be commodified, or one will focus the objection on the commodification of the child rather than of the mother.

66. Some agencies show potential receiving parents albums with pictures of applicants *and their existing children*. Some hold gatherings where several potential receiving parents can meet and look over the available contract mother applicants.

67. Though one argues that it is "a special kind of baby selling." Schuck, p. 1795.

68. Purdy, p. 12 full ref.

69. Complications about whether the sale is invalidated if its illegality comes to light do not alter the point. (The NJ Supreme Court saw itself as invalidating the sale of Baby M.)

70. Decision of Judge Sorkow, Superior Court of New Jersey, In the Matter of Baby "M"; Sistare, p. 236.

71. Note that, during slavery, if a man rented a slave woman from her "owner" and impregnated her, the resulting child belonged to the slave's "owner," not to either the genetic father or the mother. If the father wanted to keep (or sell) the child, he first had to buy "his" child from its mother's "owner." Cyril C. Means, Jr., " Surrogacy v. the Thirteenth Amendment," *New York Law School Human Rights Annual* IV (Spring 1987): 445-479, pp. 448-9.

72. John Robertson, "Surrogate Mothers: Not So Novel After All," *Hastings Center Report* 13 (October 1983); reprinted in Rem B. Edwards and Glen C. Graber, eds., *Bioethics* (San Diego: Harcourt Brace Jovanovich, 1988) p. 655. (Page reference is to *Bioethics*.)

73. Argument (4) may be seen as a version of (3) insofar as parents (including receiving parents, but not contract mothers) are restricted from selling their children.

74. Suppose the receiving parent(s) meanwhile conceive (or receive by an-

other contract) another child and no longer want this one; why not let them sell rather than reject the child? (Or, if it is rejected, why not let the contract mother put it on the market?)

75. Commissioned adoption satisfies the characterization of contract mother-hood as I proposed at the outset to use the term.

76. There is also an argument distinguishing contract motherhood from ordinary adoption on the grounds that the decision to relinquish the child is made before conception (that is the reason she becomes pregnant) whereas in ordinary adoption cases, either the pregnancy was unforeseen or unforeseen circumstances make it difficult or impossible for the pregnant woman to raise the child. In the latter case, introduction of an offer of money into the situation might induce her to relinquish the child when she otherwise would not, and that would constitute baby-selling. In the former case, the offer of money is in the picture from the beginning; it can't induce her to relinquish a child she would otherwise keep, because the child would not have existed without the contract. But, as Sarah Ketchum notes, it is odd for this point to be raised in defense of the claim that contract motherhood doesn't commodify children. "Producing a child to order seems the paradigm case of commodifying children." (Sara Ann Ketchum, "Selling Babies & Selling Bodies: Surrogate Motherhood and the Problem of Commodification," presented at Eastern Div. APA, Dec. 1987, New York. p. 6).

77. Andrews, p. 274n.

78. As Margaret Radin argues in "Market-Inalienability," *Harvard Law Review* , Vol 100, No. 8 (June 1987): 1849-1937. (Even without a widespread practice, there is symbolic commodification of other children of the parties, who may wonder whether, when, and on what terms they may be for sale. The potential harm involved is not "merely" symbolic.)

79. Of course, if the amount of payment were sufficient to be nonexploitative, this would be a very substantial financial risk to potential receiving parents, and would probably have a chilling effect on the practice. Still, if that is what it takes to prevent the buying and selling of persons, the restriction should stand, and no doubt some would still find the risk worth taking.

80. cf. Ketchum, pp. 7-8. My view differs slightly from hers. She says "Although, in giving up responsibilities, I may have a responsibility to see to it that someone will shoulder them when I go, I do not have a right to choose that person" (p. 8). In open adoption situations, the birthmother does get to choose the adoptive family (with whom she *may* have continuing contact). As I see it, she doesn't transfer her parental rights to them, and she doesn't make a gift of the baby to them. She permanently entrusts the child to them, and having done so, renounces or relinquishes her parental rights, her parental relationship to the child. In accepting the trust, the adoptive parent(s) undertake parental obligations which entail certain parental rights in order to carry them out. Full parental rights develop as the new parent-child relationship develops.

81. Schuck, Sistare, Purdy, Andrews. They note that the children involved would not exist if not for the practice, and ask whether it can be said that they would be better off not existing at all. But one doesn't have to be willing to say of

an existing child that she would be better off not existing in order to say that it is better not to create children in this way. In relation to a notional child not yet conceived, the question whether it is better off existing or not existing makes no sense to me. Purdy argues that contract motherhood is a positive benefit to some children because *they* are healthier than children who *might otherwise* have been born to parents with genetic or other health risk factors. I can't make sense of this argument either.

82. For another example, if a child was acquired by means of a contract motherhood arrangement, and the child's rearing parents deceive her into believing they are her genetic and gestational parents, and the child never finds out, the child may not be harmed, but she will have been wronged. Indeed, she might be harmed by knowing.

83. cf. Sarah Boone, "Slavery and Contract Motherhood: A Racialized Objection to the Autonomy Arguments," (unpublished manuscript); Patricia J. Williams, "On Being the Object of Property," *Signs* 12 (Autumn 1988) pp. 5-24; bell hooks, *Ain't I a Woman: Black women and feminism* (Boston: South End Press, 1981), chapter one; Carole Pateman, *The Sexual Contract* (Stanford: Stanford University Press, 1988); Means, "Surrogacy v The Thirteenth Amendment."

84. David M. Brodzinsky, "Adjustment to Adoption: A Psychosocial Perspective," *Clinical Psychology Review* 7 (1987) pp. 25-47.

85. Adrienne Asch, Report to Task Force on AID.

86. Contract children also bear increased risk of being rejected if they are born impaired.

87. See, e.g., Elizabeth Kane, *BirthMother* (New York: Harcourt Brace Jovanovich, 1988).

88. So it is when employers control every aspect of the work process to get full benefit of the labor power they have bought and to control the quality of the product, at the same time, fragmenting the work process, and thereby ignoring skills and disempowering the worker.

89. The employer buys the worker's ability to work, but when it comes time to use that capacity, it takes the actual work of the whole worker, who often goes home drained, used up. The stresses and strains, the physical and psychic insults and injuries received in the workplace are not left there, they carry over into the rest of the worker's life.

90. If neither commodification nor this total alienation of birthmother and child were involved, most of my objections to the practice would be eliminated. There would remain many potential difficulties, of course.

91. There are those, as well, who think of autonomy simply as negative liberty: absence of constraints.

92. Andrews; Sistare.

93. Barbara Andolsen, "Why a Surrogate Mother Should Have the Right to Change her Mind" in Herbert Richardson, ed., *On the Problem of Surrogate Parenthood: Analyzing the Baby M Case* (Lewiston, NY: Edwin Mellen Press, 1987) p. 50.

94. Suppose you had consented to be a kidney donor and then changed your mind; could they say "Sorry, you gave a valid consent; you were competent, informed, and not coerced; therefore, you must go through with it?"

95. American Cyanamid Willow Island case in which women were required to have themselves surgically sterilized in order to keep their jobs, which involved exposure to lead, on grounds that *if* they became pregnant, and decided to (and did successfully) carry the pregnancy to term, exposure to lead *in utero* could be harmful. See Mary Gibson, *Workers' Rights* (Totowa, NJ: Rowman and Allanheld, 1983), *Chapter One*. A similar case, *The United Auto Workers vs Johnson Controls* is currently before the Supreme Court.

96. e.g., Andrews.

97. The rationale for supporting criminal penalties for brokers but not for contract mothers or intended receiving parents is that the former promote the practice and profit from the commodification of some and the exploitation of all the others involved, while the latter act in response to personal vulnerability, pain and desperation.

98. Of course, there are many potential problems involved here, as well.

Surrogate Motherhood
and the Morality of Care

Michael Dahlem

SUMMARY. The celebrated case of *Baby M* focused public attention on the practice of surrogate motherhood. This paper examines the judicial and legislative responses and the public policy implications of surrogate parenting contracts from the perspective of a morality of care. This perspective, which owes much to the pioneering work of Carol Gilligan, elevates the bond between mother and child over the rights conferred by contract. Working with this perspective, several arguments are advanced against the granting of specific performance of surrogate parenting contracts.

In the wake of the New Jersey Supreme Court's decision in the *Matter of Baby M*[1] several states have enacted legislation declaring surrogate parenting contracts[2] to be null and void as against public policy.[3] As additional courts and legislatures address this issue, debate will focus not only on the benefits and burdens to society and to the parties involved, but also on the rights of men and women to enter into surrogacy arrangements.

In this paper, I examine legislative and judicial responses and the public policy implications of surrogate parenting contracts from the perspective of a morality of care. This perspective owes much to the pioneering work of Carol Gilligan who, in her book *In a Different Voice*,[4] explores a moral attitude based on relationships rather than rights. I contend that according to a morality of care, courts should not enforce surrogate parenting contracts which result in the termination of the birth mother's parental rights.

Michael Dahlem, JD, PhD in Philosophy from Rutgers University, is Staff Director, Montana Federation of Teachers, AFL-CIO.

THE MORALITY OF CARE

The emphasis on relationships rather than rights is central to what
Gilligan characterizes as a morality of care.[5] This emphasis is also
found in the philosophy of David Hume who argued that attach-
ments of sentiment, not obligations to universal principles, serve as
the foundation of morality.[6] It is Gilligan's position that the preference many women, and some men, display for a morality of care
has been denigrated by the adherents of traditional moral views. In
seeking to account for this preference, she cites the work of Nancy
Chodorow to suggest that because mothers experience their daughters as more like themselves, girls emerge from childhood with a
basis for empathy while boys need to separate themselves in order
to establish their individuality.[7] On this account, male gender identity is threatened by intimacy while female identity is threatened by
separation.[8] Gilligan also points to research conducted by Janet Lever
showing that boys settle disputes in games more often by an appeal
to rules while disputes in girls' games are more often settled by
taking turns because the continuation of the game is subordinated to
the continuation of their relationships.[9]

While Gilligan's account may explain some gender differences in
moral reasoning,[10] its chief virtue may lie in its challenge to traditional theories of moral development. One such theory proposed by
Lawrence Kohlberg maintains that human beings progress through
six stages of moral development, with the highest stage representing the ability to ascertain the rights of others on the basis of universal principles.[11] Gilligan responds that Kohlberg's theory measures
male moral development, but not the perspective of care which
many women share. She notes that:

> Prominent among those who thus appear to be deficient in
> moral development when measured by Kohlberg's scale are
> women, whose judgments seem to exemplify the third stage of
> his six-stage sequence. At this stage morality is conceived in
> interpersonal terms and goodness is equated with helping and
> pleasing others. . . . [H]erein lies a paradox, for the very traits
> that traditionally have defined the "goodness" of women,

their care for and sensitivity to the needs of others, are those that mark them as deficient in moral development.[12]

Gilligan's challenge might be summarized as follows: if many people conceive of morality in interpersonal terms, then on what basis can we conclude that impersonal judgments represent the highest stage of moral reasoning? This same question can be seen lurking in the disagreement between the eighteenth century philosophers Immanuel Kant and David Hume. Kant's categorical imperative requires a moral agent to "[a]ct only according to that maxim by which you can at the same time will that it should become a universal law."[13] This concern for universality underlies the morality of promise keeping which, in turn, underlies both the law of contracts and the efficacy of social contract theory.[14]

Hume, on the other hand, rejected the importance of universal moral rules. His approach to morality is based on sympathetic identification with the condition of others. At the heart of his theory is the celebration of family life and parental love. The strongest tie is the love of parents for their children.[15] It is intimate, unchosen and between unequal agents. The goal of morality, according to Hume, is not the delineation of rights, but the pursuit of social harmony.

The philosopher Annette Baier suggests that of the traditional moral theories, Hume's may come closest to expressing a morality of care.[16] His emphasis on the importance of sympathetic identification presents a strong challenge to moral theories built on abstract principles, such as universality.

In this work, I contend that a morality of care would elevate the attachment between mother and child over the rights conferred by contract. But before proceeding with this analysis, it is important to distinguish a morality of care from a right to life position which maintains that we have certain natural obligations. While a right to life position holds that all persons have a natural duty to promote human life, a morality of care position speaks of a natural connectedness between human beings. It focuses on living relationships, not on duties to promote life. From a morality of care perspective, the fact that many persons feel strong bonds with others supports the claim that it is wrong to use contractual agreements to sever these bonds. Although such bonds may resemble natural duties in some respects, they also differ from them in significant ways. Thus, while our feeling of community with others creates a sense of obligation to them, it would be incorrect to claim that this feeling generates a duty to maintain our communal ties. Friends, for example, often feel obligated to each other. But when their trust has been betrayed, they rarely feel obligated to remain friends. While proponents of a morality of care would find it wrong to interfere with communal bonds, they would not impose such a bond where it is not genuinely felt. Consequently, a morality of care cannot be used to uphold the judgement that women should be prevented from aborting their fetuses.

This pro-choice position is shared by those who support the enforcement of surrogate parenting contracts on the ground that reproductive freedom is necessary for moral autonomy. But by calling for the enforcement of surrogate parenting contracts supporters fail to respect a woman's right to choose after she has entered into the contract. When a woman changes her mind as a result of the bond she feels to her child, a society which respects personal autonomy should respect the choice to maintain the relationship with her child. This respect for autonomy and recognition of the bonds between persons provides no support for a right to life position because that position places no value on a woman's autonomy. It merely seeks to impose a duty on women to give birth and nurturance to their children, regardless of whether a woman considers other commitments to be primary.

JUDICIAL RESPONSES

Although the courts have had little opportunity to directly address the validity of surrogate parenting contracts,[17] the cases on record demonstrate strong public policy arguments against both specific performance and the payment of money for an agreement to terminate a woman's parental rights.

In *Surrogate Parenting Associates v. Commonwealth ex. rel. Armstrong*, the Attorney General of Kentucky brought suit to revoke the corporation's charter on the grounds that its promotion of surrogate parenting violated the prohibition against the sale of children.[18] Although the state supreme court found no violation of state law then in effect,[19] it did hold that surrogate parenting contracts that award custody without regard to best interests of the child are voidable.[20]

The court distinguished the consideration paid to a surrogate mother from that paid for an adoption in holding that:

> [T]he central fact in the surrogate parenting procedure is that the agreement to bear the child is entered into before conception. The essential considerations for the surrogate mother when she agrees to the surrogate parenting procedure are not avoiding the consequences of an unwanted pregnancy or fear of the financial burden of child rearing. On the contrary, the essential consideration is to assist a person or couple who desperately want a child but are unable to conceive one in the customary manner to achieve a biologically related offspring.[21]

In addition to the issue of consideration, the court was also confronted with the question of consent. In this case, Surrogate Parenting Associates (SPA) acknowledged that a surrogate's consent must be obtained five days *after* the birth of the child to be legally binding. The court agreed, noting that:

> The five days' consent feature in the termination of parental rights statute (KRS 199.601(2)) and in the consent to adoption statute (KRS 199.500(5)) take precedence over the parties' contractual commitments, meaning that the surrogate mother is free to change her mind. The policy of the [statutes] is to preserve to the mother her right of choice regardless of decisions made before the birth of the child. . . . [T]he law gives the mother the opportunity to reconsider her decision to fulfill the role as surrogate mother and refuse to perform the voluntary termination procedure.[22]

Because the court majority believed that a revocable surrogacy contract did not violate the payment or consent provisions in Kentucky law, it refused to revoke the SPA's charter. A strong dissent, however, was registered by Justice Vance who argued that "a portion of the payment is withheld . . . until her living child is delivered unto the purchaser. . . . How can it be denied that this . . . is in fact a payment for the baby, because if the baby is not delivered and parental rights not surrendered, the last part of the fee need not be paid."[23]

The court's majority did acknowledge that if "there are social and ethical problems" associated with surrogate motherhood, it should be up to the legislature to act[24] In 1988, the Kentucky Legislature took up this suggestion by amending Ky. Rev. Stat. Ann. 199.590 (Baldwin, 1989) to make surrogate parenting contracts illegal.[25]

One of the first cases involving the adoption of a child born as a result of a surrogate parenting contract was decided in 1986. In the *Matter of the Adoption of Baby Girl L.J.*,[26] the Surrogate's Court of Nassau County, New York upheld the adoption "in spite of strong reservations about these arrangements both on moral and ethical grounds."[27] In this case there was no custody contest, and the court concluded that it was in the best interests of the child to award custody to the contracting father and his spouse.[28]

The court adopted a stance similar to that of the Kentucky Supreme Court when it held that the New York Legislature did not contemplate surrogate parenting contracts when it "enacted SSL 374(6) prohibiting payments in connection with an adoption. . . . Accordingly, the court finds that this is a matter for the legislature to address. . . . "[29] Although the state legislature has yet to pass any statute on surrogacy, Governor Mario Cuomo's Task Force on Life and the Law has recommended legislation prohibiting fees for surrogates and barring surrogate brokers from operating in New York State.[30]

In New Jersey, the legality of surrogate parenting contracts was met head on in the *Matter of Baby M.*[31] In that case, the New Jersey Supreme Court held that the contract between William Stern and Mary Beth and Richard Whitehead violated state laws which (1) prohibit the use of money in connection with adoption, (2) require proof of parental unfitness before the termination of parental rights, and (3) make the surrender of custody and consent to adoption revocable in private placement adoptions.[32]

The court found "no offense to our present laws where a woman voluntarily and without payment agrees to act as a 'surrogate' mother, provided that she is not subject to a binding agreement to surrender her child."[33]

The supreme court also noted an inconsistency in the trial court's finding that the surrogate parenting contract was valid, but that custody should be determined on the basis of the child's best interest.[34] Because the contract sought to determine custody before the child was conceived, the court determined that it cannot conform to the best interests standard of New Jersey law.[35] Unlike the Kentucky and New York courts which preceded it, the New Jersey Supreme Court rejected the argument that state adoption laws do not apply to surrogate parenting contracts because the legislature did not have surrogacy contracts in mind when it passed those laws.[36] Instead, the court held that contracts to terminate a mother's parental rights cannot be enforced because they violate the state's private placement adoption statute.[37]

The court also found that the contract violates the long-held public policy in support of maintaining the parental rights of both natural parents.[38]

> The surrogacy contract guarantees permanent separation of the child from one of its natural parents. Our policy, however, has long been that to the extent possible, children should remain with and be brought up by both of their natural parents. . . . The surrogacy contract violates the policy of this State that the rights of natural parents are equal concerning their child, the father's right no greater than the mother's. . . . The whole purpose and effect of the surrogacy contract was to give the father the exclusive right to the child by destroying the rights of the mother.[39]

The court then observed that the surrogate's decision cannot be fully voluntary because she cannot know in advance the strength of her bond with her child.[40] Nor, the court held, is it possible to know in advance what are the best interests of the child.[41] The court concluded that "[t]his is the sale of a child, or, at the very least, the sale of a mother's right to her child, the only mitigating factor being that one of the purchasers is the father."[42]

According to the court, the role of money in inducing women to enter into surrogacy contracts is perhaps the most pernicious aspect of the practice. After listing a number of harms produced by the use of money, the court stated:

> There are, in a civilized society, some things that money can-not buy. In America, we decided long ago that merely because conduct purchased by money was "voluntary" did not mean that it was good or beyond regulation and prohibition (citation omitted). Employers can no longer buy labor at the lowest price they can bargain for, even though that labor is "volun-tary," (citation omitted), or buy women's labor for less money than paid to men for the same job, (citation omitted), or purchase the agreement of children to perform oppressive labor, (citation omitted), or purchase the agreement of work-ers to subject themselves to unsafe or unhealthful working conditions, (citation omitted). There are, in short, values that society deems more important than granting to wealth what-ever it can buy, be it labor, love, or life.[43]

Turning to the constitutional issues, the court denied William Stern's claim that his right to procreate includes a right to enforce a surrogate parenting contract. In *Skinner v. Oklahoma*,[44] the United States Supreme Court ruled that a statute authorizing forced sterili-zation of habitual criminals violates the Fourteenth Amendment. In interpreting this decision, the court determined that the right to pro-create extends only to natural procreation.

> There is nothing in our culture or society that even begins to suggest a fundamental right on the part of the father to the custody of the child as part of his right to procreate when op-posed by the claim of the mother to the same child.[45]

In responding to Mary Beth Whitehead's claim to a constitutional right to the companionship of her child, the court affirmed that "[t]his is a fundamental interest, constitutionally protected."[46] However, the claim was moot because the court had already invali-dated the contract as contrary to public policy.[47] In the remainder of its decision, the court addressed the matters of custody and visita-tion.

LEGISLATIVE RESPONSE

Prior to the *Baby M* decision, three states, Florida, Louisiana and Ohio, had legislation on the books prohibiting the enforcement of surrogate parenting contracts.[48] One state, Nevada, authorized surrogate contracts by excepting them from the prohibition against payment in return for consent to an adoption.[49]

In the wake of the *Baby M* decision, seventy-six separate bills were introduced in twenty-seven different states.[50] Ten states set up commissions to study the matter.[51] Eight states, Arizona, Indiana, Kentucky, Michigan, Nebraska, North Dakota, Utah and Washington, passed legislation to either criminalize the practice or to declare the contracts void as against public policy.[52] One state, Arkansas, passed legislation to uphold the validity of the contracts.[53]

In New Jersey, nine separate bills were proposed prior to the supreme court decision.[54] None of them passed, however, as the legislature chose to create the Commission on Legal and Ethical Problems in the Delivery of Health Care (Bioethics Commission). The Bioethics Commission, in turn, created a Task Force on New Reproductive Practices. Although the task force's final recommendations are still pending, a draft memorandum recommends legislation prohibiting the payment of fees to brokers or to birth mothers in connection with "the surrender or transfer of custody or relinquishment or waiver of parental rights."[55] The task force does not recommend the prohibition of non-commercial surrogacy arrangements, but does recommend that the birth mother be allowed 90 days following the birth of the child to change her mind and retain custody of the child.[56]

PUBLIC POLICY
AND THE MORALITY OF CARE

It is apparent that many of the arguments advanced against the validity of surrogate parenting contracts reflect features of a morality of care. Such a morality makes the continuation of relationships more important than the enforceability of contracts which threaten to injure or sever those relationships. As the New Jersey Supreme Court stated, there are some things that money cannot buy. With this in mind, let us examine several arguments in favor of specific performance and the payment of consideration in return for an agreement to terminate parental rights.

In the *Baby M* case, the court rejects the claim that the right to procreate includes the right to purchase the mother's parental rights. Indeed, if the mother's fundamental right to procreate can be alienated through contract it seems reasonable to maintain that she can alienate other fundamental rights, including her right to liberty. But as the court noted, there are many things which individuals may not agree to do even if the agreement is voluntary in the normal sense.

By purchasing from a woman her right to companionship with her children, surrogacy contracts threaten the most intimate bonds of family life. Not only does the practice threaten negative consequences for mother and child, it upholds a world view in which everything is subject to the terms of a contract. As the New York State Task Force on Life and the Law points out, the validity of surrogacy contracts "embodies a deeply pessimistic vision of the potential for human relationships and intimacy in contemporary society. It promotes legal obligations as the touchstone for our most private relationships instead of fostering commitments forged by caring and trust."[57]

A rights-based moral theory generally upholds the right to contract as necessary for individual autonomy. Consequently, individuals should have the right to enter into agreements as long as they do not infringe upon the rights of others. Contracts may be set aside if they are against public policy, or if obtained by fraud, undue influence, duress or mutual mistake. In the absence of one of these conditions, individuals are free to enter into a wide variety of "unequal" contracts. The Marxist critique of the labor contract is based on its inherent inequality due to the superior bargaining position of the employer. However, inequality of the bargain has rarely been sufficient to nullify it. Only in cases where contract terms are so unfair as to be unconscionable or where a party has no choice but to enter into a contract of adhesion, have courts overturned agreements on the basis of inequality.[58]

Those who support specific performance of surrogate parenting contracts argue that a ban on the right to contract would violate a woman's autonomy. Lori Andrews, for example, asserts that if the government can prevent a woman from entering into a reproductive contract, then it might also seek to curtail a woman's liberty not to reproduce. She writes that "there is considerable agreement that surrogate arrangements . . . should not be legally banned. To support such a ban would seem to acknowledge a role for government in dictating the circumstances under which a woman should be allowed to have a child and under which families may be formed."[59]

Andrews' argument against government involvement cuts both ways, however. Enforcement of surrogate parenting contracts, which Andrews endorses,[60] could just as easily lead to government efforts to control other reproductive practices. A public policy which denies specific performance seems closer to the position of non-interference which Andrews is after.

Furthermore, it does not appear that individual autonomy is violated whenever the right to contract is restricted. There are many things that cannot be contracted for because to do so would produce a generalized harm. The whole range of protective legislation, referred to by the *Baby M* court,[61] has been enacted to restrict the right to contract. What is protected by this legislation is more than the welfare of the individual who would otherwise choose to engage in the proscribed activity. All citizens have an interest that the freedom of contract not exert undue pressure on others to act similarly. In a society in which fewer opportunities are open to women in lower socio-economic classes, the lure of a surrogate contract might induce a woman to agree to something she will later regret. Where specific performance of such contracts is upheld, she will be forced to sever a relationship which did not exist at the time the contract was signed.

Supporters of specific performance also argue that the transfer of the child following birth is not a personal service and thus should be enforced.[62] However, if the transfer of the child is not viewed as a personal service, must not the child be seen as a commodity? Courts will generally order specific performance in cases involving the sale of land or nonfungible goods. But if the child is not being sold as property, how can the transaction be understood in a way which would still permit specific performance? How do we characterize the contracted termination of parental rights?

It is granted that surrogate motherhood seems to be different from either involuntary servitude or the sale of a nonfungible good. Furthermore, if the man receiving the child has contributed to its creation, then in most jurisdictions he already possesses parental rights regardless of the validity of the contract.[63]

Nevertheless, the agreement to bear a child for a fee is similar to a contract for the sale of a fungible good. In addition, an agreement to terminate a mother's parental rights is personal in the twofold sense that it both requires her to restrict her daily activities for a nine-month period and it deprives her of a personal relationship created through her efforts. Although the contractual termination of her parental rights prevents rather than enforces a particular relationship, its similarity to a personal services contract demands careful scrutiny.

In either case, there are strong legal and moral reasons not to enforce such contracts. If characterized as a contract for the sale of a good, it would violate laws against baby selling. If characterized as a personal services contract, an irrevocable agreement would violate the Thirteenth Amendment's prohibition against involuntary servitude.

In addition to the prohibition against involuntary servitude, courts have also been unwilling to grant specific performance of personal services contracts because "the mischief likely to result from the enforced continuance of the relationship incident to the service when it has become personally obnoxious to one of the parties is so great that the best interests of society require that the remedy be refused."[64]

If courts are unwilling to require parties to maintain a relationship, they should be equally wary of preventing their maintenance. It would be unheard of for a court to enforce a contract, in favor of a third person, by which two adults agree to permanently sever all ties to each other. For example, if upon a divorce, a woman contracted with her ex-husband's new wife to renounce any personal relationship with her former husband but later changed her mind, no court would specifically enforce such a contract. The reason for its refusal results from our respect for individual autonomy. Autonomy is respected only where people are accorded the right to change their minds in matters so intimate as their personal relationships.

The importance of being able to change one's mind is also reflected in state adoption laws requiring counseling before a woman can agree to give up her child[65] and in statutes preventing any adoption agreement before the birth of the child.[66] The latter requirement is particularly crucial to the debate over surrogate motherhood. What the requirement assumes is that it is difficult, if not impossible, to knowingly sever a relationship which does not yet exist. It is impossible for the mother to predict, in advance, what her feelings will be for a child who is not yet even conceived.

In response to this contention, Christine Sistare argues that it is impossible to ever know what something will be like before the time of performance.[67] She contends that if knowing how one will feel is required for informed consent, then people would never be deemed competent to "decide about their wills, their medical treatments, their marriages, even about the decision to become parents or not become parents."[68]

What Sistare ignores is that not knowing how one will feel is important in contexts where the decision is irrevocable. The examples of making a will, marrying, seeking medical treatment or becoming a parent are qualitatively different from agreeing to terminate one's parental rights to a child who is not even conceived. One can remake a will, obtain a divorce, seek a second medical opinion or abort a fetus. The decision to terminate one's parental rights by contract would be irrevocable.

One reason Sistare endorses the enforceability of surrogate parenting contracts is the potential for financial gain by women. She writes:

> What is truly feared here, is not that babies will become commodities but that women's reproductive services will no longer be cheap or available on demand. The most dreaded process of commodification is the one through which women's reproductive role will become a commodity valued in the best capitalist style: one for which the buyer must go asking and pay well.[69]

Sistare's claim that surrogate motherhood means that men will now have to pay well for what was once cheap seems to be false in two ways. One, couples who can reproduce naturally will not resort to the practice. In that case, the man will not pay well for what was once cheap. On the other hand, the wealthy infertile couple will pay well, not for something that was previously cheap, but for a child who was previously unavailable.

In another sense, Sistare's characterization of reproduction as something cheap and available on demand only reinforces the worst images of family life. While the family structure under capitalism has been far from perfect, it has imposed obligations on both parents. To suggest, as Sistare does, that the father cannot buy what is already his, implies that the child is the property of the father. It also implies that women become pregnant and give birth as a "service" to their husbands. This characterization only reinforces male domination.

But even if a woman could knowingly agree to terminate her parental rights before the birth of her child, it can still be argued that the practice would constitute baby selling.[70] For surely what is being contracted for is not simply the mother's services, but the resulting "product" of those services.[71]

To maintain that the practice is not baby selling, because the father cannot buy what is already his, ignores the fact that it is not the father who is the ultimate recipient of the mother's parental rights, but his spouse. In effect, the birth mother sells her parental rights to her child to the spouse of the father. The father already has parental rights independent of the rights of the mother.

In addition, to say that the father cannot buy what is already his assumes that the child is already the property of the father. While the father's rights are unlike traditional property rights in that persons cannot be owned as property, they may be seen as quasi-property rights because they include the right to make certain decisions for the child and the right to exclude others from interacting with the child. The right to exclude others functions like a property right. But if the mother also has parental rights which she may sell to the wife of the father, then the sale of her right amounts to the sale of a quasi-property right in the child.

At this point, one might ask, if a woman can sell her right to her unborn child, why should she not be allowed to sell her other children, especially if a loving couple offers to give them a good home and opportunities she cannot afford to provide? In other words, if surrogate motherhood is permissible, then why should we not also permit the sale of children as long as they are not sold to people who will abuse or neglect them? What difference is there, in principle, between selling children after they are born and selling them before birth?[72]

Contrary to the claims of Andrews and Sistare, the loss of freedom to profit from surrogate parenting contracts is not a real loss of autonomy. A refusal to enforce surrogate parenting contracts would invade a woman's autonomy no more than the prohibition against baby selling. Since children are not the property of the mother, the prohibition of their sale does not invade her autonomy. No one can sell what they do not own.

In sum, the claim that enforcement of the contract is necessary to support a woman's autonomy is untenable. If a woman cannot change her mind, she cannot exercise her autonomy after the contract has been signed. The purported increase in autonomy, her ability to enter into the contract in the first place, must be weighed against her loss of autonomy, the inability to sustain a relationship with her child. On balance, it seems that the "increase" cannot compensate for the loss.

Finally, proponents of surrogate motherhood insist that the fundamental right to procreate includes the right to enforce surrogacy contracts. Lori Andrews concurs with the opinion that " 'the human birthright includes the right to give birth' and infertility treatments to further that birthright are 'part of the price we pay for living together in community.' "[73]

Although courts have recognized that individuals have a fundamental right to procreate naturally, they have not extended this right to include surrogate motherhood or any of the new reproductive technologies.[74] The right has been framed in terms of a right to be free from interference with one's ability to procreate, not as a right to receive assistance in the attempt to procreate. The major problem in recognizing a positive right in this regard is that the assertion of the right will impinge upon the equal right to procreate held by the birth mother.

Stated in another way, if the right to procreate is fundamental in the sense claimed by the supporters of surrogate motherhood it is difficult to see why individuals should be allowed to alienate that right through contract. If the advocates of surrogate motherhood want procreation to be recognized as a fundamental right, they must explain why the mother's fundamental right can be compromised in favor of the father's right. They must either hold that the mother's right is less fundamental than the father's or that individuals should be free to contract away their fundamental rights.

CONCLUSION

An underlying presupposition of the care perspective appears to be that human beings develop bonds with each other which are unchosen and often between unequals. Unlike a contractarian model which presupposes voluntary agreements between free, equal, and rational agents, we often find ourselves in unchosen relationships. The most obvious example is the family. No one chose to be born into a family and yet family membership is often sufficient to bind individuals.

The importance of natural ties between persons has been devalued by a rights tradition which relies upon the freedom to contract and the harm principle to uphold individual autonomy.[75] On this view, people should be free to contract as long as they do not harm others in the process. It is not surprising, therefore, that the language of rights has been held to govern our public life, while the commitment of relationships has been relegated to the private sphere. It is this sphere to which women have been assigned as the primary care givers.

The failure of Western society to extend the care perspective to the public realm is consistent with the elevation of the rights perspective. We have the right to pursue our own conception of our good without interference so long as our pursuit does not interfere with the rights of others. We do not have the right to live in a caring community. The rights perspective assumes a form of social atomism in which individual liberty takes priority over the welfare of the community. In the end, individual rights amount to little more than the right to be free from interference.

Supporters of a morality of care, however, argue that a morality of rights cannot adequately account for the moral force exerted by our relationships. An appeal to rights cannot explain the strength of commitment we feel for our family and friends. Nor can it really explain why it is blameworthy to abandon a friend or family member in need. Yet, there is something so fundamental about these relationships that we are convinced such behavior is wrong.

Under a morality of care, we should oppose the payment of money in return for a contractual waiver of the right of a parent to the companionship of her child. Not only would such an agreement not be in the best interest of the child, it would undermine the value of all human relationships. From the point of view of the morality of care, surrogate motherhood represents an unwarranted extension of the rights-based morality into a realm hitherto governed by a morality of care. Policy makers must consider whether this extension represents such a gain for infertile couples that the potential harm to the birth mother, her family and society at large is acceptable.

Despite the claims of its proponents, we should ask if the rights perspective can fully support moral autonomy. For if abstract, universal laws become the standard for autonomy, how can human beings exercise that autonomy in contexts in which the laws can not apply without violating other commitments? The rights perspective is appealing because it chooses not to recognize the priority, and even the validity at times, of these other commitments. According to the care perspective, the desire to care for one's child should not be overridden by contract. This sense of duty accounts for the difficulty many women have in giving up their children for adoption, even when it is clear that they are unable to adequately care for them.

If a system of rights is necessary as long as disputes persist in society, is there any way in which the care perspective might insinuate itself into legal discourse and judicial decision-making? Resistance to the extension of the contract model into the realm of personal relationships only represents an attempt to hold the line against the encroachment of the rights perspective. If the morality of care is to play a critical role in our social practices, it must go much further in its critique of the rights perspective.

In analyzing this matter, it is important to keep in mind that a contract between equals, freely entered into, is the exception rather than the rule. Most people do not have, and are not likely to have in the forseeable future, equal bargaining power. The meaning of equality in society, is largely formal. To enforce all contracts as written, therefore, is to enforce the inequality between the contracting parties.

The bonds which hold families together, however, are not contractual in nature. Nevertheless, the enforcement of surrogate parenting contracts will apply a contractual standard to the most intimate of personal relationships. This standard will further weaken the family while it upholds the belief that women are valued only for their reproductive capacities.

Instead of enforcing these contracts, public policy would be better served by efforts to redefine the meaning of the family in contemporary society. While the desire for family membership is natural, it should be promoted in ways which do not forcibly sever the bonds between a birth mother and her child. Efforts to redefine the family should begin by reevaluating the traditional belief that parents and children must be genetically related. For as long as couples demand a genetic link to their children, the resort to surrogate arrangements, legal or not, will continue. If society chooses to uphold these arrangements, it will only undermine the family it wants to support.

ENDNOTES

1. *Matter of Baby M*, 109 N.J. 396, 537 A.2d 1227 (1988).

2. Surrogate parenting contracts typically require a woman to be artificially inseminated with the sperm of the contracting man, carry the fetus to full term and then surrender the child for adoption. The issue confronting the court in the *Baby M* case was whether the contractual agreement to relinquish a mother's parental rights for consideration violated the state's adoption laws. The court held that it does.

The use of the term "surrogate" in this context is quite inappropriate as the woman is the birth mother of the child and, except in cases of *in vitro* fertilization where a fertilized egg is implanted in her uterus, she is also the biological mother. If anything, the contracting father's spouse is the surrogate. A more appropriate term would be "contracted motherhood." However, because common understanding and state laws governing the practice have adopted this terminology, I will retain it for purposes of consistency.

3. See Ariz. Rev. Stat. Ann. Section 25-218 (1989), Ind. Code Ann. Section 31-8-2-1 (West 1989), Ky. Rev. Stat. Ann. Section 199.590 (3) (Baldwin 1989), Mich. Comp. Laws Sections 722.851-863 (1989) Neb. Rev. Stat. Ann. Section 25-21,000 (1989), N.D. Cent. Code Section 14-18-05 (1989), Utah Code Ann.

Section 76-7-204 (1989) and Wash. Rev. Code Ann. Section 26.26.210-260 (1989).

4. Carol Gilligan, *In a Different Voice* (Cambridge: Harvard University Press, 1982).

5. Ibid., p. 17 ff. Gilligan develops the thesis that women typically develop a moral response to conflict that is very different from that displayed by men. Rather than deciding on the basis of the "rights" of the parties, women are more likely to focus on the need to maintain relationships. Gilligan contends that researchers such as Lawrence Kohlberg discount the value of this different moral voice in developing scales of moral development because their studies focus almost exclusively on males.

Gilligan's findings have also come under fire from researchers who claim that the evidence does not support significant gender differences. See, for example, Walker, "Sex Differences in the Development of Moral Reasoning: A Critical Review," *Child Development* 55, no. 3 (June, 1984): 677-91 (finding no differences in justice reasoning tests) and Benton et al., "Is Hostility Linked with Affiliation among Males and with Achievement among Females? A Critique of Pollack and Gilligan," *Journal of Personality and Social Psychology* 45, no. 5 (November 1983: 1167-71) (citing a failed attempt to reproduce Gilligan's findings on violence). Other critics have not attacked the claim of difference, but question whether some differences might not be the product of class or religion rather than gender. See Auerbach et al., "On Gilligan's In A Different Voice," *Feminist Studies* 11 no. 1 (1985): 149-61.

For purposes of this study, it is not essential that we resolve the empirical controversy between Gilligan and her critics. It is enough to show that a morality of care has value and that it provides a viewpoint from which to criticize surrogate parenting agreements. It is not necessary to show that this moral viewpoint is strongly correlated to gender. Indeed, the argument is far stronger if it can be demonstrated that both men and women engage in this type of moral reasoning.

6. See, for example, David Hume, *Enquiries* ed. L.A. Selby-Bigge and P.H. Niddich (Oxford: Clarendon Press, 1975), p. 293: "[T]he ultimate ends of human actions can never, in any case be accounted for by reason, but recommend themselves entirely to the sentiments and affections of mankind, without any dependence upon intellectual faculties."

This distinction between rights and relationships parallels a similar dispute between communitarians such as Michael J. Sandel and Alisdair MacIntyre and liberal rights theorists such as John Rawls and Ronald Dworkin. Communitarian theory emphasizes the priority of the social good over the rights of the individual in much the same way that a morality of care insists upon a contextual morality which makes primary the bonds between persons. In contrast, rights theorists have criticized the emphasis on the good for failing to take seriously the separateness of persons. On their view, only a commitment to impartial and universal principles can support a valid moral theory.

The most representative statements of these authors can be found in the following works: Ronald Dworkin, *Taking Rights Seriously* (London: Duckworth,

1977), Alisdair MacIntyre, *After Virtue* (Notre Dame: University of Notre Dame Press, 1981), John Rawls, *A Theory of Justice* (Cambridge: Harvard University Press, 1971) and Michael J. Sandel, *Liberalism and the Limits of Justice* (New York: Cambridge University Press, 1982).

7. *In A Different Voice*, pp. 7-8, citing Chodorow, "Family Structure and Feminine Personality," *Women, Culture and Society*, eds. M.Z. Rosaldo and L. Lamphere (Stanford: Stanford University Press, 1974).

8. Ibid., p. 8.

9. Ibid., pp. 9-10, citing Lever, "Sex Differences in the Games Children Play," *Social Problems* 23 (1976): pp. 478-87.

10. See note 5 for a brief account of Gilligan's critics who claim that her findings exaggerate the gender differences in moral reasoning.

11. See Lawrence Kohlberg, *Essays in Moral Development*, vol. 1, *The Philosophy of Moral Development: Moral Stages and the Idea of Justice* (New York: Harper & Row, 1981), p. 165. There Kohlberg describes the highest stage of moral development as "Stage 6: The universal ethical principle orientation. Right is defined by the decision of conscience in accord with self-chosen ethical principles appealing to logical comprehensiveness, universality, and consistency. These principles are abstract and ethical (the Golden Rule, the categorical imperative); they are not concrete moral rules like the Ten Commandments. At heart, these are universal principles of justice, of the reciprocity and equality of human rights, and of respect for the dignity of human beings as individual persons."

12. Gilligan, p. 18.

13. Immanuel Kant, *Foundations of the Metaphysics of Morals*, trans. Lewis W. Beck (New York: Library of Liberal Arts, Number 113, 1959), p. 39.

14. In *A Theory of Justice*, pp. 344-48, Rawls argues that the principle of fidelity obligates individuals when (1) the institution which authorizes the promise is just and (2) the individual has voluntarily accepted benefits from the institution. For Rawls, the institution of promising is necessary to allow cooperative agreements for mutual advantage. Promises which are freely made in a fair bargaining position obligate the promisor.

15. Hume, *A Treatise of Human Nature*, ed. by L.A. Selby-Bigge and P.H. Nidditch (Oxford: Clarendon Press, 1978), p. 352.

16. Annette Baier, "Hume, The Women's Moral Theorist?" *Women and Moral Theory*, ed. Eva Kittay and Diana Meyers. (Totowa, New Jersey: Bowman & Littlefield, 1987), pp. 37-55.

17. Few cases would reach the court if it is true, as according to Lori Andrews, that only about one percent of the women who enter into surrogate parenting contracts change their minds about relinquishing their child. See Andrews, *Between Strangers* (New York: Harper and Row, 1989), p. 269. Of course, if most women voluntarily surrender their children, there would be even less need to grant specific performance of surrogacy contracts.

18. 704 S.W.2d 209 (Ky.1986).

19. In 1988, the Kentucky Legislature amended Ky. Rev. Stat. Ann. Section 199.590 (Baldwin 1989) to provide: "(3) No person, agency, institution, or inter-

mediary shall be a party to a contract or agreement which would compensate a woman for her artificial insemination and subsequent termination of parental rights to a child born as a result of that artificial insemination. No person, agency, institution or intermediary shall receive compensation for the facilitation of contracts or agreements as proscribed by this subsection. Contracts or agreements entered into in violation of this subsection shall be void."

Section 199.990 provides that any person who violates the above provision "shall be fined not less than five hundred dollars ($500) nor more than two thousand dollars ($2,000) or imprisoned for not more than six (6) months, or both. Each day such violation continues shall constitute a separate offense."

20. 704 S.W.2d 209, 213 (Ky.1986). Ky. Rev. Stat. 199.601(2) prevents the giving of consent to the surrender of custody and the termination of parental rights before five days following the birth of the child.

21. Id. at 211-12.

22. Id. at 213.

23. Id. at 214. Also dissenting, Justice Wintersheimer argues that,"The apparent biological father is obviously not adopting his own child but actually purchasing the right to have the child adopted by his own infertile wife. Regardless of the good intentions that may give rise to such a practice, the commercialization of this type of personal problem is exactly what KRS 199.590(2) is intended to prevent." Id. at 215.

24. Id. at 213.

25. See note 19 supra.

26. 505 N.Y.S.2d 813 (Sur. 1986).

27. Id. at 817.

28. Id. at 815.

29. Id. at 818.

30. "Surrogate Parenting: Analysis and Recommendations for Public Policy, *The New York State Task Force on Life and the Law* (1988), iv-v. Among the various recommendations of the task force are the following: "Surrogate parenting alters deep-rooted social and moral assumptions about the relationship between parents and their children. The practice involves unprecedented rules and standards for terminating parental obligations and rights, including the right to a relationship with one's own child. The assumption that 'a deal is a deal,' relied upon to justify this drastic change in public policy, fails to respect the significance of the relationships and rights at stake. . . .

"Public policy should discourage surrogate parenting. This goal should be achieved through legislation that declares the contracts void as against public policy. . . .

"The legislation proposed by the Task Force would not prohibit surrogate parenting arrangements when they are not commercial and remain undisputed. . . .

"In custody disputes arising from surrogate parenting arrangements, the birth mother and her husband, if any, should be awarded custody unless the court finds, based on clear and convincing evidence, that the child's best interests would be served by an award of custody to the father and/or genetic mother. . . . "

31. 537 A.2d 1227 (N.J. 1988).

32. Id. at 1240. N.J.S.A. 9:3-54 prohibits the payment of any consideration in the placement of a child for adoption. Termination of parental rights may be accomplished only by the surrender of the child to an approved agency or to the Department of Youth and Family Services in accordance with N.J.S.A. 9:2-16,-17; N.J.S.A. 9:3-41; N.J.S.A. 30:4C-23 or where there has been a showing of parental abandonment or unfitness. In order to terminate parental rights under the private placement adoption statute, there must be a showing of "intentional abandonment or a very substantial neglect of parental duties without a reasonable expectation of a reversal of the conduct in the future. N.J.S.A. 9:3048c (1).

33. Id. at 1235.

34. Id. at 1238.

35. Id.

36. Id. at 1238 and 1240.

37. Id. at 1240.

38. In this case, Mary Beth Whitehead provided the egg which was artificially inseminated with the sperm of William Stern. In a case where the surrogate bears no genetic relationship to the child, her claim to be the "natural" mother of the child will be more problematic.

Just this situation was recently faced in Santa Anna, California where a superior court judge awarded custody to the contracting genetic parents. See, *New York Times*, Oct. 23, 1990, at A14, col. 1. In this case, an egg from Crispina Calvert was fertilized by her husband's sperm *in vitro* and placed in the uterus of a surrogate, Anna Johnson, who carried the child to term. In awarding custody to the Calverts, Orange County Superior Court Judge Richard Parslow held that Johnson was a "genetic stranger" to the baby and did not acquire parental rights through her surrogacy. He also found that "the three natural parents contention is really not in the best interests of the child."

The case will likely be appealed and because California has no statutory or case law on this subject, it is difficult to predict the final outcome. In such a case, the morality of care would argue against specific performance by elevating the relationship established during gestation over the genetic link. However, to the extent that a genetic relationship is deemed important for parenthood, the argument for specific performance will be more forceful. Resolution of the matter will require a determination of the meaning of parenthood.

39. *Matter of Baby M* at 1246-47.

40. Id. at 1248. For an excellent review of the literature on the bonding process, see Maurice Suh, "Surrogate Motherhood: An Argument for Denial of Specific Performance," 22 *Columbia Journal of Law and Social Problems* 357 (1989).

41. Id.

42. Id.

43. Id. at 1249.

44. 316 U.S. 535 (1942).

45. *Matter of Baby M* at 1254.

46. Id. at 1255.
47. Id.
48. Fla. Rev. Stat. Ann. Section 63.212 (1) (i) (West 1989) prohibits any attempt "[t]o contract for the purchase, sale or transfer of custody or parental rights in connection with any child, or in connection with any fetus yet unborn, or in connection with any fetus identified in any way but not yet conceived, in return for any valuable consideration. Any such contract is void and unenforceable as against the public policy of this state. However, fees, costs, and other incidental payments made in accordance with statutory provisions for adoption, foster care and child welfare are permitted, . . . but the payment of such expenses may not be made conditioned upon the transfer of parental rights."

La. Rev. Stat. Ann. Article 9, Section 2713 (West 1989) simply declares contracts for surrogate motherhood to be null and void and unenforceable as against public policy.

Ohio Rev. Code. Ann. Section 5103.17 (Anderson 1989) has been interpreted by the Ohio Attorney General to allow the Department of Public Welfare to conclude that "a person or organization not licensed by the Department as a child-placing agency . . . is prohibited . . . from 1.the solicitation of women to become artificially inseminated with the sperm of men who remain anonymous to them, for the purpose of women bearing children and surrendering possession of the children and all parental rights to such men and their spouses; 2. the negotiation, for a fee, of a contract between such men and women bearing children and surrendering possession of the children and all parental rights to such men and their spouses; and 3. the arrangement for payment of the women in these transactions." OAG No. 83-001.

49. Nev. Rev. Stat. Section 127.287 (1989).
50. *Between Strangers*, p. 229.
51. Ibid.
52. Ariz. Rev. Stat. Ann. Section 25-218 (1989) provides: "A. No person may enter into, induce, arrange, procure or otherwise assist in the formation of a surrogate parentage contract. B. A surrogate is the legal mother of a child born as a result of a surrogate parentage contract and is entitled to custody of that child. C. If the mother of a child born as a result of a surrogate contract is married, her husband is presumed to be the legal father of the child. This presumption is rebuttable. D. For the purposes of this section, "surrogate parentage contract" means a contract, agreement or arrangement in which a woman agrees to the implantation of an embryo not related to that woman or agrees to conceive a child through natural or artificial insemination and to voluntarily relinquish her parental rights to the child."

Ind. Code Ann. Section 31-8-2-1 (West 1989) states: "The general assembly declares that it is against public policy to enforce any term of a surrogate agreement that requires a surrogate to do any of the following: (1) Provide a gamete to conceive a child. (2) Become pregnant. (3) Consent to undergo or undergo an abortion. (4) Undergo medical or psychological treatment or examination. (5) Use a substance or engage in activity only in accordance with the demands of another person. (6) Waive parental rights or duties to a child. (7) Terminate care, custody, or control of a child. (8) Consent to a stepparent adoption under IC 31-1-1.''

Ky. Rev. Stat. Ann. Section 199.590 (3) (Baldwin 1989) provides that "No person, agency, institution, or intermediary shall be a party to a contract or agreement which would compensate a woman for her artificial insemination and subsequent termination of parental rights to a child born as a result of that artificial insemination. No person, agency, institution or intermediary shall receive compensation for the facilitation of contracts or agreements as proscribed by this subsection. Contracts or agreements entered into in violation of this subsection shall be void.'' Section 199.990 provides for a fine of not "less than five hundred dollars ($500) nor more than two thousand dollars ($2,000)'' or imprisonment "for not more than six (6) months, or both. Each day such violation continues shall constitute a separate offense.''

Mich. Comp. Laws Sections 722.851-863 (1989) prohibit surrogate parentage contracts as contrary to public policy, awards custody in such cases on the basis of the best interests of the child and imposes misdemeanor penalties on parties who enter into such contracts for compensation except for "unemancipated minor females or a female diagnosed as being mentally retarded or as having a mental illness or developmental disability.'' The statute makes it a felony to either induce, arrange, procure or assist in the formation of a surrogate parentage contract for compensation or to enter into such a contract with an unemancipated minor female or a female with any of the diagnoses listed above.

Neb. Rev. Stat. Ann. Section 25-21,000 (1989) declares surrogate parenthood contracts to be void, but holds that "[t]he biological father of a child born pursuant to such a contract shall have all the rights and obligations imposed by law with respect to such child.''

N.D. Cent. Code Section 14-18-05 (1989) voids "[a]ny agreement in which a woman agrees to become a surrogate or to relinquish her rights and duties as parent of a child conceived through assisted conception.''

Utah Code Ann. Section 76-7-204 (1989) declares void any "surrogate parenthood agreement'' entered into between April 24, 1989 and July 1, 1991 when this section sunsets. Any "person, agency, institution or intermediary'' who is a party to any agreement for profit shall be guilty of a class A misdemeanor. Prior to January 1, 1991, an interim legislative committee will study the matter for consideration by the 1991 legislature.

Wash. Rev. Code Ann. Section 26.26.210-260 (1989) makes it a gross misdemeanor for any person to assist in the formation of a "surrogate parentage contract'' where an "unemancipated minor female'' or a "female diagnosed as as being mentally retarded or as having a mental illness or developmental disability is the surrogate.'' The statute also makes it a gross misdemeanor to assist in the formation of any such contract for compensation. Contracts entered into for compensation shall be void and unenforceable as contrary to public policy.

53. Ark. Stat. Ann. Section 9-10-118 (1989) upholds the validity surrogate parentage contracts. Under such contracts, the child shall be "of (1) the biological

father and the woman intended to be the mother if the biological father is married; or (2) the biological father only if unmarried; or (3) the woman intended to be the mother in the cases of a surrogate mother when an anonymous donor's sperm was utilized for artificial insemination.''

54. W. Marshall Prettyman, "The Next Baby M Case: The Need for a Surrogacy Statute," 18 *Seton Hall Law Review* 886, 920-21 (1988). Prettyman writes, "One bill sought to prohibit surrogate parenting by amending the New Jersey baby-selling statute to include the prohibition of payments made pursuant to surrogate agreements (footnote omitted). A second bill, aimed at making surrogate parenting contracts valid in New Jersey, was, in effect, no more than a legislative version of the trial court opinion (footnote omitted). The third bill, dealing directly with surrogate parenting, took a middle approach that would have allowed surrogacy contracts to a limited degree, strictly for infertile couples, and other strict judicial guidelines and supervision (footnote omitted). Four other bills dealt with such procedures as artificial insemination (footnote omitted), *in vitro* and *in vivo* fertilization (footnote omitted) and freezing of sperm, ova (footnote omitted) and embryos (footnote omitted).''

55. Ibid., p. 922.

56. "Bioethics Panel to Oppose Surrogate Parenting", *Newark Star-Ledger*, Nov. 8, 1990, at 30, col. 3.

57. "Surrogate Parenting: Analysis and Recommendations for Public Policy," *The New York State Task Force on Life and the Law* (1988), p. 123.

58. The test for unconscionability under the Uniform Commercial Code determines "whether, in light of the general commercial background and the commercial needs of the particular trade or case, the clauses are so one-sided as to be unconscionable. . . . The principle is one of the prevention of oppression and unfair surprise (citation omitted) and not of disturbance of allocation of risk because of superior bargaining power." Official Comment on UCC, Section 2-302.

Contracts of adhesion may also involve parties with grossly unequal bargaining power. In such cases, the weaker party is offered a good or service on a "take it or leave it" basis with no meaningful opportunity to negotiate contract terms.

59. Lori Andrews, "Alternative Modes of Reproduction," *Reproductive Laws for the 1990s*, ed. Sherrill Cohen and Nadine Taub (Clifton, N.J.: Humana Press, 1989), p. 365.

60. Ibid., p. 385. Andrews writes, "Specific performance is generally not granted for a breach of contract for personal services. . . . [I]t would be unfathomable to enforce a contract to force a surrogate to be inseminated (if she changed her mind before the insemination) or to carry the child (if she decided to exercise her legal right to an abortion).

Once the child is born, however, specific performance is a realistic possibility. The personal services of the surrogate are no longer needed so she would not be forced to provide a personal service against her will. Outside of the personal services area, specific performance is an appropriate remedy when monetary compensation is inadequate.''

61. See supra note 42 and accompanying text.

62. See supra note 57.

63. Ariz. Rev. Stat. Ann. Section 25-218 (1989) provides that the surrogate is entitled to legal custody of the child. If she is married her husband is presumed to be the legal father of the child. The presumption is rebuttable.

Mich. Comp. Laws Sections 722.851-863 (1989) provides that if there is a dispute between the parties regarding custody, "the party having physical custody of the child may retain physical custody of the child until the circuit court orders otherwise."

64. See *Fitzpatrick v. Michael*, 177 Md. 248, 9 A.2d 639, 641 (1939), citing *Fry on Specific Performance*, 5th ed., sections 110, 112.

65. In New Jersey, pre-adoption counseling is required by N.J.A.C. 10:121A-5.2(a).

66. N.J.S.A. 9:2-16 and -17 requires all formal adoptions to take place after the birth of the child.

67. Christine Sistare, "Reproductive Freedom and Women's Freedom: Surrogacy and Autonomy," *The Philosophical Forum* 19:4 (1988), p. 231.

68. Ibid.

69. Ibid., p. 237.

70. This is precisely how the New Jersey Supreme Court characterized the agreement between William Stern and the Whiteheads in the *Matter of Baby M*, 537 A.2d at 1248 (N.J. 1988). See supra note 41 and accompanying text.

71. In the *Matter of Baby M*, the contract was to pay Mary Beth Whitehead $10,000 only on the surrender of custody of the child. "As for the contention that the Sterns are paying only for services and not for an adoption, we need note only that they would pay nothing in the event the child died before the fourth month of pregnancy, and only $1,000 if the child were stillborn, even though the 'services' were fully rendered." Id. at 1241.

72. It may be argued that if the sale is restricted to early infancy the risk to the child will be minimized because the child will have no memory of the birth mother. Even if the child in such a circumstance fails to develop an interest in the birth mother at a later date, surely the other children in the birth mother's family will be subjected to potential psychological harm. They may legitimately fear that *they* might be sold at some future date.

73. Andrews, p. 388, note 123 citing Siegel, Case Study, "Baby Making and the Public Interest," 6 (4) *Hastings Center Report* 14 (August 1976).

74. See supra note 43 and accompanying text.

75. John Stuart Mill first discussed the harm principle as the basis for social interference with individual liberty in *On Liberty* (1859), ed. Elizabeth Rapaport (Indianapolis: Hackett Publishing Co., 1978), p. 73 ff.

Prenatal Harm
as Child Abuse?

Joan C. Callahan
James W. Knight

SUMMARY. Attempts to prevent prenatal harm have led to a number of court cases resulting in interference with pregnant women. These include incarceration and the imposition of medical and surgical treatments thought to prevent prenatal harm. We argue that the legal sanctions that have been used and/or are proposed for use against pregnant women in order to prevent prenatal harm are (1) morally unjustified even where they might be legal, (2) are morally and legally unacceptable because they violate important moral values captured in our legal system, and (3) are morally unacceptable and would make bad law because they would contribute to the harm they would be instituted to prevent.

Joan C. Callahan, PhD in Philosophy from the University of Maryland, is Associate Professor at the University of Kentucky. James W. Knight, PhD in Animal Science from the University of Florida, is Professor at Virginia Polytechnic Institute. They are coauthors of *Preventing Birth: Contemporary Methods and Related Moral Controversies*, University of Utah Press, 1989.

This paper has been adapted from Callahan (1986a) and Knight and Callahan (1989), Chapters 7 and 9. The authors are grateful to *Commonweal* and to the University of Utah Press for permission to adapt the material here. A version of the paper was originally prepared for the American Section of the International Association for Philosophy of Law and Social Philosophy's 1988 conference on the family, and is among selected papers from that conference to be published by Cornell University Press in a collection, *Kindred Matters: Rethinking the Philosophy of the Family*, edited by Diana Meyers, Kenneth Kipnis, and Cornelius Murphy. The authors are grateful to Cornell for permitting us to publish a slightly different version of the paper here. The authors are also grateful to Carolyn Bratt, Deborah Mathieu, Patricia Smith, and Morton Winston for their extremely helpful comments on earlier drafts.

INTRODUCTION

Potential harm to fetuses resulting from certain behaviors and decisions of pregnant women has raised several difficult questions of increasing moral urgency.[1] In what follows, we develop and defend a position on (1) whether using legal sanctions to protect fetuses from potentially harmful actions or decisions of their mothers can be morally justified and (2) whether such sanctions make good law.

We shall argue that the sanctions that have been proposed (1) are morally unacceptable even where they might be legal, (2) are morally and legally unacceptable because they violate important moral values captured in our legal system (such as the publicity condition of the rule of law which requires that persons be able to predict when their behavior might lead to sanction by the state), and (3) are morally unacceptable and would make bad law because they would be counterproductive, that is, they would contribute to the harm they would be instituted to prevent.

We cannot address the issue of prenatal harm without discussing the moral status of human fetuses, which is commonly framed as the question of fetal personhood. In discussing this question, we shall argue (1) that the most prominent secular argument for the personhood of fetuses fails, (2) that the question of personhood is a matter of decision rather than discovery, and (3) that given that we must *decide* when to commence recognition of personhood, that recognition should be set at birth, since once a viable infant emerges at birth, there is a morally crucial change in circumstances, namely, that (unlike cases involving fetuses) protecting an infant does not involve violation of its mother's rights to self-direction and bodily integrity.

It is important to note that in discussions of preventing fetal harm, moral and legal arguments often run in tandem. For example, we take it for granted that equal treatment under the law is not only a requirement of our legal system, it is a requirement of morality as well. Thus, when we argue that the policies in question are gratuitously hostile to women, and that they therefore fail to meet the requirement of equal treatment under the law, we mean to be advancing both a legal argument and moral argument against such policies. And when we argue that the policies proposed would make bad law because they would contribute to the harm they are meant to prevent, we mean to make a point about the moral justification of liberty-limiting legislation and a point about the rational construction of law.

PRENATAL PERSONHOOD:
A MATTER OF DECISION
RATHER THAN DISCOVERY

The issue that concerns us in this paper cannot be discussed without referring to the debate on the morality of legal elective abortion, which centers on the question of the moral status of the fetus. The debate commonly focuses on the personhood of the fetus. Those who hold that elective abortion is so profoundly morally wrong that it must be prohibited by law contend that the fetus is a person, having the same fundamental moral rights of any person that are protected by law.

But if fetuses are persons this is not obvious, since they lack the morally relevant characteristics of paradigm cases of persons, that is, characteristics that compel the recognition of powerful moral rights, including the right to not be killed for reasons less than self defense. Among these characteristics are certain mental ones, for example, a concept of oneself as an ongoing being with at least some kinds of plans and stakes (cf. Warren, 1975; Callahan, 1986). Fetuses simply do not have any of the characteristics that compel an immediate recognition of personhood. These characteristics emerge long after birth, and this makes the matter of accepting fetuses as persons a matter of decision rather than discovery. That is, we need to ask whether fetuses, which do not have the characteristics of paradigmatic persons, ought to be treated as persons. Since the question is one of *deciding* whether we should treat fetuses as persons, then the task is to set a convention that establishes at what point we shall recognize personhood in custom and in law.

One possible convention is to set the recognition of personhood at birth. Another is to set it at conception. Other conventions might set recognition at various prenatal stages or at various points after birth. Those who want to outlaw elective abortion insist that we must decide that personhood is to be recognized from fertilization onward. The secular argument given for this conclusion rests on the assumption that unless beings are radically different, treating them in radically different ways cannot be morally justified. The argument begins by starting with human beings everyone recognizes as having the fundamental moral rights of persons. It then points out that a person at twenty five, for example, is not radically different from one at twenty four and a half, and that person is not radically different from one at twenty four, and so on. The argument presses us back from twenty four to twenty three to twenty two, through adolescence and childhood to infancy. From infancy, it is a short step to late-term fetuses, because (the argument goes) change in location does not constitute an essential change in a being itself. Thus, change of place from the womb to the wider world is not, it is argued, sufficient to justify treating late-term fetuses and infants in radically different ways. The argument then presses us back to embryos, pre-embryos, and finally to fertilization, which is the only point in development where a clear line can be drawn between radically different kinds of beings. Logic and fairness, it is argued, force us to accept that even the human zygote is a person with the same fundamental moral rights as the mature human being (see Wertheimer, 1971). And these rights of fetuses, it is further argued, must be protected by our laws, as they are for mature persons.

One significant objection to this argument for prenatal personhood is that it turns on the assumption that we can never treat beings that are not radically different from one another in radically different ways. But if we accept this assumption we shall be unable to justify all sorts of public policies which we believe are both necessary and fair. For example, this assumption implies that we cannot be justified in setting ages for the commencement of important privileges, since withholding these privileges until a certain age unfairly discriminates against those who are close to that age: we must give the four-year-old the right to vote, the five-year-old the right to drink, the six-year-old the right to drive. But these implications show that this kind of argument for adopting a convention of recognizing personhood at fertilization is unsound (cf. Glover, 1977).

It is often objected that this criticism of the argument for prenatal personhood cannot be correct, since it not only rules out our being committed to the personhood of fetuses, it also implies that infants do not have the rights of persons, since infants are undeveloped in regard to the characteristics in question.

But this objection is not devastating. For, again, the question before us is one of deciding what convention we shall adopt. We can allow that even if infants do not yet have the characteristics that compel us to accept them as persons, there are other considerations that provide excellent reasons for taking birth as the best place to set the conventional recognition of personhood with its full range of fundamental moral and legal rights, despite the fact that infants are much more like late-term fetuses than like mature human beings who are obviously persons. Chief among these considerations is that individuals other than an infant's biological mother are able to care for the infant and have an interest in doing so (cf. Warren, 1975). Although there are intriguing physiological changes accompanying birth, there is no change in the morally relevant characteristics of late-term fetuses and infants. All else being equal, if the life of a late-term fetus is sustained, it will develop the characteristics of paradigmatic persons. But once a viable human being emerges from the womb and others are able and willing to care for it, there are radical changes in what is involved in preserving its life and otherwise protecting it. And the *crucial* change is that sustaining its life or otherwise protecting it does not violate its biological mother's rights to self-direction and bodily integrity. Thus, even though birth, unlike fertilization, is not a point at which we have a radically new kind of being, it is *not* a morally arbitrary point for commencing recognition of personhood in custom and public policy. Our suggestion, then, is that fetuses should not be treated by the law as persons with the full range of fundamental moral and legal rights attached to persons. Rather, we should take birth as the place to set the convention of recognizing personhood, even though infants do not yet possess the characteristics of paradigmatic persons. Commencing legal recognition of personhood at birth has the moral advantage of taking the actual, unequivocal personhood of women far more seriously than can setting conventional recognition of personhood at any prenatal stage.[2]

LEGAL ACTIONS FOR PRENATAL INJURY

Although United States law has traditionally not treated fetuses as persons or as rights-bearers of any sort, some recent developments in the courts reflect a movement toward recognizing prenatal rights.

Wrongful death actions. A fetus might be fatally injured as a result of someone's actions or omissions.[3] Were it not for the injury (it is assumed), an undamaged infant would have been born. In cases like this, the agent causing the damage can be held liable for the death of a viable or previable fetus. Such cases are known as 'wrongful death' cases. Traditionally, wrongful death suits have been brought under statutes designed to compensate beneficiaries for losses resulting from the death of a family member. Initially, nearly every United States jurisdiction required that an infant be born alive and then die as a result of injuries sustained prenatally for there to be a cause for legal action under a wrongful death statute. Recovery for the death of a fetus was not granted because the fetus was not considered separate from its biological mother (*Dietrich v. Inhabitants of Northampton*, 1884).

Such thinking has carried forward in some decisions.[4] But the livebirth requirement for bringing suit has been attacked because it encourages anyone who might have caused harm to a fetus to ensure that the fetus dies, since under the requirement, an injurer is only at risk of suit if a damaged infant is born. Thus, at worst, the livebirth requirement encourages anyone who might have caused injury to a fetus to kill that fetus. At best, the requirement creates an incentive for injurers to withhold any efforts to save the lives of fetuses they might have injured. For example, the livebirth requirement gives someone who has caused an accident involving a pregnant woman a reason to delay getting the pregnant woman to the hospital. Such reasons led the Minnesota Supreme Court to become the first court to allow recovery for the death of a fetus under a wrongful death statute (*Verkennes v. Corniea*, 1949).[5] In *Rainey v. Horn* (1954), the Mississippi Supreme Court accepted the inseparability thesis, but allowed recovery anyway, on the ground that since the offspring, if born, could have brought suit for injury, the parents had a rightful action for wrongful death. Although wrongful death suits involving prenatal injury have generally been limited to cases involving death after the point of viability, the trend has increasingly been toward allowing suits for prenatal death at any stage, on the ground that, but for the wrongful action(s) or omission(s), the fetus would have reached viability (Lenow, 1983).[6]

Wrongful birth actions. Wrongful birth actions are brought by parents against physicians, genetic counselors, laboratories, pharmacists, contraceptive manufacturers, or others for recovery of the costs parents incur in taking care of a disabled child, and sometimes for their pain and suffering in being burdened with such a child. Usually, these cases involve a negligent failure to warn potential parents that their children are likely to inherit a disabling condition, failure to diagnose or warn parents about the presence of such a condition in a fetus, incompetent sterilizations and unsuccessful abortions, laboratory diagnostic errors, faulty contraceptives, or pharmacist errors in filling prescriptions for oral contraceptives. The central claim in such cases is that the wrongful error of the defendant resulted in a "harmful birth" which the woman, if properly informed, could have prevented by aborting (Feinberg, 1985).

Wrongful pregnancy actions. Wrongful pregnancy actions involve unplanned pregnancies that occurred because of the error of some third party (e.g., failure of sterilization or failure of an abortion procedure). Such actions can be brought irrespective of whether a healthy infant is born. Wrongful birth and wrongful pregnancy can, in principle, be charged in the same suit (Feinberg, 1985).

Wrongful life actions. Actions for wrongful life are, as Feinberg (1985) points out, far more controversial than are the previous kinds of actions, and they have been far less successful in the courts. What distinguishes these actions from others is that they are brought, not by parents, but by the damaged child. The action for damages is not brought because the defendant caused the injuries defeating hope for a reasonably high quality of life. Rather, the claim is that the defendant wrongly allowed the child to come into existence at all, given his or her afflictions. Suits for wrongful life can be brought against physicians or genetic counselors for failure to provide to the prospective parents information that might have motivated them to avoid conceiving or to abort a pregnancy. But they can also be brought against parents for allegedly wrongfully conceiving or not aborting. The main reason that wrongful life suits have not been widely successful is that courts have had great difficulty evaluating the claim made by damaged plaintiffs that being born is itself an injury, that is, that this individual would have been better off never having been brought into existence at all (Feinberg, 1985).[7]

Actions for nonfatal prenatal injuries. The case law involving recovery for nonfatal prenatal injuries closely parallels the case law involving recovery for wrongful death, moving from the early view that the physical inseparability of the fetus from its mother precluded actions being brought in its behalf to the later view that an infant injured prenatally, but after viability, could recover damages. The first such decision, *Bonbrest v. Kotz* (1946), opened the door to wide acceptance of recovery by damaged plaintiffs for prenatal harms occurring after viability (Lenow, 1983).

But a number of courts (as happened with the development of wrongful death cases) have gone further and allowed recovery for injuries sustained prior to viability.[8] What is more, over the last decade, we have begun to see cases in which a plaintiff has recovered for injuries resulting from the actions of others prior to the plaintiff's conception. *Renslow v. Mennonite Hospital* (1977), for example, involved a child who was born suffering from hyperbilirubinemia (an excess of bilirubin in the blood that, when sufficiently high, produces visible jaundice and may cause severe neurological damage, often occurring in fetuses as a result of blood group incompatibility). The child recovered for permanent brain and nervous system damage alleged to have resulted from the hospital's twice negligently transfusing her mother with blood from the wrong blood group nine years prior to the child's birth. By allowing recovery for preconceptive harm, such decisions have helped to pave the way for controversial restrictions on allowing fertile women to work in environments that might have deleterious effects on their capacity to reproduce healthy children, a topic we take up elsewhere.[9] Today, most courts hold that the time of prenatal injury is irrelevant if a causal connection can be shown between the harm suffered and someone's actions or omissions (Glantz, 1983).[10]

Our position on recognizing personhood at birth but not before is consistent with much of the traditional treatment of prenatal injury in law and with the United States Supreme Court's abortion-liberalizing decision in *Roe v. Wade* (1973). For, as Glantz (1983) has emphasized, the court in *Roe* did *not* argue that a fetus is to be recognized as a person at viability, having the attendant moral and legal rights of other persons. On the other hand, the court also did not contend that the state has no interest in protecting even previable fetuses from injury. That is, although the *Roe* decision guarantees women the right to elective abortion through the end of the second trimester of pregnancy, a very different issue regarding protection of the fetus arises when a woman elects not to abort a pregnancy, and her actions result in the birth of a damaged child (see Mathieu, 1985; Robertson and Schulman, 1987). Indeed, the decision in *Roe* has increasingly been used in legal decisions and by legal commentators to shore up other arguments for expanding liability for prenatal harm, for restricting the behaviors of pregnant women, and for imposing medical and surgical interventions on women to protect fetuses expected to be brought to full term.[11] At least some of these commentators may be unhappy with the *Roe* decision's refusal to recognize fetuses as persons in either the moral or legal sense, and they therefore want to do whatever they can to force a legal recognition of fetal rights. However, a moral position that holds that elective abortion is acceptable and that fetuses are not persons, yet that people may be held legally liable for or may be prevented by the law from contributing to nonfatal prenatal harm because such harms involve persons can be perfectly consistent. In order to see this, we need to distinguish between actual persons, potential persons, and future persons.

PROTECTING FUTURE PERSONS

We have distinguished between (1) the time (which we've left unspecified) when a human being has developed the kinds of characteristics that compel us to recognize it as a person (we shall call these 'metaphysical' or 'actual' persons) and (2) the time to be set by convention when a human being which does not yet have these characteristics is to be accepted into the community of persons and given the full protection of the law (we shall call these 'conventional' persons). We have argued that the conventional recognition of personhood should be set at birth. Thus, infants, though not yet actual persons, are to be accepted by convention as persons and treated as such by the law. We now need to distinguish between potential persons and future persons in order to address the questions at hand.

A fetus is a potential person when it is the case that (1) it has the capacities to develop the kinds of characteristics that are relevant to compelling a recognition of a being as an actual person and (2) if its life were supported, it would be born, gaining conventional entry into the set of persons at birth. Notice that if a fetus has an anomaly that would preclude development of the characteristics that compel a recognition of personhood, it is not a potential person. That is, even if such a fetus were to be born, it could never develop the characteristics of actual persons, therefore, it is not a potential person, since it does not meet criterion (1) for potential personhood. Thus, not every fetus is a potential person.

A fetus is a future person (1) if it is a potential person and (2) it will, in fact, gain conventional entry into the class of persons through birth. All future persons are potential persons, then. But since not all potential persons will endure to reach conventional personhood (they may die because of anomalies incompatible with life, intentional abortion, or accidents), not all potential persons are future persons (cf. Langerak, 1979). The complex moral and legal issues that concern us involve fetuses as both potential and future persons. Our focus, however, will be on harm to prenatal future persons.

Central to the reasoning in decisions granting recovery for prenatal injuries is a concern to protect the interests of "liveborn persons" (Glantz, 1983). Traditionally, the class of "liveborn persons" includes *all* infants, even those with an anomaly (e.g., anencephaly, an invariably fatal condition, involving absence of the cerebral hemispheres of the brain) that precludes their ever developing the kinds of characteristics that are relevant to compelling recognition of a being as an actual person. Thus, as the class is traditionally understood, all "liveborn persons" will not qualify as members of the class of future persons, since the class of future persons does not include beings incapable of developing the kinds of characteristics that are relevant to compelling recognition of the moral rights attendant to personhood.

We shall not dwell on this distinction here, since the position we shall defend will turn out not to depend on it. Before leaving it behind, however, we should mention that the distinction between the traditional class of "liveborn persons" and the class of future persons is important and useful for dealing with other questions, particularly with questions about when infanticide might be morally permissible. For example, in 1987, Brenda and Michael Winners of Arcadia, California decided not to abort their anencephalic fetus, but to attempt to bring her to term and then keep her on life supports long enough to arrange transplants of her organs to infants in vital need of replacement organs. It is customary to not place such infants on life supports, and the decision drew criticism from a number of groups and individuals, including some ethicists who contended that going forward with the plan violated a first principle of medical ethics, namely, that the treatment of one patient must not be modified for the treatment of another patient. Other objections included the contention that treatment of the infant (i.e., sustaining her on life supports) solely for the sake of "harvesting" her organs showed lack of respect for her as a human being (Clark *et al.*, 1987). But the Winners' infant was not a potential person, since her condition made it impossible for her to ever develop the kinds of characteristics that make a characteristically human life possible and that compel a recognition of personhood. Thus, we are confronted with yet another decision regarding what conventions we shall set. Must we treat as persons beings who do not have the capacity to ever develop the kinds of characteristics that would compel recognizing them as actual persons? Recognizing infants as persons in ordinary cases is justified on the bases of (1) protecting the interests of the actual persons they will become and (2) not violating women's rights to autonomy and bodily integrity. Since anencephalic infants like the Winners' lack the capacities to become actual persons, our position allows that we need not apply the convention of recognizing them as persons at birth. It does not follow from this, of course, that anything we might do to these infants would be morally permissible, anymore than being a non-human animal (not being a person) implies that we can do just anything to it. But it does follow that treating the Winners' infant as they proposed would not involve mistreatment of a person.

Different questions arise, however, when a fetus has the capacities to become an actual person, and events taking place before it is born can seriously set back the interests it will have as an actual person. The state's concern to protect the interests of future persons was articulated in a Canadian decision, quoted in *Bonbrest* (1946):

> If a right action be denied to the child it will be compelled without any fault on its own part to go through life carrying the seal of another's fault and bearing a very heavy burden of infirmity and inconvenience without any compensation therefore. To my mind, it is but natural justice that a child, if born alive and viable, should be allowed to maintain an action in the courts for injuries wrongfully committed upon its person while in the womb of its mother. (*Montreal Tramways v. Leveille*, 1933)

This same concern is captured more succinctly by the New Jersey Supreme Court's decision in *Smith v. Brennan* (1960), which held that a child has a legal right to begin life with a sound mind and body.[12]

Such reasoning can be used to justify recovery for both nonfatal prenatal injury and wrongful life. As we have pointed out, wrongful life actions have enjoyed little success in the courts to date. But a California appellate court decision suggests that courts may be about to change that trend, not only in allowing more recoveries for wrongful life in general, but in allowing recovery from parents as well as from third parties. The case involved the failure of a laboratory (which had previously been alerted to failures in its testing) to diagnose a couple as carriers of Tay-Sachs disease (a recessive disorder characterized by progressive retardation in development, paralysis, dementia, blindness, and death by age three or four). The child's claim was recognized, and the court added this comment:

If a case arose where, despite due care by the medical profession in transmitting the necessary warnings, parents made a conscious choice to proceed with a pregnancy, with full knowledge that a seriously impaired infant would be born, that conscious choice would provide an intervening act of proximate cause to preclude liability insofar as defendants other than the parents were concerned. Under such circumstances, we see no sound public policy which would protect those parents from being answerable for the pain, suffering, and misery which they have wrought upon their offspring. (*Curlender v. Bio-Science Laboratories.* 1980, *in dictum*)

In cases where potential for a severe genetic defect is discovered prior to conception, such reasoning entails that unless potential parents practice contraception or seek abortion if they do conceive, they may well find themselves legally liable for producing a wrongful life. In cases where a severe genetic defect is discovered or a severe prenatal harm is suspected after conception, such reasoning clearly places parents in the position of choosing abortion or potentially facing legal liability for bringing a pregnancy to term. And since biological fathers (at least at present) have no legal right to interfere with a woman's right to abort or not abort a pregnancy,[13] any such liability for wrongful life must fall on women who do not abort.[14]

As regards prenatal injury more generally, there is also a rising trend toward holding women legally liable for causing prenatal harm and toward imposing medical and surgical procedures on women to prevent prenatal harm.[15] The reasoning in many of the relevant post-*Roe* cases and commentaries turns on the position that (1) if a woman has decided to carry a pregnancy to term, *ceteris paribus*, she carries what we have suggested be understood as a future person, and (2) that future person has a compelling moral right not to begin its independent life disadvantaged by avoidable harms resulting from the actions or omissions of others, including its mother; a moral right, it is further assumed, which is appropriately captured in law, as is the right of any existing person not to be harmed. This reasoning has led to using child protection statutes to impose transfusions and caesarean sections on women to protect their fetuses. It has also given rise to arguments for holding women criminally liable for acting in ways thought to cause prenatal harm during pregnancies expected to be brought full term.[16]

In one recent California action, a woman, Pamela Stewart, was criminally prosecuted when her failure to follow medical instructions (including instructions not to take amphetamines, to stay off her feet, to refrain from having intercourse, and to seek immediate medical treatment if she began bleeding) was held to have caused severe brain damage to her fetus. The infant died five weeks after birth, and Stewart was arrested for causing the death of her son. Annas (1986) reports that police officials wanted Stewart charged with murder, but that the district attorney decided instead to prosecute under a California child support statute.[17] Stewart was charged with a misdemeanor carrying a possible sentence of a year in prison or a fine of $2,000. The case was dismissed only because the defendant was able to convince the court that the 1872 law under which she was being prosecuted was intended to ensure that fathers provide child support, including (following a 1925 amendment) financial support for women pregnant by them (Annas, 1986; Brown *et al.*, 1987; Johnsen, 1987; *People v. Stewart*, 1987).[18]

THE FETUS AS PATIENT

The situation becomes even more complex as prenatal therapies, including prenatal surgical techniques, are developed. As these interventions pass from experimental status to being recognized as safe and effective treatments, we are seeing increasing support for requiring women to submit to them for the sake of future persons (see Robertson, 1982, 1985, 1986). It is not uncommon for those supportive of intrusive prenatal protection policies to suggest that recent advances in medicine that have made fetuses potential patients, somehow change their moral status, endowing them with a right to treatment (e.g., Bowes and Selgestad, 1981).

But nothing about the moral status of any organism follows from the bare fact that it can be effectively treated medically or surgically. Non-human fetuses are now able to be effectively treated medically and surgically, but we do not think that it follows from this fact that these fetuses are persons with a right to treatment (cf.

Ruddick and Wilcox, 1982). On the contrary, the question of the moral status of an organism is prior to the question of its entitlements, and those who argue from the bare fact that a human fetus can now be treated as a patient to the moral claim that human fetuses (but not non-human fetuses) have a right to treatment, fail to understand that they are simply begging the question in favor of personhood for human fetuses. It does not, then, follow from the fact that a fetus *can be* treated that it *has a right to be* treated.

Again, however, arguments for requiring women to submit to interventions for the good of their fetuses need not be based on any claim or assumption that these fetuses are already persons. All that needs to be claimed is that insofar as a fetus is a *future* person, it has a moral (and must have the legal) right not to be injured in a way that will importantly set back the interests it will have as an actual person (see Mathieu, 1985). We need, then, to ask whether the fact that a woman intends to bring a pregnancy to term justifies imposing medical and surgical interventions on her or otherwise legally restricting her behavior in the interests of a future person.

DIRECT INTERFERENCE WITH PREGNANT WOMEN AND THE ANALOGY TO PEDIATRIC CASES

Much of the case for such impositions rests on the argument that in deciding to bring a pregnancy to term, a woman thereby waives her legal right to abortion and thereby takes on a set of special, legally enforceable moral duties of care toward a fetus as the current embodiment of a future person. But, in fact, a woman never waives her right to abortion (Smith, 1983; Annas, 1987). She may decide not to exercise that right, but this does not count as a waiver of the right itself any more than the decision not to buy a certain kind of car amounts to a waiver of the right to buy that kind of car. Given the decision in *Roe*, a woman retains a legal right to elect abortion for any reason through the end of the second trimester of pregnancy, and even after the second trimester if the pregnancy is sufficiently threatening to her health.

Further, those who argue for the view in question assume that in making the decision not to abort, a pregnant woman waives both her moral and legal rights to bodily integrity in favor of a future person (see Mathieu, 1985; Green and Brill, 1987). But waiving a right involves voluntarily relinquishing it, and in just the kinds of cases that concern us (i.e., cases in which a woman refuses an intervention thought to prevent prenatal harm or in which a woman acts in a way that is thought to cause prenatal harm) we find women who clearly have *not* voluntarily relinquished their moral or legal rights to bodily integrity. As Smith (1983) has rightly pointed out, the concept working here is not one of waiver at all. It is, rather, the concept of forfeiture. Felons, for example, forfeit, but do not waive, their moral and legal rights to be at liberty in the community. The argument, then, is one from forfeiture of moral and legal rights; and once this is understood, the picture is substantially altered to a far less benign one than one in which a woman voluntarily relinquishes legal protection of her bodily integrity to protect the interests of a future person. The pregnant woman becomes analogous to the felon who can no longer demand that he or she not be interfered with by the state. Indeed, in arguing for the position that impingements on a pregnant woman's bodily integrity to protect a future person are justified, legal commentators often point out that bodily seizures and bodily intrusions without a person's consent are not unknown to the law (see Bowes and Selgestad, 1981; Mathieu, 1985). The examples given include imposing prison sentences, execution, forced medical and surgical treatment, forced feeding for the sake of prison discipline, and imposing surgery to retrieve evidence of a crime (Robertson, 1982, 1985, 1986; Robertson and Schulman, 1987). The analogy is chilling. Pregnant women are not felons,[19] nor are they, to use another example in the literature, incompetents who may be ordered by courts to submit to bodily invasions to aid others because they are not capable of making such judgments for themselves.[20]

The argument from presumed waiver of a pregnant woman's moral and legal rights generally includes (explicitly or implicitly) analogizing the prenatal cases to ordinary pediatric cases. It is widely accepted that the state may interfere with parents to provide needed medical treatment for a child or to provide for other fundamental needs of a child. Although it is generally recognized that there is an important difference between the prenatal and pediatric cases (since preventing harm in prenatal cases necessarily involves providing treatment through the woman's body or otherwise directly interfering with a woman's behaviors and pediatric cases do not), recommendations for when women might justifiably be imposed upon tend to be discussed in terms of comparing the risks of harm to the woman attendant to the bodily invasion (or other interference) and the risks of prenatal harm to a future person if there is no intervention. But the move to the pediatric model is too quick; and the presumption of waiver of rights accompanying it is mistaken, as we have already seen, and too strong, as we shall see shortly.

The very serious problem with all the arguments for imposing prenatal treatment on a woman or forcibly interfering with a woman's behavior to prevent prenatal harm is the failure of proponents of these arguments to address the issue from the point of view of pregnant women (cf. Whitbeck, 1983; Johnsen, 1987; Levi, 1987). Using the pediatric model to resolve the prenatal cases fails precisely because preventing pediatric harm does not involve the violations of autonomy or bodily integrity involved in the prenatal cases. What is more, the obligation not to harm proposed for the prenatal cases involves much more than what is involved in ordinary cases of avoiding harming other persons, even one's own children. The duty to avoid harming others is generally dischargeable by simply refraining from running them over with cars, avoiding dropping things on them, and so on. But, as Bolton (1979) has observed, if pregnant women have a duty to avoid causing prenatal harm, this requires actually nurturing a future person. Although this makes the prenatal cases unlike most cases of not harming others, it does make them somewhat like the pediatric cases because we do recognize that parents have special positive duties of nurturing and aiding their children. But to avoid speciousness, proponents of the analogy must be willing to hold that morality requires court-ordered invasions of the bodily integrity of parents for their children's welfare, as well as severe restrictions on parental behaviors when those behaviors are believed to be damaging to children. Once the movement is made to comparing the potential harms to parents resulting from intervention with the potential harms to children resulting from nonintervention, it follows from the analogy that parents could be forcibly taken to medical centers to donate blood, bone marrow, or even transplantable organs, such as eyes or kidneys. And since it is well known that substance abuse in parents is severely psychologically harmful to children, the position requires that the state must attempt to ensure that no such abuse goes on in families.

Rather than so dramatically interfere with individual lives, however, we have not allowed such forcible interventions. Where parents grossly fail to nurture their children, or where their behaviors otherwise seriously harm their children, the acceptable intervention is physical removal of the children from the family. In the prenatal cases, however, protecting previable future persons requires taking custody of pregnant women, and separation involves forcible removal of viable fetuses, a draconian measure not even the most strident supporters of prenatal protection have explicitly endorsed, although the cases involving forced caesarean sections are *extremely* close to this.[21]

The implications of making the prenatal and pediatric cases analogous are, we submit, simply too morally costly. In the pediatric cases, upholding the analogy would require applying the doctrine of forfeiture of rights to autonomy and bodily integrity and giving to the state a right to extreme and constant interference with parental behavior. In the prenatal cases, it would involve giving the state the right to take a pregnant woman into custody, disable her, and induce labor in her or cut her open against her will to rescue her viable fetus. We describe the implications of the analogical argument this way, not as an exercise in inflammatory rhetoric, but to make evident the very harsh realities for women and for parents more generally that follow from accepting the analogy. And we submit that confronting these realities lucidly should make it evident that the moral costs of giving such intrusive powers to the state are just too high. Thus, overriding a woman's right to control what will be done to or through her body for the sake of a future person cannot be morally justified on the basis of an argument from the analogy between prenatal and pediatric cases, which is the only argument that holds out any real hope of justifying the kinds of impositions on pregnant women that are currently being proposed. As Rothman (1986) argues, then, pregnant women may not be treated as mere "maternal environments"; as Annas (1986) argues, neither may they be treated as mere "fetal containers" that may be opened and shut or otherwise forcibly manipulated for the protection of future persons.

LEGAL SANCTIONS FOR WOMEN WHO CAUSE PRENATAL HARM?

One suggested alternative to allowing direct interference with pregnant women is to apply sanctions to them after they have caused prenatal harm, relying on the deterrent value of the criminal law to help prevent prenatal harm (Parness, 1985, 1986). The analogy to the pediatric cases fails to justify direct interference with pregnant women, but it has been argued that child protection statutes might be interpreted in such a way that women who cause prenatal harm could be charged with crimes. For example, Leiberman *et al.* (1979) argue this way, contending that since pregnant women are the natural guardians of fetuses, it is logical to construe rejection of a potentially lifesaving prenatal intervention (which does not put the woman's life at comparable risk) as a felony, and they suggest that physicians should be able to warn a pregnant woman who refuses such an intervention that she is committing a felony. Parness (1983) suggests that a woman who risks addicting to heroin a fetus she intends to bring to term could be deemed to have undertaken both tortious and criminal conduct. And the Pamela Stewart case is just one of several recent attempts to interpret an existing statute as making criminal a pregnant woman's behavior. We believe that the arguments against the justifiability of directly interfering with women also show that criminal sanctions should not be used against women to prevent prenatal harm, since such sanctions would coerce women into submitting to intrusive interventions. But there are also other problems with this use of the criminal law that need to be pointed out.

First, it needs to be realized that the movement to criminality by interpreting existing statutes to include prenatal harm caused by pregnant women is just too quick. If we are to make women who act (or refuse to act) in the ways at issue into criminals, this requires that we enact new statutes or revise existing statutes to expressly and unambiguously make criminal the behaviors and refusals of medical or surgical interventions in question. In the United States, crimes (unlike torts) do not emerge through case law. Common law crimes were abolished many years ago (see *In re Greene*, 1892), and it is now a well-established principle in law that crimes must clearly be identified as such so that people are provided with advance notice that engaging in certain behaviors will mark them as enemies of the community and may justify the state's removing them from the community. Thus, unless criminal codes are revised to amply warn pregnant women who intend to continue their pregnancies to term that behaviors thought to cause prenatal harm and refusals of prenatal medical or surgical interventions are now crimes, criminal prosecution of women under existing statutes (be they child protection statutes or more general criminal neglect or battery statutes) violates the publicity condition of the rule of law and, therefore, cannot be legally or morally justified.

Rewriting criminal codes to expressly protect fetuses has been suggested (Parness, 1985). And if we take Leiberman *et al.* (1979) seriously, at least some medical/surgical intervention refusals ought to be felonious. But felonies are crimes punishable by death or imprisonment. What would be a morally acceptable and legally appropriate punishment for felonious refusals of medical and surgical interventions believed to prevent prenatal harm? Laying the possibility of execution aside, imprisonment of nonconsenting women is neither morally nor legally justifiable, since such women cannot reasonably be construed as societal menaces.

In cases where a woman's behaviors or omissions lead to prenatal harm, criminal sanctions are equally unacceptable. Prenatal harm resulting from maternal behaviors or omissions nearly always involves low birthweight and/or fetal drug addiction. Low birthweight is a major cause of infant mortality and has been identified as the single greatest hazard for surviving infants, since it results in heightened vulnerability to various developmental problems and substantially increased risk of death from common childhood diseases (National Academy of Sciences, 1985; Hartmann, 1987). Low birthweights are associated with poor prenatal nutrition, pregnancy in the very young, smoking tobacco and drinking alcohol during pregnancy, and other kinds of drug use, including use of crack, the extremely potent form of cocaine, which is thought to account for a twenty percent rise in infant deaths in at least one United States community in 1986 (Monmaney *et al.*, 1987). That community is the impoverished black community in Harlem, New York, which has a high rate of teenage pregnancy, and in which, like many similar communities, prenatal education and prenatal care have not been readily available.

The Harlem example is a telling one, and proponents of holding women criminally responsible for prenatal harm need to realize that the harms they seek to prevent are neither justifiably nor effectively dealt with by bringing the massive powers of the state to bear against women to coerce medical or surgical intervention or by treating as criminals women (often teenaged women) who frequently know very little about proper prenatal care. The often interrelated problems of pregnancy in the very young, chemical abuse, poor nutrition, ignorance, and poverty are social problems, appropriately and most effectively dealt with by positive measures that enhance the social, economic, and intellectual position of the least well-off members of society and of women generally. Treating women as mere uterine environments that can be invaded or punished involves the kind of blaming the victim that can only seem correct when one flatly ignores the complex social conditions that typically give rise to the evil that is to be avoided, in this case, the evil of prenatal harm. As Annas (1986) argues, the best chance the state has for protecting prenatal future persons is through positive actions that benefit pregnant women, rather than by cutting funds for maternal education, health care, and nutrition and then assailing often resourceless women for not doing the best that can be done for their future children (cf. Henifin *et al.*, 1987; Johnsen, 1987).

The use of civil sanctions against women who cause prenatal harm is equally unacceptable; although holding a woman financially responsible for the costs associated with caring for a child who is handicapped as a result of her actions or omissions seems, in principle at least, to involve no violation of a woman's moral or civil rights. But one problem here is that such sanctions seem pointless, since parents with the resources to support their children are already commonly required to support them, therefore, adding specific sanctions for pregnant women who cause prenatal harm is redundant. And requiring full support from parents without the necessary resources is as futile in these cases as it is in other cases where children of impoverished parents require special care.

Further, adding any sanctions directed against women seems gratuitously hostile to women and violative of equal treatment under the law, since they ignore the fact that fetuses are begotten by fathers, and fathers often encourage precisely the kinds of behaviors that may cause prenatal harm (e.g., alcohol and other drug use). Part of the case against Pamela Stewart was that she had intercourse with her husband after being advised to refrain from doing so. Yet her husband was not prosecuted (Annas, 1986).

Other problems with any sort of legal sanctions applicable to pregnant women include worries about abuse, for example, by fathers who want to retaliate against or control women. And many women fearing prosecution or lawsuit would be easily intimidated into accepting unnecessary interventions. Further, many medical and surgical interventions are unproven, and this should make us *very* reluctant to press women into accepting them out of a fear of legal reprisal. That physicians tend to overestimate the need for intrusive interventions to prevent prenatal harm is demonstrated by a number of cases involving attempts to force caesarean deliveries on women who subsequently successfully delivered vaginally (see *Jefferson v. Griffin Spalding County Hospital Authority*, 1981; *North Central Bronx Hospital v. Headley*, 1986; Rhoden, 1986).

Finally, allowing direct interference with pregnant women or the use of legal sanctions against pregnant women will surely encourage precisely those pregnant women most likely to cause prenatal harm (particularly those using teratogenic drugs) to avoid the medical establishment, leading to hidden pregnancies, births away from needed medical assistance, and increased abandonment of infants, making such policies patently counterproductive (cf. Johnsen, 1987; Gallagher, 1989). One need not be a jurist to realize that laws which are likely to increase the harms they are instituted to prevent are bad laws.

CONCLUSION

Our conclusion, then, is that a woman's bodily integrity must never be impinged upon for the sake of a prenatal future person, even if an intervention that is not seriously risky for her will clearly prevent substantial damage to a future person. Nor should a woman whose behavior is believed to cause prenatal harm be a candidate for forcible interference or criminal prosecution. The proper policy is to find the political will to take positive action to reduce the ignorance that often (though not always) underpins maternal refusals of prenatal medical and surgical interventions (Shriner, 1979; cf. Leiberman *et al.*, 1979), and the ignorance that so often leads to poor prenatal nutrition. The task is to introduce and sustain policies that will increase, rather than decrease, the welfare of pregnant women (Annas, 1986, 1987), and to encourage (through education and the ready availability of prenatal services, substance abuse counselling and supports, contraceptive aids, and abortion services) the avoidance of pregnancy and childbirth among those who are not prepared to be committed to the welfare of the future persons whose interests will be so closely tied to their behaviors and decisions during pregnancy.

NOTES

1. We shall use the term 'fetus' to refer to the developing organism at all prenatal stages. Technically, the appropriate terms are 'conceptus' through the first two weeks of gestation, 'embryo' between weeks two and six of gestation, and 'fetus' from week six of gestation through birth. These stages are also commonly calculated from the first day of a pregnant woman's last menstrual period, which adds roughly two weeks to their calculation, making the conceptus stage weeks one to four, the embryonic stage weeks four to eight, and the fetal stage week eight through birth.

2. For expanded discussions of the morality of abortion, see Callahan (1986a,b) and Knight and Callahan (1989), Chapter 7.

3. Whether omissions are properly understood as causes is a question beyond the scope of this inquiry, and we shall ignore it here. For discussions of this question, see Fitzgerald (1967); Foot (1967); Harris (1974); Rachels (1975); Mack (1976, 1980); Benjamin (1979); Green (1980); Husak (1980); Feinberg (1984); Callahan (1988).

4. See *Libbee v. Permanente Clinic* (1974); *Salazar v. St. Vincent Hospital* (1980); *Vaillancourt v. Medical Center Hospital of Vermont* (1980).

5. See also *Chrisafogeorgis v. Brandenberg* (1973).

6. From a scientific perspective, suits for wrongful death are problematic, especially when they involve previable fetuses. Since as many as 75 percent of human pregnancies may spontaneously abort (Lauritsen, 1982), it is extremely difficult to establish a causal connection between some external event and a prenatal death, particularly when the death is early in pregnancy.

7. See *Speck v. Finegold* (1979); *Phillips v. United States* (1980).

8. See *Hornbuckle v. Plantation Pipe Line* (1956); *Bennett v. Hymers* (1958); *Smith v. Brennan* (1960).

9. Knight and Callahan (1989), Chapter 9.

10. Again, there are hard questions here regarding how such a causal connection can be demonstrated. See note 7.

11. See *Jefferson v. Griffin Spalding County Hospital Authority* (1981); Bowes and Selgestad (1981); Parness and Pritchard (1982); Robertson (1982, 1985, 1986); the discussion in Lenow (1983); Dougherty (1986); Mathieu (1985); Parness (1985, 1986, 1987); Green and Brill (1987).

12. This judgment has been reiterated in other cases, e.g., *Womack v. Buckhorn* (1976); *Berger v. Weber* (1978); *In re Baby X* (1980).

13. But see *Taft v. Taft* (1983), in which the husband of a woman in her fourth month of pregnancy sought a court order giving him authority to require that she submit to a surgery involving suturing her cervix (a cerclage or "purse string" operation) to minimize her risk of a miscarriage, a surgery the woman had refused on religious grounds. The lower court appointed a guardian *ad litem* for the fetus, and granted the husband authority to consent to the surgery. Although the Massachusetts Supreme Court reversed the decision, it did so only because no legal precedent ordering such a submission to protect a previable fetus was cited by the husband or found by the court and because no facts had been presented to show that the surgery would be a genuinely life-saving one as opposed to a merely precautionary one. The reasons for the reversal leave it open that the original decision might have been upheld in another case. The court makes this explicit in saying, "We do not decide whether, in some circumstances there would be justification for ordering a wife to submit to medical treatment in order to assist in carrying a child to term." Even more recently, in the well-publicized "Baby M Case," which involved a custody battle for a child conceived by Mary Beth Whitehead, via artificial insemination with the sperm of William Stern, the court's reasoning implies that biological fathers have what seem to be property rights in offspring containing their genetic material. Whitehead argued that the arrangement she had agreed to, which included her being paid $10,000 when she turned the child over to Stern, involved selling a baby. In reply, Judge Harvey Sorkow of the New Jersey Superior Court claimed:

> The fact is, however, that the money to be paid to the surrogate is not being paid for the surrender of the child to the father. . . . The biological father pays the surrogate for her willingness to be impregnated and carry his child to term. At birth, the father does not purchase the child. It is his own biological genetically[-]related child. He cannot purchase what is already his. (*New York Times*, 1987)

Notice that such an arrangement cannot coherently be construed as a contract for a service rather than as a contract for a product, since the arrangement makes payment contingent on the delivery of a product, i.e., "the surrender of the child to the father." Notice, too, how the label "surrogate" diminishes the role and authority of the woman in such cases and favors the biological father's authority over the fetus and child. But Whitehead is not a surrogate mother at all, she is the baby's biological mother, a fact that was recognized by the New Jersey Supreme Court (*In re Baby M*, 1988).

14. Wrongful life cases and the growing emphasis on prenatal testing raise a number of concerns. Pregnant women are increasingly pressured to undergo such testing and increasingly face the expectation that they will abort a pregnancy if test results suggest prenatal damage. Such pressures foster an already worrisome societal attitude which disenfranchises the disabled (see Blatt, 1987; Henifin, 1987; Henifin *et al.*, 1987; Saxton, 1987).

15. See *Application of President and Directors of Georgetown College* (1964); *Raleigh Fitkin-Paul Morgan Memorial Hospital v. Anderson* (1964); *People v. Estergard* (1969); *Jefferson v. Griffin Spalding County Memorial Hospital Authority* (1981); *Taft v. Taft* (1983); Leiberman *et al.* (1979); Bowes and Selgestad (1981); Parness and Pritchard (1982); Robertson (1982, 1985, 1986); Shaw (1983); Mathieu (1985); Parness (1985, 1986, 1987); Mackenzie and Nagel (1986); Johnsen (1987).

16. See Leiberman *et al.* (1979); Bowes and Selgestad (1981); Annas (1982, 1986); Parness (1982, 1985); Johnsen (1987).

17. Cal. Penal Code, Sec. 270 (West Publishing Company, 1986).

18. Cases like this raise some additional puzzles. For example, if physicians in such cases fail to so advise women, should *they* be subject to prosecution? What medical advice must be explicitly stated and what may be left up to "common sense?" Must a woman be told about *all* the drugs and other potentially hazardous chemicals (e.g., those in some cat litters) that could possibly harm her fetus and advised to avoid them; must she be advised not to sky-dive, etc.?

19. In saying this, we certainly do not mean to approve all the kinds of impingements on individual autonomy and bodily integrity that have been allowed against criminals. There are, for example, serious moral questions raised by force feeding prisoners, and serious moral and constitutional questions raised by forcible surgical interventions on prisoners to gain evidence in criminal cases. And it should go without saying that execution is extremely difficult to justify in a society which has the resources to effectively protect innocent persons from those who have murdered.

20. See *Strunk v. Strunk* (1969) and *Hart v. Brown* (1972) where kidney transplants from incompetents were ordered to save the life of a sibling, and the argument from these examples in Bowes and Selgestad (1981). See, too, the discussion of court-ordered bodily invasions in Mathieu (1985).

21. Also see Parness's (1983) discussion of taking custody of prospective parents, with examples of several attempts by states to take custody of fetuses by taking custody of pregnant women. And see Robertson and Schulman (1987), who seem to be in favor of accepting the implications of making the analogy to the pediatric cases work. Although there is some slippage, Robertson and Schulman also attempt to keep the protection of women's liberty and bodily integrity as the considerations to be balanced against the prevention of prenatal harm. However, this raises another pair of problems, namely, how to decide when a potential harm to a future person outweighs the rights to noninterference and bodily integrity of an existing person, and the question of who should make such decisions.

REFERENCES

Annas, George J. 1987. "Letters." *Hastings Center Report* 17/3: 26.

Annas, George J. 1986. "Pregnant women as fetal containers." *Hastings Center Report* 16/6: 13.

Annas, George J. 1982. "Forced cesareans: The most unkindest cut of all." *Hastings Center Report* 12/3: 16.

Application of President and Directors of Georgetown College. 1964. 331 F 2d 1000 (DC Cir.). Cert. den. 337 U.S. 978.

Benjamin, Martin. 1979. "Moral agency and negative acts in medicine." In: *Medical Responsibility: Paternalism, Informed Consent, and Euthanasia.* Ed. Robison, Wade and Pritchard, Michael. Clifton, NJ: Humana, pp. 170-80.

Bennett v. Hymers. 1958. 101 NH 483, 147 A 2d 108.

Berger v. Weber. 1978. 82 MI App 199, 267 NW 2d 124.

Blatt, Robin J. R. 1987. "To choose or refuse prenatal testing." *Genewatch* 4: 3.

Bolton, Martha Brandt. 1979. "Responsible women and abortion decisions." In: *Having Children: Philosophical and Legal Reflections on Parenthood.* Ed. O'Neill, Onora and Ruddick, William. New York: Oxford University Press, pp. 40-51.

Bonbrest v. Kotz. 1946. 65 F. Supp. 138.

Bondeson, William B., Engelhardt, H. Tristram, Jr., Spicker, Stuart F., and Winship, Daniel H., eds. 1983. *Abortion and the Status of the Fetus.* Boston: D. Reidel.

Bowes, Watson A., Jr. and Selgestad, Brad. 1981. "Fetal versus maternal rights: Medical and legal perspectives." *Obstetrics and Gynecology* 58: 209.

Brown, Edward, Hackler, Chris, Kuhse, Helga, and Thomson, Colin. 1987. "The latest word." *Hastings Center Report* 17/2: 51.

Callahan, Joan C. 1988. "Acts, omissions, and euthanasia." *Public Affairs Quarterly* 2/2: 21.

Callahan, Joan C. 1986a. "The fetus and fundamental rights." *Commonweal* 11 April: 203. Revised, expanded version in *Abortion and Catholicism: The American Debate.* Ed. Shannon, Thomas A. and Jung, Patricia B. New York: Crossroads, 1988, pp. 217-30.

Callahan, Joan C. 1986b. "*The Silent Scream:* A new, conclusive argument against abortion?" *Philosophy Research Archives* XI: 181.

Chrisafogeorgis v. Brandenberg. 1973. 55 IL 2d 368, 304 NE 2d 88.

Clark, Matt, King, Patricia, Buckley, Linda, and Springen, Karen. 1987. "Doctors grapple with ethics." *Newsweek* 28 December: 62.

Cohen, Sherrill and Taub, Nadine. 1989. *Reproductive Laws for the 1990s.* Clifton, NJ: Humana Press.

Curlender v. Bio-Science Laboratories and Automated Laboratory Sciences. 1980. 165 CA Rpt 477.

Dietrich v. Inhabitants of Northampton. 1884. 138 MA 14.

Dougherty, Charles. 1986. "The right to begin life with sound body and mind: Fetal patients and conflicts with their mothers." *University of Detroit Law Review* 63/1-2: 89.

Feinberg, Joel. 1985. "Comment: Wrongful conception and the right not to be harmed." *Harvard Journal of Law and Public Policy* 8: 57.

Feinberg, Joel. 1984. *Harm to Others.* New York: Oxford University Press.

Fitzgerald, P. J. 1967. "Acting and refraining." *Analysis* 27: 133.

Foot, Philippa. 1967. "The problem of abortion and the doctrine of double-effect." Oxford *Review* 5: 5.

Gallagher, Janet. 1989. "Fetus as patient." In: Cohen and Taub, eds., *supra*, pp. 185-235.

Glantz, Leonard. 1983. "Is the fetus a person? A lawyer's view." In: Bondeson et al., eds., *supra*, pp. 107-17.

Glover, Jonathon. 1977. *Causing Death and Saving Lives.* New York: Penguin.

Green, 0. H. 1980. "Killing and letting die." *American Philosophical Quarterly* 17: 195.

Green, Willard and Brill, Charles. 1987. "Letters." *Hastings Center Report* 17/3: 25.

Harris, John. 1974. "The Marxist conception of violence." *Philosophy and Public Affairs* 3: 192.

Hart v. Brown. 1972. 29 CT Supp. 368, 289 A 2d 386 (CT Sup. Ct.).

Hartmann, Betsy. 1987. *Reproductive Rights and Wrongs: The Global Politics of Population Control and Contraceptive Choice.* New York: Harper & Row.

Henifin, Mary Sue. 1987. "What's wrong with 'wrongful life' court cases?" *Genewatch* 4: 1.

Henifin, Mary Sue, Hubbard, Ruth, and Norsigian, Judy. 1989."Prenatal screening." In: Cohen and Taub, eds., *supra*, pp. 155-183.

Hornbuckle v. Plantation Pipe Line. 1956. 212 GA 504, 93 SE 2d 727.

Husak, Douglas. 1980. "Omissions, causation, and liability." *Philosophical Quarterly* 30: 318.

In re Baby M. 1988. 217 NJ Super. 313 (1987), rev'd in part, 525 A.2d 1128, 1988 W L 6251, Silp Op A-39-87, decided 3 Feb. 1988.

In re Baby X. 1980. 97 MI App 111, 293 NW 2d 736.

In re Greene. 1892. 52 F 104 (CCW OH).

Jefferson v. Griffin Spalding County Hospital Authority. 1981. 247 GA 86, 274 SE 2d 457.

Johnsen, Dawn. 1987. "A new threat to pregnant women's autonomy." *Hastings Center Report* 17/4: 33.

Knight, James W. and Callahan, Joan C. 1989. *Preventing Birth: Contemporary Methods and Related Moral Controversies.* Salt Lake City: University of Utah Press.

Langerak, Edward A. 1979. "Abortion: Listening to the middle." *Hastings Center Report* 9/5: 24.

Lauritsen, J. G. 1982. "The cytogenitics of spontaneous abortion." *Research in Reproduction* 14/3: 3.

Leiberman, J. R., Mazor, M., Chaim, W., and Cohen, A. 1979. "The fetal right to live." *Obstetrics and Gynecology* 53: 515.

Lenow, Jeffrey L. 1983. "The fetus as patient: Emerging legal rights as a person?" *American Journal of Law and Medicine* 9: 1.

Levi, Don S. 1987. "Hypothetical cases and abortion." *Social Theory and Practice* 13: 17.

Libbee v. Permanente Clinic. 1974. 268 OR 258, 518 P 2d 636. Reh'g. den. 268 OR 272, 520 P 2d 361. App. dismissed. 269 OR 543, 525 P 2d 1296.

Mack, Eric. 1980. "Bad samaritanism and the causation of harm." *Philosophy and Public Affairs* 9: 230.

Mack, Eric. 1976. "Causing and failing to prevent." *Southwest Journal of Philosophy* 7: 83.

Mackenzie, Thomas B. and Nagel, Theodore C. 1986. "When a pregnant woman endangers her fetus: Commentary." *Hastings Center Report* 16/1: 24.

Mathieu, Deborah. 1985. "Respecting liberty and preventing harm." *Harvard Journal of Law and Public Policy* 8: 19.

Monmaney, Terrence, Hager, Mary, Springen, Karen, and Drew, Lisa. 1987. "A black health crisis." *Newsweek* 13 July: 53.

Montreal Tramways v. Leveille. 1933. 4 Dom. LR 337.

National Academy of Sciences. 1985. *Preventing Low Birthweight.* (Prep. by the Committee to Study the Prevention of Low Birthweight, Institute of Medicine.) Washington: National Academy Press.

New York Times. 1987. "Excerpts from the ruling on Baby M." 1 April: 13.

North Central Bronx Hospital v. Headley. 1986. No. 1992-85. NY Sup. Ct. 6 January.

Parness, Jeffrey A. 1987. "Letters." *Hastings Center Report* 17/3: 26.

Parness, Jeffrey A. 1986. "The abuse and neglect of the human unborn." *Family Law Quarterly* 20: 197.

Parness, Jeffrey A. 1985. "Crimes against the unborn: Protecting and respecting the potentiality of human life." *Harvard Journal on Legislation* 22: 97.

Parness, Jeffrey A. 1983. "The duty to prevent handicaps: Laws promoting the prevention of handicaps to newborns." *Western New England Law Review* 5: 431.

Parness, Jeffrey A. and Pritchard, Susan K. 1982. "To be or not to be: Protecting the unborn's potentiality of life." *University of Cincinnati Law Review* 51: 257.

People v. Estergard. 1969. 457 P 2d 698 (CO S.Ct.).

People v. Stewart. 1987. No. M508197, San Diego Mun Ct, 23 February.

Phillips v. United States. 1980. 508 F.Supp. 537 (D.S.C).

Rachels, James. 1975. "Active and passive euthanasia." *New England Journal of Medicine* 292: 78.

Rainey v. Horn. 1954. 222 MS 269, 72 S 2d 434.

Raleigh Fitkin-Paul Morgan Memorial Hospital v. Anderson. 1964. 42 NJ 421, 201 A 2d 337 (NJ S.Ct.).

Renslow v. Mennonite Hospital. 1977. 67 IL 2d 348, 369 NE 2d 1250.

Rhoden, Nancy K. 1986. "The judge in the delivery room: The emergence of court-ordered caesareans." *California Law Review* 74: 1951.

Robertson, John A. 1986. "Legal issues in prenatal therapy." *Clinical Obstetrics and Gynecology* 29: 603.

Robertson, John A. 1985. "Legal issues in fetal therapy." *Seminars in Perinatology* 9: 136.

Robertson, John A. 1982. "The right to procreate and in utero fetal therapy." *Journal of Legal Medicine* 3: 333.

Robertson, John A. and Schulman, Joseph D. 1987. "Pregnancy and prenatal harm to offspring: The case of mothers with PKU." *Hastings Center Report* 17/4: 23.

Roe v. Wade. 1973. 410 U.S. 113.

Rothman, Barbara Katz. 1986. "When a pregnant woman endangers her fetus: Commentary." *Hastings Center Report* 16/1: 25.

Ruddick, William and Wilcox, William. 1982. "Operating on the fetus." *Hastings Center Report* 12/5: 10.

Salazar v. St. Vincent Hospital. 1980. 95 NM 150, 619 P 2d 826 (NM Ct.App.).

Saxton, Marsha. 1987. "Prenatal screening and discriminatory attitudes about disability." *Genewatch* 4: 8.

Shaw, Margery W. 1983. "The destiny of the fetus." In: Bondeson et al., eds., *supra*, pp. 273-79.

Shriner, Thomas L. 1979. "Maternal versus fetal rights — A clinical dilemma." *Obstetrics and Gynecology* 53: 518.

Smith, Holly M. 1983. "Intercourse and responsibility for the fetus." In: Bondeson et al., eds., *supra*, pp. 229-45.

Smith v. Brennan. 1960. 31 NJ 353, 157 A 2d 497.

Speck v. Finegold. 1979. 268 PA Sup 342, 408 A 2d 496.

Strunk v. Strunk. 1969. 445 SW 2d 145 (KY Ct.App.).

Taft v. Taft. 1983. 338 MA 331, 446 NE 2d 395.

Vaillancourt v. Medical Center Hospital of Vermont. 1980. 139 VT 138, 425 A 2d 92.

Verkennes v. Corniea. 1949. 229 MN 365, 38 NW 2d 838.

Warren, Mary Anne. 1975. "On the moral and legal status of abortion." In: *Today's Moral Problems*. Ed. Wasserstrom, Richard A. New York: Macmillan, pp. 120-36.

Wertheimer, Roger. 1971. "Understanding the abortion argument." *Philosophy and Public Affairs* 1:67.

Whitbeck, Caroline. 1983. "The moral implications of regarding women as people." In: Bondeson et al., eds., *supra*, pp. 247-72.

Womack v. Buckhorn. 1976. 384 MI 718, 187 NW 2d 218.

Punishment and Welfare:
Crack Cocaine
and the Regulation of Mothering

Lisa Maher

SUMMARY. This paper will attempt to situate the current discourse on 'crack pregnancies' within the context of a broader regulatory discourse.[1] It will argue that defining and locating state intervention solely within the confines of formal legal discourse not only privileges the criminal law, but (1) occludes recognition of the ways in which regulation and control are effected by administrative law and welfare policy and (2) fails to specify the role of the welfare state in the construction and reproduction of dominant cultural norms of womanhood and mothering. The paper draws on feminist literature and fieldwork-in-progress to suggest that many of these women are already subject to substantial mechanisms of social control and cultural reproduction. In concluding, it is suggested that the construction of this debate to date has served to deflect attention away from the fissures of gender, race and class that render these women's lives as publicly problematic.

I went home to Australia this summer. "J" was eight months pregnant and smoking crack when I left. By the time I returned, her eight pound infant had been taken from her and placed in foster care along with her two elder children. "J" is currently homeless and without support. She continues to smoke crack. The essay that fol-

Lisa Maher, PhD Candidate ABD in Criminal Justice at Rutgers University, is currently doing ethnographic research on women who use crack cocaine in three Brooklyn (New York) neighbourhoods.

The author is indebted to the women who have shared their stories and their lives with her and to Richard Curtis and Ansley Hamid. The author also thanks Marie Adrine, Kathleen Daly, David Dixon, and Andrew von Hirsch.

lows cannot be disconnected from her life and the lives of many women who find themselves in similar positions.

This paper is primarily concerned to elaborate the nature of regulatory state responses to women like "J." Although current estimates suggest some 375,000 infants are born annually in the United States with traces of illegal drugs in their bloodstreams (Chasnoff, 1989), the approximately fifty criminal prosecutions since 1987 (ACLU, 1989) tend to suggest that the function of the formal criminal law has, to date at least, been primarily symbolic. Within the broader context of legal developments during the twentieth century, where it can be argued that the primary tool of state control shifted from criminal law to modes of administrative regulation, this paper will focus on the control aspects of welfare intervention in relation to crack pregnancies and the regulation of mothering. Specifically, it is concerned to explore how, in this instance, welfare or administrative controls overlap and intersect with traditional criminal justice controls and simultaneously function as an independent and gender-specific form of punishment and regulation. It will be argued that welfare sanctions against women who use crack can be viewed as more than a judgmental mode of regulation insofar as they constitute a set of interventions which both visit censure and have real effects in terms of material deprivations.

INTRODUCTION

Contemporary debates about drugs and drug policy and, in particular, as concerns crack cocaine, have tended to centre on the role of the criminal law. This is not surprising given the fact that the criminal law provides concrete identifiable events such as the passing of legislation and the conduct of criminal trials which make issues public and visible. Similarly, historical studies have concentrated on the sources and production of criminal statutes regulating the consumption and sale of drugs (Musto, 1973). However these studies have tended to be based on the assumption that an examination of the debates around drug legislation provides not only the key to understanding societal reactions to drugs, but also the precise forms of regulation adopted to deal with particular drug problems.

While this approach has been valuable in illuminating the racist and classist assumptions that have historically undergirded regulatory strategies, the focus on criminal law has served to mask distinctions as to the actual modes or specific forms of state regulation. As a result of concentrating on those forms of regulation which are derived from or associated with the criminal law, this perspective has not only marginalized gender, but has also distorted the effects of other key variables, such as race. These variables do not operate independently of each other but rather are articulated together. By systematically ignoring the gendered nature of regulatory controls, the interactive effects of gender, race, class and offense categories/ social constructions of deviance in producing particular forms of regulation, have gone largely unexamined (offense see, Daly 1988).

This paper will attempt to explore the implications of such a thesis in terms of the interconnections between the current debate on crack cocaine and the criminalization of pregnancy, and the relations between law, science and the state in regulating and controlling women's lives. By treating law and science as forms of cultural discourse engaged in the production of historically specific, ideologically embedded and profoundly gendered knowledges, the paper will attempt to situate recent attempts to criminalize the pregnancies and regulate the lives of women crack users within a complex of ideological dynamics that have broader meanings beyond the current war on drugs. It will elaborate the specific forms through which dominant norms of womanhood and mothering are imposed on a particular group of women whose lifestyles do not appear to conform to the cultural beliefs and social practices which undergird and legitimate the state's power to punish.

However even within the law, this power to punish is not situated in a particular realm or locale but rather is dispersed throughout a range of sites which can be broadly defined as constituting formal and informal strategies of state intervention. Utilizing the distinction between formal regulation and control effected by the substantive criminal law and the informal ends realized by administrative law and policy under the auspices of the welfare state, I will demonstrate that the focus on formal legal regulation epitomized by the rhetoric of 'criminalizing pregnancy' is problematic. The legal discourse on the criminalization of pregnancy has tended to obscure the fact that certain groups of women who use certain kinds of drugs are already subject to harsh deprivations by administrative means of state intervention and regulation. By extending the notion of punishment to encompass unpleasant and arguably unjust practices and deprivations for norm violations visited outside the criminal law, this essay seeks to draw attention to some of the processes by which the "power of law" (Smart, 1989) already extends to control the bodies of poor women and women of colour.

Such a perspective also suggests that the concept of punishment can not be fully understood within the confines of traditional legal discourse, the formal justice system and the categories of the criminal law. Rather, it suggests a need to examine the processes by which specific modes of informal deprivations are visited on those who are perceived as having deviated from [gender-specific] culturally assigned roles. Although the formal punishment and incarceration of women is to a large extent predicated on sentencer's perceptions of women as wives, mothers and daughters (Carlen, 1988:10; see also Daly, 1987a, 1987b), these same cultural constructions of womanhood in general and motherhood in particular, make certain groups of women particularly good candidates for informal or administrative justice. Women's candidacy for administrative justice is enhanced by the welfare state's leverage over poor and minority women by virtue of their status vis-à-vis the public patriarchy (Brown, 1981). As Stang Dahl (1987) has suggested, the three areas of law which affect women most concern the administration of welfare benefits, maintenance and child support laws and the formulation of policy and guidelines by administrative agencies.

CONTROLLING WOMEN: THEORY

The creation and transmission of societal norms are effected through a number of social control mechanisms which range from formal punishments authorized by the law and imposed by the criminal justice system to the informal sanctions meted out by agents of the welfare state. There are two sets of problems in relation to societal norms that come to mind from an examination of the traditional literature. The first is that not all individuals within a given society necessarily subscribe to a universal set of values and secondly, as

Goode (1960) has pointed out, variations in the social positioning of individuals give rise to differentials in the ability to effect norm compliance. However a third set of problems which is only partially visible in the literature concerns the role of the state in constructing and enforcing norms based on gender distinctions, in articulating and effecting the social roles of women and men.

Mainstream social scientists have long viewed gender distinctions as a combination of biological fact and individual socialization. The social divisions between women and men have been legitimated by this tendency to regard sex differences as somehow more natural than other types of difference. Feminist scholarship has sought to demonstrate the extent of formal and informal state coercive power in maintaining these gender distinctions (Smart, 1976; Stang Dahl and Snare, 1978) and in doing so, has highlighted the fallacy of assumptions that the state is neutral where the interests of women are concerned. This exposé has taken two forms. First, the examination of specific instances whereby coercive state policies and practices can be seen to be undergirded by gender distinctions (Smart, 1976; Collier et al., 1982; Stone, 1979; Walkowitz, 1980; MacKinnon, 1982, 1989) and second, by drawing attention to more covert forms of regulation and control and, in particular, by pointing out how the state has failed to prevent the use of force against women (eg. Bart, 1981; Russell, 1982; Stanko, 1985; Hanmer and Maynard, 1987; Hanmer, Radford and Stanko, 1989).

However the role of the state extends to finer distinctions beyond defining and regulating women as women. One of these finer distinctions is through the definition and construction of some women as mothers. Within western cultures, a much romanticized idealized notion of the family has formed the basis of a model for the regulation and control of women. As Lasch (1977) has pointed out, it is the idealization of a particular form of family which has enabled the state to construct variations [others] as deviations. Similarly, the idealized construct of woman as mother has led to distinctions between good and bad mothers based on deviations from the ideal. As Ehrenreich and English (1979) have pointed out, the concept of the ideal mother is rooted in a cultural and scientific shift at the beginning of the twentieth century whereby mothers began to be held responsible and accountable in terms of the end product of their child-bearing and rearing. Davin's (1978) analysis of this same period in British history illustrates how this shift served not only to create a powerful ideology of motherhood, but further how the "doctrine of maternal fault" served to occlude the structural effects of poverty and environment. High infant mortality rates were attributed to maternal inadequacy and maternal ignorance (Davin, 1978).

> Motherhood was so powerful a symbol that often class differences disappeared, along with the realities of working class life. All the individual real mothers were subsumed into one ideal figure, the Queen Bee, protected and fertile, producing the next generation for the good of the hive. . . . The family was such an accepted symbol for the state that its actual disparate identities were forgotten. (Davin, 1978:53)

That this kind of 'mother-blaming' has pre-occupied subsequent social science research is illustrated by Caplan and Hall-McCorquodale's (1985) review of clinical journals. And as Chodorow and Contratto (1982) have pointed out, some feminists, by focussing on the exclusive nature of the mother-infant relationship have contributed to this idealization of the fantasy of the perfect mother.

> This creates the quality of rage we find in the 'blame-the-mother' literature and the unrealistic expectation that perfection would result if only a mother would devote her life completely to her child and all impediments to her doing so were removed. Psyche and culture merge here and reflexively create one another. (Chodorow and Conratto, 1982:65)

Feminist anthropologists have led the challenge to dominant cultural ascriptions of the family and mothering (Medick and Sabean, 1984). By deconstructing dominant assumptions of the family as a universal cross cultural and natural entity, feminist anthropological accounts have enabled a wide array of social scientists to begin the task of reconstructing the family as an historically and culturally situated social unit, "as ideology, as an institutional nexus of social relationships and cultural meanings" (Rapp, 1978). As Collier et al. (1982) have pointed out:

The Family (thought to be universal by most social scientists today) is a moral and ideological unit that appears, not universally, but in particular social orders. The Family as we know it is not a 'natural' group created by the claims of 'blood' but a sphere of human relationships shaped by a state that recognized families as units that hold property, provide care and welfare, and attend particularly to the young. (Collier et al., 1982:33)

However some feminists have been reluctant to abandon the universals of women's oppression (see Fraser and Nicholson, 1990 for review) and in particular, its situatedness in family life. Rossi's (1977) biosocial model of parenting posits the uniqueness and biologically determined basis of the mother-child bond, and Chodorow's analysis of mothering is suggestive of an essential womanhood which can be located in the singular activity of mothering. As Fraser and Nicholson have summarized:

It claims that the difference thus generated between feminine and masculine gender identity causes a variety of cross-cultural social phenomena, including the continuation of female mothering, male contempt for women, and problems in heterosexual relationships. (Fraser and Nicholson, 1990:30)

However it is problematic to assume that categories like sexuality, mothering, reproduction and the like have universal cross cultural significance. As Fraser and Nicholson see it, "for a theorist to use such categories to construct a universalistic social theory is to risk projecting the socially dominant conjunctions and dispersions of her own society onto others, thereby distorting the important features of both" (1990:31). However it is not only cross cultural essentialism that much feminist theory needs to take on board. Perhaps the more interesting political and epistemological question is whether one can make generalizations in relation to different groups within specific societies and historical periods (see hooks, 1981, 1984; Moraga and Anzaldua, 1981; Lorde, 1984; Spelman, 1988; Anzaldua, 1990).

[White, Western] Feminist theory has yet to deal with recent challenges of essentialism and exclusion by women of colour, working class women and lesbian women. What these hitherto unheard voices suggest is the need to treat gender as one axis of domination among many, including class, race, ethnicity and sexual orientation. As Fraser and Nicholson (1990) have argued, one way of doing this is to genealogize social institutions such as the family in terms of their historical and cultural specificity, prior to universalizing them. Within the current context however, dominant cultural ascriptions of motherhood remain largely uncontested (for an exception see Hill, 1990). Moreover, little mention has been made of the ways in which powerful Western ideologies of mothering undergird the covert regulation and control of women. Despite the fact that women who break the law are dealt with not on the basis of the seriousness of their infractions, but rather, in accordance with judicial perceptions of them (Eaton, 1986; Daly, 1987a, 1987b; Carlen and Worrall, 1987), few attempts have been made to explore the specificity of this contention, to analyze the ways in which the dominant cultures' construction of women is interpreted by rule-makers and rule-enforcers and the concrete effects on women's lives (see Worrall, 1990 on 'offending women').

If one looks to the law, women who use crack cocaine are obstensibly punished for the same set of offenses that men who use this illegal drug are also subject to. However additionally, attempts have been made to criminalize the conduct of women, based on the assumption that the use of illegal drugs during pregnancy harms foetuses. Whilst this represents a critical development, it is one that has been extensively catalogued elsewhere (see this volume). My point is rather, that the very terms of reference of the current debate, the rhetoric of criminalizing pregnancy, serves to illustrate the "power of law" to disqualify and define the truth of events (Smart, 1989). Yet law's power is not solely defined in reference to, nor can it be entirely situated within, the formal criminal law. In fact it is the tendency of formal legal discourse to dominate over other forms of knowledge that perhaps leads us to concentrate on criminalization at the expense of less overt, less formal and arguably less 'just' responses. Although for the purposes of this paper, formal sanctions are those constructed on the traditional terrain of the criminal law as punishment whereas informal sanctions encompass various noncriminal administrative forms of intervention not formally denominated as punishment, in reality these boundaries are fluid. Formal and informal interventions interlock and overlap. And although they are often contiguous, their meanings and consequences vary according to the nature of the intervention and the context in which it is deployed. Many of the women interviewed in the course of this research regard administrative interventions as more significant in terms of the degree of intrusion and long range consequences than the criminal justice system. Such a perspective can be arguably viewed as rational were one faced with the choice between spending a short period at Rikers Island for possession of a crack stem or surrendering a child to the foster care system.

CONTROLLING WOMEN: COURT DECISIONS

There is no doubt that the new woman is a more interesting companion than her predecessors, and that she has made great progress in the arts and sciences, in trades and professions, but the question of questions is — is she a better mother of the race? Does, for instance, her knowledge of mathematics, or even her efficiency in athletics, make her intrinsically a better mother than the natural, bright, intelligent girl interested in frills, dances and flirtations? (R. Murray Leslie, 1911; cited in Davin, 1978:20)

Garland (1985) has defined eugenics as "the study and deployment of agencies under social control for the purpose of improving the 'racial qualities' of future generations, either physically or mentally" (1985:142). There were two paradigms within the eugenics movement in Britain at the turn of the century. Positive eugenics spoke to those concerned with the falling birth rate and its implications for the maintenance of the empire and new developments in industrial capitalism. It sought to promote the fertility of the 'better classes' and the production of white, Anglo-Saxon and preferably male offspring. Negative eugenics, on the other hand, was concerned to circumscribe the "prolific fertility" of the unfit. In the United States, it was negative eugenics that left its mark on political, scientific and legal discourses.

At the height of the eugenics movement, sections of the American scientific community believed that criminality or criminogenic characteristics were hereditary. Approximately 60,000 women were sterilized in the United States between 1900 and 1950 (Stefan 1989). Perhaps the most notorious case is that of *Buck v. Bell* decided by the Supreme Court in 1927 (274 U.S. at 200 [1927]). In upholding a Virginia statute that provided for the involuntary sterilization of both criminals and the 'feeble-minded', the Court upheld states' power to circumscribe the right to procreate, on the basis of IQ level. As Justice Holmes surmised:

> It is better for all the world, if, instead of waiting to execute degenerate offspring for crime, or let them starve for their imbecility, society can prevent those who are manifestly unfit from continuing their kind. . . . (ibid. at 207)

Although the frameworks of legal and scientific knowledges have changed considerably since the days of *Buck v. Bell*, many of the same ideological forces are embedded in the ongoing construction and affirmation of the roles ascribed to women and institutions like the family and motherhood in Western cultures. As Garland (1985) has pointed out in the British context, eugenics was more than a temporary aberration. "Many of its strategies, techniques and proposals were in fact to become inscribed in the new complex of social and penal regulation [the British welfare state], though usually without acknowledgement, and on terms which are less embarrassingly explicit" (1985:142-3). Similarly, the work of Rafter (1988) in the United States has revealed how the eugenics family studies shaped subsequent constructions not only of social policy, but of crime and deviance. This work illustrates how family studies researchers used literary techniques to construct powerful negative images of deviant families as threats to the social order. By cataloging the impact that these depictions had on the eugenics movement, Rafter effectively demonstrates the linkages between science and the construction and definition of deviance (Rafter, 1988).

The same discursive devices utilized by the Progressive Era eugenics movement are evident in contemporary legal notions of the 'unfit.' Decisions concerning the sterilization of mentally retarded women continue to be based on phallocentric and paternalistic values and standards. Assumptions that mentally retarded women are unfit to mother, that they are unable to comprehend the consequences of sexual activity, would be adversely affected by the trauma of pregnancy and are unwilling and unable to care for their children, continue to pervade American judicial reasoning. As Stefan has argued:

> The factors used by the courts, those specifically rejected, those tacitly acknowledged and those that are altogether ignored form as fascinating a rendering of society's current picture of mentally retarded [sic] people as Justice Holmes' angry vision of incompetence sapping the strength of the state does of his day's attitudes. (Stefan, 1989:422)

Legal discourse in relation to women's responsibility and culpability at law has historically been constructed in and around masculinist notions of women's bodies (see Walkowitz, 1980; Edwards, 1981; Smith, 1981; Allen, 1987). Both legal and medical discourses have sought to reduce women's corporality to their reproductive functioning (Smart, 1989). Although Foucault's works revealed how the human body serves as a locus for the convergence of a number of disciplinary discourses, it is Smart's (1989) gendering of the Foucauldian analysis that facilitates the recognition that law is and has always been intrinsically concerned with the regulation of female bodies as "specific sites of activity over which the law should have jurisdiction" (1989:92-93).

However, in some instances it may not be enough simply to recognize the significance of the gendered (i.e., constructed) female body. A more complete analysis may necessitate an exploration of the ways in which characteristics such as race, class, religion and other variables such as technology and changing social constructions of deviance mediate the construction of gendered bodies as the subjects of regulatory discourse. That these interactive effects are fundamental to any analysis of judicial reasoning can be illustrated by an examination of court decisions concerning the right to privacy in the United States.[2]

In 1973 the United States Supreme Court held that a statute which criminalized abortions bar those to save the life of the woman, violated the constitutional right to privacy (*Roe v. Wade*, 410 U.S. 113 1973).[3] The *Roe* decision effectively legalized abortion in determining that a woman's right to terminate her pregnancy is fundamental and entitled to protection under the equal protection clause of Fourteenth Amendment. While the Court declined to recognize the foetus as a person, it attempted to articulate a standard for balancing the competing interests between mother and foetus by what has become known as the trimester approach. The point at which state interest becomes compelling is the point of foetal viability. Such determinations are to be made "in the light of present medical knowledge" (ibid. at 163). The trimester approach has effectively meant that a woman's right to an abortion is contingent on the length of her pregnancy (see Annas, 1989 for review). By declining to define the point at which life or viability [insofar as the state's compelling interest is concerned] begins, the Supreme Court has retained the power to restrict the scope of women's access to abortion in accordance with prevailing medical technology.[4]

On July 3, 1989 the United States Supreme Court held, in *Webster v. Reproductive Health Services* (109 S. Ct. [1989]), that individual states have the authority to limit women's access to abortion by prohibiting the performance of abortions in public facilities (see *Women's Rights Law Reporter*, Vol. 11 (3&4) Fall/Winter, 1989). Moreover, the preamble to the Missouri statute at issue in the *Webster* case declared that life begins at conception and that unborn children, "at every stage of development" have "all the rights, privileges and immunities available to other persons" (as cited in Steinmann, 1990). Unlike the decision in *Roe* however, the *Webster* decision did not overtly extend to an analysis of women's constitutional rights in the interests of maintaining privacy, autonomy and bodily integrity.

However such 'rights' as arguably existed (see MacKinnon, 1987), had already been severely encroached upon by the 1986 decision in *Bowers v. Hardwick* (106 S. Ct [1986]), where the United States Supreme Court held that the right of privacy only extends to limited areas of family, marriage and procreative choice. Such a restrictive interpretation has, in effect, given the state the power to regulate private relations which extend beyond the narrow confines of traditional concepts of family. The Court's decision to vest the 'right' to privacy in a social institution (i.e. the traditional family) has rendered certain forms of consensual sexual activity subject to state scrutiny and intervention. This line of reasoning is problematic even if one takes a limited view of the nature of what are regarded as fundamental liberties. However it becomes highly problematic when one considers the historical abuses of privacy in the context of the patriarchial family. It is a rather romantic view of 'rights' indeed which is derived from a legal doctrine that has served to shield the subordination and victimization of women and children from public view. As Stang Dahl and Snare have noted:

> Linked to the close supervision women experience is the legal conception of the sacred character of private life and the non-intervention practice of social agencies in cases of family violence and conflicts. . . . (Stang Dahl and Snare, 1978:22)

However, despite the apparent coherence and clarity of these court decisions with respect to women, they display considerable fragmentation when one considers their significance in terms of legitimating and extending the material, as opposed to symbolic, regulation of women. Both the fields and the actual modes of regulation are diverse, not only in terms of the degree of control extended and the deprivations visited, but with respect to the degree of incorporation of extra-legal knowledges which empower law, but are effected by auxillary discourses such as medicine and welfare. However the autonomy of certain groups of women and certain types of families has not always been, as Hirst (1981) has pointed out, contingent on law or right, but rather on competence (1981: 73-4). Freedom from regulation is extended only to the degree that the individual or institution involved satisfies the norms of the dominant culture. Thus while there is clearly a patterning of legal discourse, it is the historically connected nature of certain shared logics that continues to shape popular conceptions which in turn affect official practices. It is not only the enforcement of laws as such but the construction and affirmation of norms derived from particular configurations of values and their inscription in the practices of medical and welfare agents, housing authorities and so on that result in particular configurations of the power to punish.

THE VEIL OF FOETAL RIGHTS:
A KINDER, GENTLER CONTROL?

> Law reaches every silent space. It invades the secrecy of wom-
> en's wombs. It breaks every silence, uttering itself. Law-lan-
> guage, juris-dic-tion. It defines. It commands. It forces.
> (Ashe, 1989:355)

It is only really since 1973 that United States law has officially
acknowledged a state interest in the foetus per se (*Roe v. Wade*, 410
U.S. 113, 161-2, 1973). Prior to that the foetus was a legal non-
entity by virtue of the born alive rule at common law which required
that foetuses be born alive in order to attain the status of legal personhood. Contemporary trends toward a recognition of 'foetal
rights' present as problems for existing legal conceptualizations of
mother and child in utero as one under law. The prospective separation of mother and foetus at law raises the spectre of maternal and
foetal 'rights' as conflicting interests to be balanced against one
another (see Gallagher, 1987; Kahn, 1987).

However as Ehrenreich and English have observed, medical concerns for foetal well-being have long served to imprison women in
their own bodies (Ehrenreich and English, 1978). It is the extension
of law into medical terrain which makes the issue of foetal health
problematic. Punishing pregnant women for the good of the foetus
is not only paternalistic, but demonstrates how concerns such as
public health which are conceived of as virtually devoid of negative
consequences can have a very punitive downside. As Smart has
argued, despite the potentially oppressive consequences of incorporating historically specific desires/wishes/values into legal frameworks (Sevenhuijsen, 1986), "Arguing against legislation to enforce health measures is like arguing against virtue" (Smart,
1989:99).

Couched in terms of the legal discourse of rights, the use of illegal drugs by pregnant women posits an unnatural and certainly un-
healthy conflict between the 'rights' of women and those attributed
to foetuses. Foetal rights advocates claim that regardless of issues
such as access to health care and/or abortion, once a woman has
decided not to abort, she has a legal and moral duty to give birth to a
healthy child (see Fleischman, 1989; Robertson, 1989). According

to this kind of logic, women who 'chose' not to abort should be held legally accountable for voluntary conduct which harms their foetuses. However the notion that women's autonomy is expendable in the interests of foetal well-being is extremely problematic (see McNulty, 1988, 1989; Manson and Moralt, 1988; Bigge, 1989; Gallagher, 1987; King, 1989). As King has pointed out, "mothering has long been celebrated as the paradigm benevolent relationship between human beings" and pregnancy does carry certain [cultural] moral obligations on the part of the pregnant woman to her foetus (1989:395). However such obligations as are arguably owed a foetus also have to be considered in light of the obligations that individual women perceive as owing themselves and others.

Moreover, the imposition of additional burdens, moral or legal, on pregnant women may actually encourage them to terminate their pregnancies (King, 1989:398). Neither the dictation of cultural standards that impose moral obligations for pregnant women to act in the interests of their foetuses or the translation of moral obligations into legal compulsions serves the interests of healthy women and children. In fact it is precisely the interpretation of dominant cultural ascriptions of womanhood and mothering by agents of the welfare state that result in stories like "J's." Deconstructing this notion of motherhood as the paradigm benevolent relationship constitutes the crux of feminist analysis. As Willis has recently argued:

> What right-to-lifers are really demanding is that we make an exception for foetuses—or rather, continuing making the exception that's always been implied in women's traditional obligation to nurture life regardless of their own needs. It's feminists who are insisting that the treatment of a class of people—women—be brought in line with accepted standards of human rights. (Willis, 1989:92)

If, as right-to-lifers claim, the purpose of legal regulation is to ensure the health and safety of the foetus/child, the state would surely be better advised to adopt a course of preventive intervention through the provision of adequate and proper prenatal health care for women. A more detailed analysis of the right-to-lifer's claim serves to illuminate the motivations behind the invocation of a duty which would obstensibly require women to abrogate their 'rights' in favour of those accorded their foetuses. Even if one accepts the premise of foetus saving, the arguments for regulating women in the interests of the foetus remain problematic. As the detailed analysis of the elevation of motherhood provided by Davin (1978) and the work of Brophy and Smart (1985) attest, the rhetoric of 'child saving' has a long, complex and troublesome history. As I have argued elsewhere (Maher, 1990), neither the foetal rights movement or current attempts to criminalize pregnancy are in any sense directed at improving anyone's health and certainly not at eradicating engendered experiences of poverty, ill-health or drug addiction. Symbolically, they represent the potential to effect a much greater degree of regulation of all women's lives. Materially, what they are about is rendering certain groups of women contingent by shifting the control of their pregnancies and their experiences of mothering to legal, medical and welfare agents.

THE JURIDOGENIC POWER OF LAW

Cultural constructions of motherhood and women's sexuality are located at the intersection of productive and reproductive relations (Eisenstein, 1979; Jaggar, 1983) and project powerful images which are at the very core of gender relations in American society. As noted previously, legal discourse in relation to women's responsibility and culpability has historically been constructed in and around phallocentric notions of women's bodies. The advent of sophisticated new reproductive technologies which enhance not only the viability of the foetus but its visibility (see Petchesky, 1987) threaten to amplify the tendency of legal discourse to reduce women to their bodies and thus exacerbate the pervasive inequality of existing gender relations. The introduction of these new reproductive technologies into a society ridden with social and economic inequalities not only constrains the reproductive choices of low income women, but possesses the potential to exacerbate existing social conflicts.

Attempts to define these issues exclusively in terms of the formal legal discourse of regulation and control via the rhetoric of 'rights' encourages individualization and in effect, privatization and the attendant disqualification from public discourse and political agendas. By framing these social issues in terms of individual reproductive rights we not only occlude the social and cultural origins of such problems [and the role of the state in defining and reproducing them], but encourage the disparity that results from private solutions. Rothman points this out rather nicely in her examination of the difficult issues raised by amniocentesis tests and selective abortions. Women who abort damaged or defective foetuses, she argues, are not villains, but rather

> victims of a social system that fails to take collective responsibility for the needs of its members, and leaves individual women to make impossible choices. We are spared collective responsibility, because we individualize the problem. We make it a woman's own. She 'chooses,' and so we owe her nothing. Whatever the cost, she has chosen, and now it is her problem, not ours. (Rothman, 1986:189)

Both the criminalization and medicalization of social problems are problematic insofar as both approaches are based on control models which seek to individualize social problems (see Noble, 1990). However current attempts to regulate and control the pregnancies of women who use illegal drugs cannot be reduced to questions of the hegemony of one discourse over the other, but rather must be viewed as the product of a process whereby law has extended its terrain to incorporate these new medical knowledges. As Smart (1989) has described it:

> Through the appropriation of medical categorizations and welfare oriented practices rather than judicial practices, law itself becomes part of a method of regulation and surveillance. Law therefore has recourse to both methods, namely control through the allocation of rights and penalties, and regulation through the incorporation of medicine, psychiatry, social work and other professional discourses of the modern episteme. (Smart, 1989:96)

The collusion between medical and legal discourse in relation to new reproductive technologies presents the potential for a more persistent intrusion into women's lives. As more areas of women's lives are colonized by medical interventions, they are also staked out as legal territory. However it is not medical colonization per se that gives these developments their punitive edge, but rather as Smart (1989) suggests, the appropriation of medicine by law, and in particular reproductive medicine and advances in foetal science. It is law which "seals the fate" of these new medical knowledges. By incorporating the new terrain colonized by medicine, law reasserts and strengthens its own status, attesting to the historical interconnections between law, medicine and patriarchy (Smart, 1989).

The interrelation between the current discourse surrounding crack pregnancies and historical attempts to regulate and control women's lives through their bodies serves to illustrate the "juridogenic" power of law. As Smart has recently argued, "The idea that law has the power to right wrongs is persuasive. Just as medicine is seen as curative rather than iatrogenic, so law is seen as extending rights rather than creating wrongs" (Smart, 1989:12). While Smart's recent "warning to feminism to avoid the siren call of law" (1989:160) provides a timely reminder of the consequences of legal cures, she also urges feminists to focus on the power of law to disqualify and define the "truth of events" and to offer alternate counter-interpretations and [feminist] redefinitions (Smart, 1989:164-65). Moreover, Smart points out that feminists are increasingly engaged in deconstructive projects which challenge "naturalistic, overgeneralized and abstract assumptions about the social world" (1989:68) and further, are involved in "analysing the micro-politics of power, and the everyday oppressions of women which are invisible to the grand theorist" (1989:68). It is these insights, gained from being witness to the "everyday oppressions" of women who use crack cocaine, that permit me to make the following observations.

JURIDOGENIC FOR WHOM AND HOW?

Prosecutors have selected women whom society views as undeserving to be mothers in the first place. . . . Society is much more willing to condone the punishment of poor minority women who fail to meet the middle class ideal of motherhood. (Roberts, *New York Times*, 1990)

The current debate over the criminalization of pregnancy is framed almost exclusively in terms of scientifically mandated legal truths on one side and women's 'rights' on the other. By privileging this form of formal legal discourse over other knowledges, not only do we fail to de-centre law, but further, serve to obscure the reality that the power of law is already deployed in a number of covert and perhaps more acceptable ways to intervene in some women's lives. Utilizing a less inquisitorial mode and less formal proceedings, informal state interventions into women's lives are usually conducted under the auspices of administrative law and welfare policy. Although welfarism has been revealed as a judgemental mode of regulating certain classes (Wilson, 1977; Donzelet, 1980), administrative law seeks to utilize the rhetoric of welfarism to present intervention as benevolent, unproblematic and not warranting the procedural safeguards of formal justice. In general, when contrasted with formal sanctions, informal sanctions offer less protection for weaker parties and especially those who fail to conform to dominant social values (Bottomley, 1985:184).

The modes of informal justice subsumed under the heading of administrative law have long been recognized but not in their specificity. The failure to recognize to whom and under what conditions informal sanctions are extended is highlighted by an examination of Davis's (1971) pioneering work on discretionary justice which sought to expand jurisprudential analysis to encompass administrative law. The bodies in Davis's volume are distinctly male and in fact, the only time he mentions women, apart from thanking his wife in the acknowledgements section, is to use the feminine to illustrate three hypothetical cases concerning 'undesirable' tenants in public housing, a disturbed social worker and AFDC applicants. There is no mention, let alone analysis, of the differential conditions and processes by which women are present in these and other scenarios of informal or discretionary justice.

An examination of the nature and forms by which women who use crack are subject to informal regulation and control by virtue of their status as women and mothers necessitates a consideration of the relations between women and the modern state. Whilst it is important to recognize that the state is not a monolithic singular entity, it is clear that the state and its policies have a significant impact on the social position of women in Western societies. The state's role in defining gender ideologies which serve to promote particular forms of sexuality, family and mothering and which are enforced via economic, political and legal practices clearly affects the degree of control that individual women have over their bodies and their lives.

This is not to suggest that state policies and practices are inevitably and specifically designed to oppress all women, but rather that they both shape, and are shaped by, prevailing assumptions and ideologies about the role of women and in particular, as this role relates to the dominant model of the family and the reproduction of male/female relations. Such a perspective suggests that some state policies will be contradictory. These contradictions can be elaborated by an examination of the ideologies and beliefs which underpin specific forms of state policy. As noted previously, regulation with the ostensible aim of protecting mothers and children may discriminate harshly against those women whose lives do not conform to the assumed set of social practices from which these policies are derived.

It does not necessarily follow that we can analyze state institutions and policies and their relation to women as a group/homogenous analytical category. The assumption that all women will be affected by the state in the same way occludes recognition of the differential ways in which race, class, religion, ethnicity and sexual orientation both structure and mediate given relations between sets of women and the state. Rather than attempt to speak of women as a group we need to highlight the specificity of particular relations between women, as social agents located within particular and historically specific social formations, and the state (see Bryan, Dadzie and Scafe, 1986). This permits an exploration of the spaces in which the state seeks to intervene in order to mediate conflicts of interest based on critical social divisions such as gender, class and race. It allows us to move beyond an analysis of the formal state apparatuses of power to the legal and ideological conditions which constitute specific forms of state agency. By highlighting the administrative apparatus of the modern state and its bureaucratic/legal/coercive order, we are able to demonstrate how the state acts to structure and restructure relations between itself and certain groups within society and to specify the nature of gendered relations.

The differential impact of legal and ideological systems on particular groups of women can be elaborated further by the theoretical distinction provided by Pateman (1989) in relation to the sexually divided nature of the modern welfare state (1989:179). Pateman argues that welfare policies in the United States support the patriarchial structure of familial relations (1989:183). The sexual divisions in the welfare state have established a two-tier system in the United States whereby benefits are available to men as public persons on the basis of contributions by virtue of their participation in the market and to women as private persons who by virtue of their lack of contributions are means-tested and defined as dependent (Pateman, 1989:188).

The social welfare programs in the first category are in effect social insurance schemes. Benefits are earned on the basis of contributions and therefore deserved. As a consequence of this status, they also have less burdensome requirements in terms of eligibility, qualification, and maintenance. Women's welfare, on the other hand, is neither earned nor deserved but viewed as state largesse. These 'handouts' are subject to far more intrusive controls and surveillance. Recipients need to be monitored so as to ensure that the benevolence of the state is neither abused nor taken for granted. Recipients are constructed as clients rather than as purchasers or consumers and are given in-kind benefits rather than cash (re this distinction see Fraser, 1989:151-2). In return, the state gains considerable leverage over these women's lives, over how they will live, where they will live and who will live with them.

Within this two-tiered system which legitimates state intervention into many women's lives, dominant cultural norms in relation to the family, womanhood and mothering are central to conceptions of eligibility and deservedness. The imposition and regulation of approbated motherhood on welfare clients is based on the dominant ideological model of the family, the dual parent single family household. However as Stack's (1974) study of the domestic arrangements of poor Black welfare recipients indicates, both familial and household form are subject to considerable diversity. Stack found that within this community, the basis of domestic life was a cluster of "kinspeople" who are primarily related through children but also through friendship and marriage ties. Stack's work illustrates how domestic units are not necessarily constructed around the concept of biological mothers and their children, and how this in turn affects the differential construction of the concept of mothering. Contrary to dominant cultural assumptions, there is no universal and immutable mother-child bond produced by sheer virtue of biological fact (Stack, 1974). In fact, it may be as Strathern has suggested, that in Western cultures, precisely because women are associated with the natural, with children and with the domestic, that they are constructed as "less than persons" (Strathern, 1984:17). Within the confines of the modern welfare state, women clients are certainly less than citizens or political subjects in the traditional sense of political and philosophical discourse (Pateman, 1989).

This complex interface between the welfare state and the imposition of dominant norms of womanhood and mothering can be elaborated by research which examines the differential treatment and regulation by the state of those women whose lifestyles do not appear to conform to the cultural beliefs and social practices which undergird legal practices and welfare state policies. The actual nature of regulation and control can be differentiated by utilizing the distinction between formal and informal sanctions to analyze just who is being regulated and how. As Bryan et al. (1986) point out in relation to Black women's lives in Britain:

> There is no single area of our lives which better exposes our experience of institutionalized racism than our relationship with the various welfare services. Here we deal regularly with people who are vested with the power to control, disrupt and intervene in our lives on behalf of the State. Any Black woman who has ever spent a day at the DHSS office trying to claim benefit or who has had a child taken into care quickly learns that once contact with the welfare agencies is made, her life is no longer her own. (Bryan et al., 1986:110-11)

It is suggested that, in relation to poor minority women who are mothers who use drugs, a substantial component of the state's power to punish can be located in administrative law and welfare policy. My own field work has made this abundantly clear. While I have interviewed both women who smoke crack and are mothers and pregnant women who have subsequently given birth to babies with positive toxicologies [considered presumptive evidence of neglect in New York State], to the best of my knowledge none of them have been subject to the criminal prosecutions that the bulk of the literature concentrates on. However this does not mean they are exempt from regulation and control. These women are subject to an array of harsh sanctions imposed by the administrative welfare system: their babies are taken from them at birth and often a positive toxicology on a newborn will subsequently lead to the placement of other older children into foster homes. Their welfare benefits are often reduced, and many lose their eligibility for subsidized housing. Going into treatment to deal with their drug problems can often bring about the same set of disastrous consequences.

These deprivations constitute punishment. Punishment by welfare, by the infliction of administrative sanctions on women who use crack cocaine, is inherently discriminatory and unjust for a number of reasons. First, there is the fact that these forms of regulation and control can only be effected by virtue of these women's status as welfare clients. The state has considerable leverage over these women that it does not have over other women by virtue of their social situation. This leverage is not subject to any of the usual requirements of due process or procedural safeguards. Second, the same social situation of low-income and minority women that gives the state leverage over their lives, effectively denies them access to health care and in particular, prenatal care (Hughes et al., 1986). Research conducted for the period 1984-85 indicates an overall decline in maternal and infant health in the United States. However, maternal mortality rates for Black women are almost four times higher than that of white women, and one out of every two Black women failed to receive adequate prenatal care (Children's Defense Fund, 1988).

Third, adequate drug treatment for these women is non-existent (Chavkin, 1989). The fact that most substance abuse programs have emanated from a male-centred treatment model compounds the neglect of gender differentials in meeting the needs of women with substance abuse problems. The lack of child care provision often means that women addicts seeking residential treatment are faced with the "choice" of placing their children in state care in order to protect their own health and if pregnant, that of their foetus (McNulty, 1988:301; and more generally, Rosenbaum, 1981). There is also a considerable reluctance on the part of drug treatment centres to accept pregnant women because of fear of obstetric mal-practice suits (Perkins and Stoll, 1987). Fourth, the lack of ade-quate programs and facilities for women experiencing drug prob-lems is compounded by fears that seeking any form of medical treatment may lead either to criminal charges or even more intrusive forms of welfare intervention and regulation. A study conducted in 1974 revealed that 75 percent of pregnant drug addicts did not con-sult a physician at any stage during their pregnancies (Finnegan and MacNew, 1974), and recent research conducted in New York City suggests that maternal cocaine users are seven times less likely to receive prenatal care than non-drug users (Drucker, 1990). How-ever research indicates that women in receipt of proper prenatal care who continue to use drugs during pregnancy have improved birth outcomes over women who do not have prenatal care and use drugs during pregnancy (MacGregor et al., 1989).

Fifth, there is the issue of how these women are treated during the actual birthing and hospitalization experience. I have spoken to many women who smoke crack who refuse to give birth in public hospitals, which are often the only options open to them. Within the public hospital system, the stereotypes that are attendant to their definition as welfare clients are compounded by racist stereotypes of drug use and the fear of AIDS. As a result, these women are almost always drug tested and are often subject to other forms of discriminatory and degrading treatment. As "K" who is 24 years old and has given birth to two children since she has been using crack puts it:

> Bad . . . they treat you bad. . . . That was like I had my daughter, when the nurse came, and I was having the stomach pain and my stomach was killing me. I kept callin and callin and callin. She just said you smokin that crack, you smoke that crack, you suffer. . . . Man I want to hit that lady so bad. I broke and then my mother came, yeah my mother said regard-less of what she do, if she in pain, then thats what ya'all get paid for an ya'll help her. (fieldnotes, 1990)

What it comes down to is that these women experience blatant racial and economic bias. Research indicates that despite similar rates of substance abuse, Black women are at least twice as likely to be reported to government authorities. This rate reflects a testing ratio ten times higher than that for white women (NAPARE, 1989). Since 1987 there have been about 50 prosecutions against women who use drugs during pregnancy. The great bulk of these defendants have been Black and poor (see also ACLU, 1989). However Black women are not targetted for testing and prosecution because they are more guilty of foetal abuse, but rather because of the combination of racism and poverty which renders them visible and vulnerable (Roberts, 1990). As Bryan et al. (1986) have argued, it is the institutionalization of these biases that render Black women vulnerable to the excesses of the state. By pointing out how the Thatcherite state constructs Black women as parasites and scroungers, "as having a child-like dependence upon a benevolent caring (white) society" (1986:111), these authors draw attention to the ways in which social and economic factors are systematically obscured, and Black women's contributions to British society ignored. They also point out how this construction makes it easier for the welfare state to "rely on loose assumptions and loaded stereotypes of us rather than try seriously to address the root cause of our problems. These assumptions become justifications for everything from secret files and surveillance to direct intervention of the most destructive kind" (Bryan et al., 1986:112).

CONCLUSION

How is that? You don't even know me.
I've worked and I'm a good mother.
That doesn't matter, says the system.
You use drugs, brother.
—And that the real deal.
So out of the clear blue sky
This obnoxious, unidentifiable, anonymous creature
Elopes with my son.
But that's alright says Uncle Sam,
You defaulted your rights
The moment you picked up

—Daisy Oatman, homeless poet, 1990.

The obstensible aim of the state in mandating child neglect and abuse reporting is to protect children. In New York City, child abuse and neglect petitions before the Family Court containing allegations of drug abuse quadrupled in the three year period 1986-1989 (Fink, 1990). The great bulk of these notifications are filed on the basis of positive toxicologies performed on newborn infants in public hospital facilities. In addition to the fact that women who give birth in public hospitals hardly constitute a random sample, toxicology tests carry the usual risks of false positives and false negatives (Cherukuri et al., 1988). Positive toxicology screens on newborns also indicate very little about the conduct or lifestyle of the woman/mother other than that she ingested drugs within the week preceding delivery (Frank et al., cited in Lockwood, 1990). They do not indicate (a) harm to the infant, (b) evidence that the woman is a drug addict, or (c) that the woman is unfit to be a parent. Moreover, the mandatory reporting of these positive toxicology screens and their basis as evidence of neglect or abuse is problematic even by traditional legal standards developed to ensure consent and confidentiality. The notion of informed consent would appear to warrant that where positive toxicologies are utilized as evidence in relation to potential criminal prosecution or administrative proceedings such as may result in deprivation of custody, the consequences of consent should be known to the patient prior to drug testing.

The assumption of a causal connection between perinatal exposure to illegal drugs and harm is also highly problematic when one considers the difficulties in controlling for a host of high risk factors associated with adverse birth outcomes such as alcohol abuse, prescription drug use, cigarette smoking and factors generally associated with poverty such as poor diet and nutrition and inadequate prenatal care (Koren et al., 1989; see also Drucker, 1990). However the link between perinatal exposure to illegal drugs and an inability to parent is even more tenuous. Is evidence of prenatal exposure to drugs in and of itself, independent of any other harm or perceived future harm, sufficient justification for state intervention and sanction? Does parental drug use warrant the removal of infants from their mothers? Are substance users inherently incapable of adequate parenting? Surely the deprivation of custody under such conditions, before women have even had the opportunity to demonstrate their ability to care for their infants, amounts to the punitive sanctioning of women based on culturally loaded predictions as to their future conduct as mothers.

And what about the 'best interests' of the children? The current overloading of the foster care system and the shortage of shelter facilities has given rise to the phenomenon of boarder babies in many large hospitals and institutions (Bussiere and Shauffer, 1990). Removing children from parental care and custody when substitute homes are not available would not appear to serve the best interests of the child in the absence of strong evidence that the child is at serious risk of harm. The psychological and physical harm potentially engendered by the institutionalization of these infants (Bussiere and Shauffer, 1990) would appear to render such a practice irresponsible at best.

To date, the debate over criminalizing pregnancy and regulating motherhood has been conducted within the privileged terms of legal discourse. Talk of rights and harms pervade public debate and legal consideration of this issue. The almost exclusive focus on the criminal law tends to overshadow the power to punish that less visible administrative forms of regulation and control vest in the welfare state. The notion of criminalizing pregnancy, by definition, suggests that law's power can be located in its formal, criminal component and that efforts to redefine and address this issue need to be constructed within the confines of a legalist discourse.

This inevitably leads us to arguments about 'rights,' and in particular those rights of privacy, autonomy and bodily integrity which tend to suggest that sexuality, fertility and mothering are and somehow always have been, inherently private concerns beyond the realm of state intervention. Well, maybe for some. What this paper has intended to reveal is that when one casts aside the posturing of legal rhetoric couched in terms of the rights of women, children or foetuses, it becomes apparent that recent attempts at criminalizing pregnancy and regulating motherhood are coterminous with an historical litany of attempts to regulate and control certain groups of women and in particular, with some women's current experiences of pregnancy and mothering. The underlying logic between these recent developments and the 1927 case of *Buck v. Bell* is identical; those women who are judged unfit to be mothers must be prevented from having children and where this is already too late, separated from the children they do have.

The problematic nature of the current practice of relying on toxicology screens as evidence of neglect or abuse renders judgements as to women's ability to parent tantamount to punishing women who fail to conform to dominant cultural ascriptions of mothering. If you are a female drug user, and in particular, a poor minority woman who uses crack, then you must be a 'bad' mother. Targetting and sanctioning these women for transgressing white middle class fantasies of the ideal mother, whether formally or informally, represents the contemporary equivalent of the doctrine of maternal fault (Davin, 1978) and like its predecessor, does absolutely nothing to enhance collective social responsibility for healthy women and healthy children.

The New York City Health Department maintains that births to substance abusing women have increased some 3,000 percent over the last ten years (French, 1989). Access to health care for uninsured women has diminished greatly over the same ten year period because of funding cuts (McNulty, 1990). The United States currently ranks last in infant mortality among twenty industrialized nations, and Black infant mortality rates are on the increase (Children's Defense Fund, 1988). Over 85 percent of adult females with AIDS are Black or Hispanic. Over 90 percent of babies and young children with AIDS are Black or Hispanic (Farber, 1989). Meanwhile, "J" is still smoking crack and living by her wits on the streets of Flatbush. Later this month, "J" will return to the Family Court. Her caseworker has told her she has one more chance to enter a treatment facility and deal with her drug problem. Otherwise the judge will put her kids up for adoption.

> My caseworker told me, you cant make an excuse one more, this is you last chance. . . . C'mon, I know I'm a fuckin junkie. I deserve to be hung. . . . All I want is somebody, you know what I'm sayin to you. Thats all I want, I'm lonely, I have no one—no friends, no family . . . thats for me to suffer in life you know. (fieldnotes, 1990)

Surely it is at the very least arguable whether the complex of relations encapsulated by the social phenomena of women's crack use either can or should be dealt with by legal regulation and intervention, or for that matter, any form of unitary proscriptive approach. A contextual examination of the lives of women who use crack suggests that historically and culturally specific forms of difference in social life, gender, class, race, ethnicity, sexuality, are constructed and mediated in interrelation with each other. Specific conjunctures of these properties specify both the nature of relations between women and the state and particular forms of state responses to particular constructions of 'woman.'

NOTES

1. As the title implies, the work of Garland (1985) and Garland and Young (1983) has had a major influence. In particular, the recognition that punishment is not a "singular unitary phenomenon" and that to treat it as such is to ignore its plurality and complexity (Garland and Young, 1983:15). Drawing on the insights provided by Garland's analysis of the relation between punishment and social structure and the relation between power and knowledge, the paper is concerned to articulate the ways in which "the penal" and "the social" overlap and interpenetrate with respect to the regulation of crack pregnancies.

2. These interactive effects are also evident in an examination of the recent resurgence of court-ordered medical interventions in the form of forced caesareans. Over the past five years at least 24 women have been compelled by the state to undergo caesarean sections in the United States, and the majority of these women have been minority and foreign born women, many of whom have non-mainstream religious beliefs (Kolder et al., 1987; see also Annas, 1989).

3. This right had been previously established as a constitutional principle in *Griswold v. Connecticut,* U.S. 479 [1965] but see also *Meyer v. Nebraska,* 262 U.S. 390, [1923] for enumeration of the right to "privacy, autonomy and bodily integrity."

4. Note also that the Court held in *Harris v. McRae* (448 U.S. 297 [1980]) that this right did not extend to funding of abortions under the federal Medicaid program. As MacKinnon has pointed out, this decision highlights the contradictions of the capitalist state insofar as it funds continuing conceptions whilst simultaneously denying funds to discontinue them (MacKinnon, 1987;1989).

REFERENCES

American Civil Liberties Union. (1989). Reproductive Freedom Project, New York.

Allen, H. (1987). *Justice unbalanced: Gender, psychiatry and judicial decisions.* Milton Keynes, Open University Press.

Annas, G. (1989). Predicting the future in pregnancy: How medical technology affects the legal rights of pregnant women. *Nova Law Review*. 13(2):329-354.

Anzaldua, G. (1990). (Ed). *Making face, making soul (Haciendo Caras): Creative and critical perspectives by women of color.* San Francisco, Aunt Lute Foundation.

Ashe, M. (1989). Zig-zag stitching and the seamless web: Thoughts on 'reproduction' and the law. *Nova Law Review*. 13 (2):355-384.

Bart, P. (1981). A study of women who were both raped and avoided rape. *Journal of Social Issues*. 37(4):123-37.

Bigge, E. (1989). The fetal rights controversy. *UMKC Law review*. 57:261-288.

Bottomley, A. (1985). What is happening to family law? A feminist critique of conciliation. In J. Brophy and C. Smart (Eds). *Women in law*. London, Routledge and Kegan Paul.

Brophy, J. and Smart, C. (1985). (Eds). *Women in law*. London, Routledge and Kegan Paul.

Brown, C. (1981). Mothers, fathers and children: From private to public patriarchy. In Sargent (Ed). *The unhappy marriage of marxism and feminism.* London, Pluto Press.

Bryan, B.,Dadzie, S. and Scafe, S. (1986). *The heart of the race: Black women's lives in Britain.* London, Virago.

Bussiere, A. and Shauffer, C. (1990). The little prisoners. *Youth Law News*. 11(1):22-26.

Cain, M. (1990). Towards transgression: New directions in feminist criminology. *International Journal of the Sociology of Law*. 18:118.

Caplan, P. and Hall-McCorquodale, I. (1985). Mother-blaming in major clinical journals. *American Journal of Orthopsychiatry*. 55(3):345-613.

Carlen, P. and Worrall, A. (1987). (Eds). *Gender, crime and justice*. Milton Keynes, Open University Press.

Carlen, P. (1988). *Women. crime and poverty*. Milton Keynes, Open University Press.

Chasnoff, (1989). *Women and Health*. Vol. 15(3):1-3.

Chavkin, W. (1989). "Help, don't jail addicted mothers." *New York Times*, July 18.

Cherukuri et al. (1988). A cohort study of alkaloidal cocaine ('crack') in pregnancy. *Obstetrics and Gynecology*. 72:147.

Chesler, P. (1986). *Mothers on trial: The battle for children and custody*. Seattle, Seal Press.

Children's Defense Fund (1988). *The health of America's children: Maternal and child health data book.* Institute of Medicine.

Chodorow, N. (1978). *The reproduction of mothering: Psychoanalysis and the sociology of gender*. Berkeley, University of California Press.

Chodorow, N. and Contratto, S. (1982). The fantasy of the perfect mother. In Thorne and Yalom (Eds). *Rethinking the family*. New York, Longman.

Cohen, S. and Taub, N. (1988). (Eds). *Reproductive laws for the 1990s*. Clifton, N.J.: Humana Press.

Collier, J. F., Rosaldo, M. Z. and Yanagisako, S. (1982). Is there a family? New anthropological views. In Thorne and Yalom (Eds). *Rethinking the family*. New York, Longman.

Collins, P. Hill. (1990). Black feminist thought: *Knowledge, consciousness and the politics of empowerment*. Boston, Unwin Hyman.

Daly, K. (1987a). Structure and practice of familial-based justice in a criminal court. *Law and Society Review*. 21(2):267-290.

Daly, K. (1987b). Discrimination in the criminal courts: Family, gender and the problem of equal treatment. *Social Forces*. 66(1):152-175.

Daly, K. (1988). The social control of sexuality: A case study of the criminalization of prostitution in the Progressive Era. *Research in Law, deviance and social control*. Vol. 9:171-206.

Davin, A. (1978). Imperialism and motherhood. *History Workshop*. 5:9-65.

Davis, K. C.(1971). *Discretionary justice: A preliminary inquiry*. Chicago, University of Illinois Press.

Diesenhouse, S. (1989). "Punishing pregnant addicts: Debate, dismay, no solution" *New York Times*, September, 10.

Dobash, R.E. and Dobash, R. (1979). *Violence against wives: A case against patriarchy*. New York, Free Press.

Donzelet, J. (1980). *The policing of families*. London, Hutchinson.

Drucker, E. (1990). Children of war: The criminalization of motherhood. *The International Journal on Drug Policy*. 1(4).

Eaton, M. (1986). *Justice for women? Family, court and social control*. Milton Keynes, Open University Press.

Edwards, S. (1981). *Female sexuality and the law*. Oxford, Martin Robertson.

Ehrenreich, B. and English, D. (1979). *For her own good*. London, Pluto Press.

Eisenstein, Z. (1979). Developing a theory of capitalist patriarchy and socialist feminism. In Z. Eisenstein (Ed). *Capitalist patriarchy and the case for socialist feminism*. New York, Monthly Review Press.

Farber, J. (1990). AIDS: Words from the front. *Spin*. October. pp.73-75.

Fink, J. R. (1990). Reported effects of crack cocaine on infants. *Youth Law News*. 11(1):37-39.

Finnegan, L. P. (1972). Comprehensive care of pregnant addicts and it's effect on maternal and infant outcome. *Contemporary Drug Problems*. 1(4):795.

Finnegan and MacNew (1974). Care of the addicted infant. *American Journal of Nursing*. 74:685.

Fleischman, A.R. (1988). The fetus is a patient. In S. Cohen and N. Taub (Eds). *Reproductive laws for the 1990's*. Clifton, N.J.: Humana Press.

Foucalt, M. (1978). *The history of sexuality: An introduction*. New York, Pantheon.

Foucault, M. (1979). *Discipline and punish: The birth of the prison*. New York, Vintage Books.

Foucault, M. (1985). *The use of pleasure: The history of sexuality*. Vol. 2, New York, Vintage.

Fraser, N. (1989). *Unruly practices: Power, discourse and gender in contemporary social theory*. Minneapolis, University of Minnesota Press.

Fraser, N. and Nicholson, L. J. (1990). Social criticism without philosophy: An encounter between feminism and postmodernism. In L. J. Nicholson (Ed). *Feminism/postmodernism*. New York, Routledge.

French, H. (1989). Rise in babies hurt by drugs is predicted. *New York Times*. 18 October, 1989.

Fullilove, M. T. and Fullilove, R.E. (1989). Intersecting epidemics: Black teen crack use and sexually transmitted disease. *JAMWA*. 44(5).

Gallagher, J. (1987). Pre-natal invasions and interventions: What's wrong with fetal rights. *Harvard Women's Law Journal*. 10:9.

Galliher, J.F. and Walker N. (1978). The politics of systematic research error. *Crime and Social Justice*. 10:29-33.

Garland, D. (1985). *Punishment and welfare: A history of penal strategies*. London, Gower.

Garland, D. and Young, P. (Eds). (1983). *The power to punish: Contemporary penalty and social analysis*. Heinemann, London.

Goode, William J. (1960). Norm commitment and conformity to role-status obligations. *American Journal of Sociology*. 66:248-258.

Gordon, C. (Ed). (1980). *Power/knowledge: Selected interviews and other writings 1972-1977 By Michel Foucault*. New York, Pantheon.

Guttmacher Institute. (1987). *Blessed events and the bottom line: Financing maternity care in the United States*. New York, Alan Guttmacher Institute.

Guttmacher Institute. (1980). *Safe and legal: Ten years experience with legal abortion in New York state*. New York, Allan Guttmacher Institute.

Hanmer, J. and Maynard, M. (Eds). (1987). *Women, violence and social control*. London, Macmillan.

Hanmer, J., Radford, J. and Stanko, E. (Eds). (1989). *Women, policing and male violence*. Routledge, New York.

Hamid, A. (1990). The political economy of crack-related violence. *Contemporary Drug Problems*. 17(1):31-78.

Harding, S. (1986). *The science question in feminism*. Ithaca, Cornell University Press.

Harding, S. (1986). The instability of the analytical categories of feminist theory. *Signs: Journal of Women in Culture and Society*. 11(4):645-664.

Hirst, P. (1980). Law, socialism and rights. In P. Carlen and M. Collinson (Eds). *Radical issues in criminology*. Oxford, Martin Robinson.

Hirst, P. (1981). The genesis of the social. In *Politics and power*. Vol. 3. London, Routledge and Kegan Paul.

hooks, b. (1981). *Ain't I a woman: Black women and feminism*. Boston, South End Press.

hooks, b. (1984). *Feminist theory: From margin to center*. Boston, South End Press.

Hughes, Johnson, Rosenbaum and Simmons (1986). The health of America's mothers and children: Trends in access to care. *Clearinghouse Review*. 20:473-474.

Jaggar, A. (1983). *Feminist politics and human nature*. Totowa, N.J., Rowman and Allanheld.

Kahn, J. (1987). Of woman's first disobedience: Forsaking a duty of care to her fetus—Is this a mother's crime? *Brooklyn Law Review*. 53:807.

King, P. (1989). Should mom be constrained in the best interests of the fetus? *Nova Law Review*. 13(2):393-404.

Kirp, D. (1989). "Prosecuting crack mothers won't help." *The Los Angeles Daily Journal*, July 11.

Klein, D. (1983). Ill and against the law: The social and medical control of heroin users. *Journal of Drug Issues*. 13:1.

Klein, D. and Kress, J. (1976). Any woman's blues: A critical overview of women, crime and the criminal justice system. *Crime and Social Justice*. 5:34-49.

Kolder, Gallagher and Parsons. (1987). Court-ordered obstetrical interventions. *New England Journal of Medicine*. 1192:316. Cited in King, Op. cit.

Koren, G., Graham, K., Shear, H. and Einarson T. (1989). Bias against the null hypothesis: The reproductive hazards of cocaine. *The Lancet*. Dec. 16., pp. 1440-1442.

Lasch, Christopher (1977). *Haven in a heartless world: The family besieged*. New York, Basic Books.

Lockwood, S. E. (1990). What's known—and what's not known—about drug-exposed infants. *Youth Law News*. 11(1):15-18.

Lorde, A. (1984). *Sister outsider*. California, The Crossing Press.

MacGregor et al. (1989). Cocaine abuse during pregnancy: Correlation between prenatal care and perinatal outcomes. *Obstetrics and Gynecology*. 74:882.

MacKinnon, C. (1982). Feminism. marxism, method and the state: An agenda for theory. *Signs: Journal of Women in Culture and Society*. 7(3):515-54.

MacKinnon, C. (1987). *Feminism unmodified: Discourses on life and law*. Cambridge, Mass., Harvard University Press.

MacKinnon, C. (1989). *Toward a feminist theory of the state*. Cambridge, Mass., Harvard University Press.

McLanahan, S. S., Sorenson, A. and Watson D. (1989). Sex differences in poverty, 1950-1980. *Signs: Journal of Women in Culture and Society*. 15(1):102-122.

McNulty, M. (1988). Pregnancy police: The health policy and legal implications of punishing pregnant women for harm to their fetuses. *New York University Review of Law and Social Change*. 16(2):277-319.

McNulty, M. (1989). Combatting pregnancy discrimination in access to substance abuse treatment. *Clearinghouse Review*. 23:21-25.

McNulty, M. (1990). Pregnancy police: Implications of criminalizing fetal abuse. *Youth Law News*. 11(1):33-36.

Maher, L. (1990). Criminalizing pregnancy: The downside of a kinder gentler nation. *Social Justice*. 17(3).

Maher, L. Fieldnotes for Ph.D. Dissertation, School of Criminal Justice, Rutgers University.

Malveaux, J. (1990). Gender difference and beyond: An economic perspective on diversity and commonality among women. In D.L. Rhode (Ed). *Theoretical perspectives on sexual difference*. New Haven, Yale University Press. pp. 226-238.

Manson, R. and Marolt, J. (1988). A new crime, fetal neglect: State intervention to protect the unborn — Protection at what cost? *California Western Law Review*. 24:161-182.

Medick, H. and Sabean, D. W. (1984). (Eds). *Interest and emotion: Essays on the study of family and kinship*. Cambridge, Cambridge University Press.

Moraga, C. and Anzaldua, G. (1983). (Eds). *This bridge called my back: Writings by radical women of color*. New York, Kitchen Table: Women of Color Press.

Moss, K. L. (1990). Legal issues: Drug testing of post-partum women and newborns as the basis for civil and criminal proceedings. *Clearinghouse Review*. 23:1406-1414.

Musto, D. (1973). *An American disease: Origins of narcotic control*. New Haven, Yale University Press.

National Association of Perinatal Addiction Research (1989). (Pinellas County, Fla. Study).

Nicholson, L. J. (Ed). (1990). *Feminism/postmodernism*. New York, Routledge.

Noble, A. (1990). Criminalize or medicalize?: Social and political definitions of substance abuse during pregnancy. A Report prepared for the Maternal and Child Health Branch of the Department of Health Services.

Oatman, Daisy (1990). Notes from the underground: Prose and poetry by homeless and formerly homeless writers. *Crossroads*. September. p. 31.

Paltrow, L. M. (1990). When becoming pregnant is a crime. *Criminal Justice Ethics*. 9(1):41-47.

Pateman, C. (1989). *The disorder of women: Democracy, feminism and political theory*. Stanford, California, Stanford University Press.

Pearce, D. (1978). Farewell to alms: Women's fare under welfare. In J. Freeman (Ed). *Women*. (1988; 4th Edition). Mountain View, CA., Mayfield.

Perkins and Stoll. (1987). Medical Malpractice: A 'crisis' for poor women. *Clearinghouse Review*. 20:1277-78.

Petchesky, R. P. (1984). *Abortion and woman's choice: The state, sexuality and reproductive freedom*. New York, Longman.

Petchesky, R. P. (1987). Foetal images. In M. Stanworth (Ed). *Reproductive technologies: Gender, medicine and motherhood*. Minneapolis, University of Minnesota Press.

Raff, B. Guest Editorial. *Women and Health*. 15(3):1-3.

Rafter, N.H. (1988). *White Trash: The eugenics family studies, 1877-1919*. Boston, Northeast University Press.

Rapp, R. (1978). Family and class in contemporary America: Notes toward an understanding of ideology. *Science and society*. 42:278-300.

Raymond, J. (1987). Preface. In G. Corea, J. Hanmer, B. Hoskins, J. Raymond, R.D. Klein, H. B. Holmes, M. Kishwar, R. Rowland and R. Steinbacher (Eds). *Man-made women: How the new reproductive technologies affect women*. Bloomington, Indiana University Press.

Roberts, D. (1990). The bias in drug arrests of pregnant women. *New York Times*. August, 11.

Robertson, J. A. (1989). Reconciling offspring and maternal interest during pregnancy. In Cohen and Taub (Eds). Reproductive laws for the 1990's. Clifton, N.J.: Humana Press.

Rosaldo, M.Z. (1974). Women, culture and society: A theoretical overview. In M. Rosaldo and L. Lamphere (Eds). *Women, culture and society*. Stanford, California, Stanford University Press.

Rosenbaum, M. (1981). *Women on heroin*. New Brunswick, N.J., Rutgers University Press.

Rosenbaum, M., Murphy, S., Irwin, J. and Watson, L. (1990). *Women and crack: What's the real story?* Unpublished paper, Institute for Scientific Analysis, San Francisco, CA.

Rossi, A. (1977). The biosocial basis of parenting. *Daedalus*. 106:1-31.

Rothman, B. K. (1984). The meaning of choice in reproductive technology. In R. Arditti, R.D. Klein and S. Minden (Eds). *Test- tube women: What future for motherhood?*. New York, Viking.

Rothman, B. K. (1986). *The tentative pregnancy*. New York, Viking.

Rothman, B. K. (1989). Motherhood: Beyond patriarchy. *Nova Law Review*. 13: 481-486.

Rowland, R. (1987). Technology and motherhood: Reproductive choice reconsidered. *Signs: Journal of Women in Culture and Society*. 12:512-28.

Rowland, R. (1987). Motherhood, patriarchial power, alienation and the issue of 'choice' in sex preselection. In G. Corea, J. Hanmer, B. Hoskins, J. Raymond, R. D. Klein, H. B. Holmes, M. Kishwar, R. Rowland and R. Steinbacher (Eds). *Man-made women: How the new reproductive technologies affect women*. (pp.74-87). Bloomington, Indiana University Press.

Russell, D. (1982). *Rape in marriage*. New York, Macmillan.

Scott, L. A. (1988). The Pamela Rae Stewart case and fetal law. *Harvard Women's Law Journal*. 11:227-245.

Sevenhuijsen, S. (1986). Fatherhood and the political theory of rights: Theoretical perspectives of feminism. *International Journal of the Sociology of Law*. 14(3/4):329-40.

Smart, C. (1976). *Women, crime and criminology: A feminist critique*. Boston, Routledge and Kegan Paul.

Smart, C. (1989). *Feminism and the power of law*. New York, Routledge.

Smart, C. (1990). Law's power, the sexed body and feminist discourse. *Journal of Law and Society*. 17(2):194-210.

Smith, R. (1981). *Trial by medicine*. Edinburgh, Edinburgh University Press.

Spelman, E. V. (1988). *Inessential woman: Problems of exclusion in feminist thought*. Boston, Beacon Press.

Spillinger, C. (1989). Reproduction and medical interventionism: An historical comment. *Nova Law Review*. 13(2):385-392.

Stack, C. (1974). *All our kin: Strategies for survival in a Black community*. New York, Harper & Row.

Stang Dahl, T. and Snare, A. (1978). The coercion of privacy: A feminist perspective. In C. Smart and B. Smart. (Eds). *Women, sexuality and social control*. London, Routledge and Kegan Paul.

Stang Dahl, T. (1987). *Women's law: An introduction to feminist jurisprudence*. Oxford, Oxford University Press.

Stanko, E. A. (1985). *Intimate intrusions: Women's experience of male violence*. London, Routledge and Kegan Paul.

Stanworth, M. (1987). Reproductive technologies and the deconstruction of motherhood. In M. Stanforth (Ed). *Reproductive technologies: Gender, motherhood and medicine*. Minneapolis, University of Minnesota Press.

Stefan, S. (1989). Whose egg is it anyway/ Reproductive rights of incarcerated, institutionalized and incompetent women. *Nova Law Review*. 13(2):405-456.

Steinmann, R. (1990). Does the foetus of an incarcerated pregnant inmate have any constitutional rights under the Missouri abortion law? Paper presented at the Annual Meetings, Academy of Criminal Justice Sciences. March.

Stone, L. (1979). *The family, sex and marriage: In England 1500-1800*. New York, Harper.

Strathern, M. (1984). Domesticity and the denigration of women. In D. O'Brien and S. Tiffany (Eds). *Rethinking women's roles: Perspectives from the Pacific*. Berkeley, University of California Press.

Walkowitz, J. (1980). *Prostitution and Victorian society*. Cambridge, Cambridge University Press.

Weeks, J. (1984). *Sex, politics and society: The regulation of sexuality since 1800*. London, Routledge and Kegan Paul.

Willis, E. (1989). From forced pregnancy to forced surgery: The wrongs of fetal rights. In *Feminism lives!* North Carolina, Radical Feminist Organizing Committee.

Wilson, E. (1977). *Women and the welfare state*. London, Tavistock.

Woliver, L. R. (1989). The deflective power of reproductive technologies: The impact on women. *Women & Politics*. 9(3):17-47.

Women's Rights Law Reporter. Vol. 11 (3&4). Fall/Winter 1989.

Worrall, A. (1990). *Offending women: Female law breakers and the criminal justice system*. New York, Routledge.

Working Group of the Project on Reproductive Laws for the 1990's. (1989). Introduction to symposium on reproductive rights. *Nova Law Review*. 13(2): 321-328.

Women and Fetus: The Social Construction of Conflict

Wendy Chavkin

SUMMARY. An emerging social theme positions a pregnant woman as antagonist to the fetus if she deviates from medically, socially, or legally sanctioned behavior. This is particularly devastating for low income women and women with stigmatized problems. These policies convey a vision of an errant pregnant woman whose antagonism to the fetus must be constrained by outside intervention. Autonomy, bodily integrity, and constitutional status are all at stake. Ironically, these policies may well undermine fetal as well as maternal health by deterring women from involvement with medical care. Moreover, the focus on the individual plays the diversionary role of distracting attention from the societal failure to enable women to be healthy and have healthy babies.

The Johnson Controls Company, a battery plant, has instituted a policy excluding all fertile women from jobs with lead exposure on the grounds that such exposure would be "fetotoxic" were they ever to become pregnant. In 1987, A.C., a terminally ill young woman, was subjected to a court ordered caesarean section on behalf of her 25-week fetus. Both died in the post-operative period. In

Wendy Chavkin, MD, MPH, is a Perinatal Research Associate with the Chemical Dependency Institute at Beth Israel Medical Center. She is also Associate Professor of Clinical Public Health and Obstetrics-Gynecology at Columbia University School of Public Health.

The author acknowledges the Rockefeller Foundation for its support and Catholics for a Free Choice who have graciously permitted publication here. This paper is based on a talk given at their Annual Conference in June 1989 in Washington, DC.

1989, Jennifer Johnson was convicted of the felony drug charge of having transported an illicit substance to a minor, via the umbilical cord in the seconds after childbirth, prior to the clamping of the cord. In 1987, S.B. enrolled in a prenatal care access program for medically indigent women. She experienced a fetal demise at 32 weeks gestation after a pregnancy complicated by hypertension and was discharged from the program after a postpartum visit.[1,2]

What unites these cases is an emerging theme which considers a pregnant woman's welfare only in relation to the "maternal environment" she provides for the fetus. While this tendency can be located in the larger societal convulsion over the changing role of women, of which the abortion debate is the most obvious manifestation, it has medical and public health implications in addition to the social and political ones.

Taken to its extreme this emerging trend in the social perception of women positions a pregnant woman as antagonist to the fetus whenever she asserts her own primacy. This has direct implications for the delivery of health services to women, especially low income women. At least two sets of interests, woman as protector of the fetus and woman as adult decision-maker, are brought into conflict in this formulation.

This theme of maternal-fetal antagonism has had various manifestations and a long history. Feminist historians of reproductive politics have commented on protective labor legislation designed to protect the "vessels of the race" with the criminalization of contraception and abortion as some of these manifestations. At the present time, legal and medical discourse establishes this antagonism clearly in issues ranging from consideration of the woman's welfare only insofar as it impacts on the "maternal environment" she provides for the fetus, to constraining her behavior and penalizing her for certain activities during pregnancy, to overt coercion.

What forces converge to create our current social perception of maternal-fetal antagonism? In the United States, societal supervision of maternal behavior has historically been closely linked to public health efforts on behalf of children. In 1921, the Shepherd Towner Act provided for preventive health care for pregnant women and children and introduced a mechanism for State supervision of poor mothers through the persons of public health nurses.

Interestingly, the resources offered by the State were meager and of short duration as the Act was repealed within eight years of passage.[3]

More recent attempts at the supervision of mothers differ sharply in their focus on the fetus rather than the child. At least three strands converge to explain this emphasis on "the unborn." One obvious component is the current controversy over abortion. A second component, which in turn contributes to the first, are recent dramatic technological accomplishments in neonatal care, the development of perinatal medicine, and the emergence of fetal therapy. The third component is the medical malpractice crisis. As long as parents of "imperfect" babies have no recourse to resources except through legal suit, obstetricians will continue to defensively increase medical surveillance of pregnant women.

All of these developments must be set against the backdrop of societal uneasiness over the growing participation in paid employment by pregnant women and mothers of very young children. Here too, the battle over women's changing role has been cast in terms relating to fetal viability and welfare. Since gender is no longer a legally permissible reason for exclusion from employment, in the last decade major companies have implemented "fetal protection" policies whereby "potentially pregnant" women have been excluded from (previously sex segregated) jobs involving "fetotoxic" exposures.[4] Corporations cite fear of liability as the reason for excluding fertile women from worksites deemed "fetotoxic." Hostility towards working mothers is also manifest in the recent controversies over pregnancy disability since the United States has no national policy guaranteeing job retention for women who take leave from work in relation to childbirth.[5]

This ideological stance toward the pregnant woman has translated into policies and programs with a wide range of manifestations. Attempts have been made in recent years to penalize women for activities undertaken during pregnancy which were believed to be harmful to fetal health. In 1980, a Michigan court held that a boy could sue his mother for taking antibiotics during her pregnancy, allegedly resulting in the discoloration of the child's teeth.[6] Another Michigan court decided that evidence concerning a woman's "prenatal abuse" of her fetus could be obtained by reviewing her medical records without her consent.[7] A well-known such case is that of Pamela Stewart, a San Diego woman who faced criminal charges for not following doctor's orders to stay off her feet during pregnancy, abstain from taking amphetamines, and summon medical assistance when she went into labor.[8] Women have not only been penalized after the fact but coercion involving medical practice has been exercised in the interest of "fetal health." Court orders have been obtained for caesarean sections in eleven states, for hospital detentions in two states, and for intra-uterine transfusions in one state.[9]

Women have also been denied services for failure to promise compliance with all possible medical regimens. Several obstetrical services in New York City have refused prenatal care to women who are Jehovah's Witnesses (a religious group comprised largely of low income blacks), on the grounds that women might refuse a blood transfusion if one were ever to be deemed necessary.[10]

The socially constructed perception of maternal-fetal conflict is clearly apparent in the case of the woman who uses drugs during pregnancy. Evidence demonstrates that drug use among pregnant women has significantly increased in the last several years.

There have been three major categories of societal response to this problem. The one that has attracted the most media attention, but is the rarest, has been the criminal prosecution of new mothers for their use of illicit drugs during pregnancy. Since the law does not recognize the fetus as a person, these cases have had to employ novel legal arguments. In California, in the Reyes case of 1977 and the widely publicized Stewart case of 1986, prosecutors charged these two women with criminal child abuse. Since the fetus is not recognized as a child, the statutes were deemed inapplicable and the cases dismissed. Subsequently the local prosecutor in northern California's Butte County announced his intention of using a positive newborn toxicology screen in the baby as evidence of maternal illicit drug use, a prosecutable offense. Since Jennifer Johnson's conviction for transferring a controlled substance to a minor, similar cases have been brought against more than a dozen pregnant women around the country.[11]

The second major category of response has been invocation of the child neglect apparatus. Some states consider parental *habitual* drug use as prima facie evidence of child neglect. In New York City, for example, it has become widespread practice to screen neonatal urine for the presence of illicit drugs when maternal substance use is suspected. Criteria for suspicion vary and are often based on either clinical or demographic characteristics. A single positive toxicology screen is interpreted as evidence of maternal *repeated* illicit substance use, and therefore of neglect, and triggers the involvement of the local child protective service agency. Because of the increasing numbers of such cases and limited supply of foster homes, the system has become overwhelmed. Consequently hundreds of babies "board" in hospital or city sponsored group institutional care pending investigation and disposition of their cases.[12,13,14]

The third category of societal response is to offer drug treatment and prenatal care for addicted women. Various federal agencies and the Surgeon General have extensively documented this nation's failure to provide prenatal care for all who need it.[15] Unfortunately, the situation regarding drug treatment for pregnant women is even worse. A 1989 survey of drug treatment programs in New York City documented categorical exclusion of pregnant women (particularly those on Medicaid and addicted to crack), and lack of coordination between drug treatment programs, prenatal care, and childcare. Yet lack of child care is a major obstacle to participation in drug treatment for many women as the National Institute for Drug Abuse (NIDA) documented a decade ago.[17]

Even programs that appear to benefit women are limited and deformed by this ideology. Take, for example, programs that appear beneficent, such as the public health initiatives to decrease infant mortality. They, too, have succumbed to a vision that values maternal welfare only insofar as it will benefit the fetus. The pregnant woman is considered of interest in her capacity as a vessel. This is illustrated clearly by the titles of the programs which have developed across the nation to decrease infant mortality by increasing enrollment of women into prenatal care: Washington, D.C.'s *Better Babies* Project, Boston's *Healthy Baby* Program, Virginia's *Beautiful Babies* Program, Utah's *Baby Your Baby*, Detroit's *961-Baby* hotline, Ohio's *Thanks, Mom* hotline, Massachusett's *Healthy Start*, New Jersey's *Health Start*, Missouri's *Great Expectations*, and North Carolina's *Baby Love* programs.[19]

As evidenced by these names, the focus is on the baby-to-be. Missing from these programs are services for other reproductive health care needs of women, overlooking the fact that access to family planning and abortion services is critical in lowering both infant and maternal mortality. Indeed, evidence indicates that access to family planning and legalized abortion yields direct benefits to women's health. Data for the United States indicate that since abortion was legalized there has been a significant decrease in maternal and infant mortality rates.[19] Indeed, reductions in maternal mortality rates have long been associated with the increased availability of family planning as well as legal abortion worldwide.

The United States lags behind other developed nations in terms of maternal as well as infant mortality, and failed to meet the Surgeon General's 1990 objectives for maternal mortality. The maternal mortality rate for black women is almost four fold higher than for white women.[20]

Despite continuing evidence that maternal and child health is best advanced through facilitating women's use of a *wide* variety of services, most local initiatives are focusing strictly on providing prenatal care. Indeed, family planning and abortion are avoided even in the context of perinatal AIDS. Policy initiatives to counsel and test women for HIV in reproductive health care settings have side-stepped family planning and abortion.[21] Ironically, some of the contradictions involved in the politics of the abortion debate explode here. If a poor, drug-using woman is tested for HIV antibody, found to be positive, and decides to abort, she will be unable to do so in most of the United States. More than eighty percent of United States counties have no abortion provider, and the *Webster* decision presages further restrictions on access for public patients.[22]

The public education campaigns that accompany these prenatal care initiatives imply that the responsibility for poor neonatal outcome sits squarely with the individual pregnant woman. This individualistic and blaming message diverts attention from the larger social context, the United States' poor profile regarding maternal-infant health status.

Not only has the United States consistently performed worse than other developed nations regarding maternal and infant health indicators, but in this decade the disparities among different races and socio-economic groups within the United States have widened. Black infants are twice as likely as white infants to be of low birth weight and to die in the first year of life. Approximately seventeen percent of reproductive age women have no health insurance, and in the 1980s the proportion of women receiving inadequate prenatal care increased to almost one third.[23]

What impact is the formulation of maternal-fetal conflict having on pregnant women, especially on low income minority women and on women with stigmatized problems? The assumptions translated into policy described here add up to a vision of the errant pregnant woman whose antagonism to the fetus must be constrained by outside intervention. This has profound implications for all women. Autonomy, bodily integrity, and constitutional status-of-and-for herself are all at stake. Ironically, these assumptions may well undermine fetal as well as maternal health by deterring these women from involvement with medical care.

The advocates of forced interventions have focused on the legal status of the fetus in late gestation. Opponents, however, argue that the more salient issue is the woman's constitutional right to self determination and bodily integrity. Compared to the protection now afforded to many vulnerable groups, the decisions of pregnant women to refuse medical treatment have been overridden. Opponents of forced caesareans, for example, state that the pregnant woman is being treated in a distinct manner: her judgement and autonomy are abrogated on behalf of the fetus whereas the bodily integrity of criminal defendants, mental incompetents, minors, and competent adults are protected. These various policies hold in common a vision of woman as a mother/fetal vessel whose existence is on behalf of another and not for herself. While the autonomy of all women is threatened by this formulation, the harshest consequences have been felt by the most vulnerable: the poor and the outcast (drug users and HIV positive pregnant women).

Almost all the pregnant women involved in court actions described earlier have been from minority groups, and all were poor. Eighty-one percent of the women involved were black, Hispanic or Asian; forty-four percent were unmarried; twenty-four percent did not speak English as their first language; all were public patients.[24] Similarly, women losing custody of newborns because of drug use allegations have been public patients, often from minority groups.

Pregnancy is a paradox. It presents us with the central mystery of two in one, or one person in the process of becoming two. How do we understand the obligations of the pregnant woman toward herself and toward the future other? And who is to make these decisions? Different players have been ascendant at different historical moments in wielding authority over reproduction. *Roe v. Wade* established women and physicians as the decision-makers, with a limited role for the state. Fathers and churches have sought to regain ascendancy. The construction of maternal-fetal conflict represents one such attempt. It is an attempt enacted within a symbolic arena. The struggle over the rights, status, and existential nature of the fetus obscures the root controversy over the rights, status, and existential nature of women.

The argument about abortion, maternal-fetal conflict, and the social significance accorded the fetus takes place in code, only we have lost the key. I submit that, decoded, the struggle is over our social understanding of women as female roles change in the society. The innocence ascribed to the fetus and the punitive anger expressed toward the pregnant woman considered to be its selfish adversary, express metaphorically the pain and rage of those who no longer find the family to be a "haven in a heartless world," and who perceive the loss of the mother as central to family dissolution (rather than structural changes in the economy).

The focus on the errant pregnant individual also serves a diversionary role. It becomes a sleight of hand to distract attention from the societal failure to provide resources to enable women to be healthy and to have healthy babies. This magic trick is a serious one, with deadly consequences. The inequities we do not challenge leave women and babies in jeopardy. The drug and AIDS epidemics underscore the urgency of providing positive responses, not only the travesty of offering those in great need choices between rocks and hard places.

REFERENCES

1. McNulty, M. Pregnancy Police: The Health Policy and Legal Implications of Punishing Pregnant Women for Harm to their Fetuses, *NYU Review of Law and Social Change* XVI(2), 1987-88.

2. Paltrow, L. Case overview of arguments against permitting forced surgery, prosecution of pregnant women or civil sanctions against them for conduct or status during pregnancy. Memorandum ACLU Reproductive Freedom Project, NYC 1989.

3. Rothman, S. *Woman's Proper Place*, Basic Books, NYC 1978.

4. Scott, J. Keeping Women in their Place: Exclusionary Policies and Reproduction in *Double Exposure: Women's Health Hazards on the Job and at Home*, Ed. W. Chavkin, Monthly Review Press, NYC 1984.

5. Kamerman, S. *Maternity and Parental Benefits and Leaves: An International Review*, Impact on Policy Series Monograph No.1, Columbia Center for Social Sciences, NYC 1980.

6. *Grodin v. Grodin* 102 Mich App 396, 301 NW 2nd 869 1980.

7. Johnson, D. The Creation of Fetal Rights: Conflicts with Women's Constitutional Rights to Liberty, Privacy and Equal Protection, *Yale Law Journal* 95(3) January 1986.

8. Gallagher, J. Prenatal Invasions and Interventions: What's Wrong with Fetal Rights, *Harvard Women's Law Journal* 10, Spring 1987.

9. Kolder, V., Gallagher, J. and Parson, M.T. Court Ordered Obstetrical Interventions, *New England Journal of Medicine* 316:1192-6, 1987.

10. Reported by staff of Pregnancy Healthline, Mini Department of Health, Pregnancy Testing Program, Bureau of Maternity Services and Family Planning, New York City Department of Health 1985, 1986, 1987.

11. Paltrow, L. op. cit.

12. Chavkin, W. Testimony before House Select Committee on Children, Youth and Families. Washington, DC, April 27, 1989.

13. Driver, C., Chavkin, W. et al. Survey of Infants Awaiting Placement in Voluntary Hospitals, Bureau of Maternity Services New York City Department of Health, May 1987.

14. Office of the Comptroller, New York City. *Whatever Happened to the Boarder Babies?* January 1989.

15. Children's Defense Fund. *Maternal and Child Health Data Book* 1986.

16. Chavkin, W. Drug addiction and pregnancy: Policy crossroad, *American Journal of Public Health* 80:483-87, 1990.

17. Beschner, G. and Thompson, P. *Women and Drug Abuse: Needs and*

Services, National Institute for Drug Abuse Services Research Monograph Series DHHS No (ADM) 84-1057, 1981.

18. Chavkin, W., St. Clair, D. Beyond prenatal care: A comprehensive vision of reproductive health, *Journal of American Medical Women's Association* 45:55-57, 1990.

19. Cates, W., Tietze, C. Standardized Mortality Rates Associated with Legal Abortion, *Family Planning Perspectives* 10:109, 1987.

20. Koonin, L. et al. Maternal Mortality Surveillance, US 1980-1985 MMWR 37 No.SS-5:19-29, 1989.

21. Donovan, P. AIDS and Family Planning Clinics: Confronting the Crisis, *Family Planning Perspectives* 19(3), 1987.

22. Henshaw, S. K., Forrest, J. D., Van Vort, J. Abortion Services in the United States 1984, 1985, *Family Planning Perspectives* 19(2), 1987.

23. Brown, S. *Reaching Mothers, Reaching Infants*, Washington, DC: Institute of Medicine 1988.

24. Kolder, V. et al., op. cit.

Mothers and Children, Drugs and Crack: Reactions to Maternal Drug Dependency

Drew Humphries
John Dawson
Valerie Cronin
Phyllis Keating
Chris Wisniewski
Jennine Eichfeld

SUMMARY. This paper discusses the criminalization of pregnancy. Prosecutors have charged drug-using pregnant women with drug trafficking and child abuse. However health care providers, bound to report suspected cases of drug use among pregnant women, have brought far more women into family court where they risk forfeiting their children to congregate or foster care. The paper reviews the lack of drug treatment programs for women and concludes by recommending community-based drug treatment that keeps families together and provides full range of social services.

Fear that prosecutors are making pregnancy a crime rests on a handful of highly publicized cases. Brenda Vaughan, an African-

Drew Humphries, PhD, in Criminology from University of California Berkeley, is Associate Professor of Sociology at Rutgers University, Camden. John Dawson, Valerie Cronin, Phyllis Keating, Chris Wisniewski, and Jennine Eichfeld are sociology majors at Rutgers University. Lisa Devonshire, Cheryl Herda, Beth Ezekiel, Laura Houston, Carol Staiger, and Heather McDermott contributed to this research.

This paper is a revised version of one presented at the American Society of Criminology Conference, November 10, 1990.

American woman, was charged with and convicted of second-degree theft for check forgery in Washington, D.C. Although probation is the normal sentence for first-time offenders like Vaughan, the judge decided to imprison the pregnant woman after she tested positive for cocaine. "I'm going to keep her locked up until the baby's born," said Judge Peter Wolf at the time of sentencing (Churchville, 1988:A1). No drug charges were brought against Vaughan nor did the prosecution seek a trial on possession or use of illegal drugs. Vaughan's attorney worked to amend the sentence (Churchville, 1988).

When she was charged with and convicted of two counts of delivering drugs to a minor, the prosecution alleged that Jennifer Johnson, an African-American woman, had passed cocaine to her newborn child through the umbilical cord after the baby was delivered, but before the cord was cut (Curriden, 1990). Prosecutor Jeff Deen defended the move: "We needed to make sure this woman does not give birth to another cocaine baby. The message is that this community cannot afford to have two or three cocaine babies from the same person" (Curriden, 1990:51). The Florida court gave Johnson fifteen to twenty-four years probation, mandatory drug rehabilitation, drug and alcohol prohibitions, and required her to report subsequent pregnancies to her probation officer and to enter a court-approved prenatal care program (Curriden, 1990; Sherman, 1989). The American Civil Liberties Union and fourteen other public interest and public health groups appealed the drug trafficking conviction in the Florida District Court of Appeals (Sherman, 1989).

In Rockford, Illinois, Melanie Green, African-American, became the first woman to be charged with manslaughter for the death of her two-day old infant due allegedly to her cocaine use during pregnancy. Apparently, doctors at the hospital where Green gave birth reported that the child had tested positive for cocaine (Curriden, 1990; Sherman, 1989). When an Illinois grand jury refused to indict Green, the charges were dropped.

Pamela Rae Stewart, a white woman, was arrested under a California child support statute when she delivered a brain-damaged baby that died soon after birth. She had failed to "follow her doctor's advice to stay off her feet, to refrain from sexual intercourse, to refrain from taking street drugs, and to seek immediate medical attention if she experienced difficulties with the pregnancy" (Paltrow, Fox, Goetz, 1990:1). The San Diego Municipal Court dismissed the charges, declaring that "California's criminal child support statute was not intended to apply to the actions of a pregnant woman and does not create a legal duty of care owed by a pregnant woman to her fetus" (Paltrow, Fox, Goetz, 1990:1).

In other words, pregnancy combined with drug use, especially cocaine use, has been made grounds for punitive sentencing and novel application of criminal and child protection statutes. These developments give meaning to the phrase criminalizing pregnancy. This paper reviews practices which make pregnancy a crime. Because the prosecutions are a response, we begin with the perceived problem, drug-dependent mothers. We then return to reactions, both legal and medical, before discussing treatment and policy issues.

MATERNAL DRUG USE
AND COCAINE-EXPOSED CHILDREN

The perceived problem consists of (1) the presumably large number of infants born to drug-using mothers, (2) the damaging effects of drug use on fetal and infant development, and (3) the fear that the long-term needs of these infants will overwhelm social, health, and educational systems.

Maternal Drug Use: The widely publicized claim that 375,000 babies are born annually to mothers who use drugs[1] is the basis of fears about crack and crack-addicted babies. The 375,000 figure, reported by Chasnoff,[2] a leading researcher in the field of perinatal drug exposure, represents about eleven percent of births in the United States. It has been extrapolated from case studies of urban hospitals where one might expect that drug use, especially the use of illicit drugs, might be relatively high (Chasnoff, 1988, 1987). A Los Angeles study cited by Chasnoff reported that nine percent of the births surveyed involved neonatal withdrawal due to maternal drug use (Chasnoff, 1988). Another case study conducted at Harlem Hospital in New York City showed that ten percent of the newborns (3,300) tested positive for cocaine in their urine

(Chasnoff, 1987). By 1988, trends suggested that maternal drug use was on the increase. In New York City, it increased from eight percent in 1980 to 30 percent in 1988, affecting from 20 to 25 percent of all women giving birth (Drucker, 1989).

Cocaine use is of special concern. Not only have estimates of cocaine use spawned a moral panic; the awareness that women, including pregnant women, use cocaine and crack contributes to the medical and legal reactions. The National Drug Control Strategy Report, the key source for President Bush's war on drugs, singled out pregnant cocaine users estimating that 100,000 cocaine babies[3] are born each year (Kusserow, 1990). This figure is consistent with the results of an eight-city survey conducted by the U.S. Department of Health and Human Services (Kusserow, 1990). The eight-city survey found that 9,000 babies had been born addicted to crack in 1989.

Effects of Exposure: There is ample evidence that maternal cocaine use adds avoidable risks to pregnancy (Chasnoff, 1986). Cocaine increases maternal blood pressure and the risk of stroke. When used by a pregnant woman, the drug crosses the placenta, exposing the fetus which cannot excrete the foreign substance quickly enough. Cocaine stimulates fetal movement, increasing the risk of miscarriage during the first trimester and risking premature labor during the last trimester. Cocaine has been associated with an abstinence syndrome (Chasnoff, 1987). If the mother abruptly stops taking the drug, the fetus experiences withdrawal-like symptoms. Shortly after birth, the cocaine-exposed infant experiences withdrawal symptoms which can persist for two to three weeks (Chasnoff, 1988). Symptoms include wakefulness, irritability, trembling, body temperature variations, rapid breathing, hyperactivity, exaggeration of reflexes, and increased muscle stiffness. Neonates suffer diarrhea, sweating, respiratory distress, runny nose, apneic attacks (failure to breathe), and failure to gain weight. The babies have a high-pitched persistent cry, are painfully sensitive to sound, cannot suck properly, and are very difficult to comfort (State of Oregon, 1985).

In addition to withdrawal symptoms, infants delivered to mothers who used cocaine during pregnancy are smaller in size, tend to be shorter, and have lower birth weights. Their smaller than normal head size, indicative of growth retardation, is thought to result from cocaine-induced constriction of the blood supply to the uterus. Babies born addicted to cocaine can develop convulsions and strokes. They are also at significantly higher risk for Sudden Infant Death Syndrome (Chasnoff, 1988).

While no one would dispute the toll maternal cocaine use may take, two points require attention. First, the studies reviewed for this paper point out that the women in question are polydrug users, using among other drugs, heroin, methadone, marijuana, tobacco, alcohol, and over-the-counter medications. Polydrug use makes it difficult to trace all but a few newborn symptoms to cocaine, these being irritability and the risk of premature delivery (Chasnoff, 1986, 1987). Other effects, like low birth weights or growth reductions, may have social roots in the lack of prenatal and health care, or can be traced to other illicit or licit drugs.

Second, Koren et al. recently reported what they call "the bias against the null hypothesis" in the literature on cocaine effects. In other words, studies that fail to show that cocaine has adverse effects on pregnancy tend to be ignored (Koren et al., 1989). Of 58 abstracts on fetal outcomes following exposure to cocaine that were submitted for presentation at the Society of Pediatric Research conference, nine reported no effects and 28 reported adverse effects. Only one of the abstracts reporting no effects was accepted for presentation, despite the fact that these studies verified cocaine use and used control cases more often than the other studies. Reviewers, however, accepted over half of the abstracts reporting adverse effects. Findings led researchers to conclude that there may be a "distorted estimation of the teratogenic risk of cocaine" (Koren et al., 1989:1440).

Long-Term Needs: Predictions about the long-term needs of cocaine-exposed infants are dire. According to a 1989 survey by the U.S. Department of Health and Human Services, the cost of caring for 9,000 crack-addicted children from infancy through age five would be 500 million dollars (Kusserow, 1990). To mitigate this cost, the U.S. Department of Health and Human Services recommends that state and local governments provide prenatal care for pregnant women at risk for addiction. It further recommends revising laws on child custody to make it easier to place "boarder babies" in foster care and adoptive homes. The report also estimates that the additional cost of preparing the 9,000 crack babies for school could exceed one and a half billion dollars. With confirmation of the national estimate of 100,000 crack babies a year, the annual cost could come to ten billion dollars.

It may be difficult to reconcile spending such sums on children thought to have suffered permanent, irreversible damage, including emotional detachment, inability to relate to others, and neurological impairment. The results of long-term studies are not yet in. But whatever their outcome, one thing is clear: investments that improve a child's environment pay off in minimizing drug-related damage. Environment, not drugs, has the larger influence on development. A two-year study of three groups of newborns (opiate addicted, nonopiate addicted, and a control group) showed a downward trend in mean developmental scores, a phenomenon not uncommon in infants from low socio-economic circumstances (Chasnoff, 1986). A study of methadone-exposed infants from birth to four years of age produced similar findings (Kaltenbach and Finnegan, 1984). The strongest correlates of developmental status were again social factors. Biological risk, researchers concluded, is either attenuated or potentiated by the child's social environment. The point is, biological risk including drug related ones can be minimized.

CRIMINALIZATION, DRUG TRAFFICKING AND CHILD ABUSE

State and federal prosecutors have argued that pregnant women who use drugs are engaging in illegal activity, and that they ought to be arrested, prosecuted, and convicted. The purpose, they claim, is to stop maternal drug use by incarcerating the women or by forcing them into drug treatment. Patricia Toth[4] of the National Center for the Prosecution of Child Abuse says, "Prosecutors seem to agree that the ultimate solution is not criminal prosecutions, but prevention and treatment" (Curriden, 1990:53). Lynn Paltrow of the American Civil Liberties Union's Reproductive Freedom Project argues however, that these prosecutions, in effect, "criminalize" pregnancy. She asserts that "none of these women have been arrested for the crime of illegal drug use or possession. Instead, they are being arrested for a new and independent crime, becoming pregnant while addicted to drugs" (Paltrow, 1990:41-42).

Clearly, the debate over how to handle the problem of maternal drug abuse has aroused passionate feelings on both sides of the issue. Those who favor prosecution state that women must be held accountable for prenatal conduct that may injure the fetus. Those who oppose it feel that the creation of a "prenatal police force" would only succeed in driving the problem underground, preventing many women from obtaining the help that they desperately need (Paltrow, 1990). In examining this issue, it is important to outline the theories behind the prosecutions and explore the consequences of prosecuting pregnant addicts.

Of the more than forty cases reported around the country in the past three years, over half are based on the mother's alleged violation of drug trafficking laws (Paltrow, Fox, and Goetz, 1990). In the case of Jennifer Johnson, the state of Florida succeeded in convicting her of passing cocaine to her newborn through the umbilical cord (Curriden, 1990). Prosecutors have argued in similar cases that delivery of the controlled substance occurs during the sixty to ninety seconds after birth, before the cord is severed (Kolbert et al., 1990). A drug trafficking conviction can carry with it a prison sentence of up to ten to fifteen years. Only three women have been successfully prosecuted on these grounds and all three cases have been appealed at the state level.

Other methods of prosecution center on the issues of child abuse or infant neglect. This is the instance in nearly every case cited in the American Civil Liberties Union's summary of criminal proceedings involving pregnant women (Paltrow, Fox, and Goetz, 1990). Prosecutors allege that maternal drug use during pregnancy imposes serious health risks on the developing fetus or can result in postnatal trauma including narcotic withdrawal and physical and mental defects (Chasnoff, 1987). This type of prosecution is more likely to result in a conviction, although these decisions are also later appealed since most states do not have child abuse statutes that pertain to prenatal conduct.

Civil and women's rights advocates have denounced these proceedings and offer many reasons why they may be considered unethical, unproductive, and in some ways, unconstitutional. First and foremost, there are the problems of legislative intent and due process of law. Specifically, it is argued that prosecutions based on drug trafficking go beyond the expressed intention of the law. In other words, these laws are designed to apply to the sale or exchange of controlled substances between "born persons." Arbitrarily using them to convict pregnant women violates due process since there has been no notice that these laws are applicable to this situation (Paltrow, 1990). Using existing child abuse statutes also falls under this criticism. Since the fetus is not legally defined as a child, these types of prosecutions violate due process rights of the mother. While evidence concerning the negative effects of drug use during pregnancy exists, prosecutors are not always able to prove that the mother's drug use is the cause of specific postnatal defects, if indeed such defects occur at all.[5]

The child abuse issue leads us into the area of "fetal rights." In her article, "Fetal Rights: A New Assault on Feminism," Katha Pollit discusses the problems created by placing the interests of the unborn above those of the mother. Not only does this kind of action violate the constitutionally guaranteed right to privacy, she argues, it also places an undue burden, a "duty of care" on the pregnant women (Pollit, 1990). Prosecutors, like University of Texas law professor John Robertson, insist that "if the pregnant woman decides to go to term, she takes on additional responsibilities so the child will be born healthy" (Curriden, 1990:52). But Pollit (1990) insists that the emphasis on the woman's responsibility is merely a convenient way of dismissing the multitude of factors which affect pregnancy but which are beyond the ability of the woman to control.[6] If prosecutors succeed in establishing fetal rights, she argues, women will come to be seen as "incubators," unable to control pregnancies or maintain bodily integrity.

Prosecuting drug-addicted pregnant women leads inevitably

down a "slippery slope." Lynn Paltrow suggests that "prosecutions . . . cannot rationally be limited to illegal conduct because many legal behaviors cause damage to developing babies. Women who are diabetic or obese, women with cancer or epilepsy who need drugs that could harm the fetus, and women who are too poor to eat adequately or to get prenatal care could all be categorized as fetal abusers" (Paltrow, 1990:7). She also points out that the more than 900,000 women who suffer still births and miscarriages each year could be subject to these same types of criminal proceedings (Kolbert et al., 1990).

The overwhelming majority of prosecutions involve poor women of color. The criminal justice system may accentuate the class-racial bias, but it originates in the requirement that medical providers report drug use among pregnant women. Cases normally come to the prosecutor's office from the police, but few maternal drug-use cases come to prosecutors this way. This is what makes Brenda Vaughan's case unusual. She entered the system through conventional channels: she was arrested for and charged with forgery, her pregnancy and drug use were discovered in the course of criminal processing. In contrast, most of the women against whom prosecutors have pressed charges enter the system through hospitals and clinics.

MEDICALIZATION: REPORTING CHILD ABUSE

The wave of prosecutions described in the introduction began not with drug arrests, but as doctors or other health workers started to report the positive results of drug tests for women who, like Melanie Green and Pamela Rae Stewart, had just delivered babies. Such practices reflected medical providers' belief that without law enforcement assistance, they could do little to halt the increasing numbers of drug-exposed infants (Goetz, Fox, and Bates, 1990). They supported the "reporting laws" which by the mid-eighties had already imposed a legal and ethical duty on medical providers to report infants born addicted to drugs (Angel, 1988). The purpose of such laws, according to Catherine Tracy of Los Angeles County Children's Services, was to prevent child abuse, child neglect, or health endangering situations (Angel, 1988). But in creating a "duty," reporting guidelines, even in states without applicable child abuse statutes, turned health care providers into medical police officers (McNulty, 1988).

The procedures developed to implement child abuse statutes require medical providers to report evidence of abuse or neglect to social service agencies with the authority to remove the infant from the mother's custody. Evidence of neglect consists of the mother's admission of drug use, positive drug screens for the mother, and positive drug screens for the newborn (Chasnoff, 1990).

When the mother admits to drug use, the medical provider has a duty to report. The admission, which is in other circumstances a condition for getting help, jeopardizes the mother's custody of the newborn and, depending on local prosecutors, places her at risk for criminal prosecution. The focus of reporting is unrelated to maternal health or illness. If it were, the U.S. Supreme Court's definition of drug addiction as an illness would bar prosecution (Chavkin, 1989). Instead, the duty to report arises from the newborn's exposure to drugs. So in addition to the mother's admitted use of drugs, courts accept the positive results of drug tests on mothers or newborns as evidence of abuse.

Drug testing, however, has limited value in identifying the drug-exposed newborns protected by the abuse laws. It is important to understand what drug tests can and cannot tell us (see Chasnoff, 1990). What drug tests can tell is that a drug was ingested by the mother within the last twenty-four to seventy-two hours (Moss and Crockett, 1990). They do not indicate the quantity of drug nor do they reveal the prevalence of its use (Chasnoff, 1990). They cannot discriminate between the habitual and the occasional user. They cannot determine whether miscarriage, neonatal death, or early childhood illness or injury are due to maternal or paternal drug use (American Public Health Association, n.d.). Finally drug tests do not always tell exactly what drug was used. In one case, a woman tested positive for an illegal substance which was actually an antihistamine (Moss and Crockett, 1990). Laboratory technicians are not infallible, and false positives can occur.

Nonetheless, drug testing takes place. In public hospitals drug testing is periodic or routine (Chavkin, 1989; Moss and Crockett, 1990), but many private hospitals test only when drug use is suspected (Angel, 1988). Guidelines like those established in South Carolina (Goetz, Fox, and Bates, 1990) reveal the circumstances that justify testing: no prenatal care, late prenatal care, incomplete prenatal care, abruptio placentae, intrauterine fetal death, preterm labor, intrauterine growth retardation, previously known drug or alcohol abuse, or unexplained congenital abnormalities. Some criteria pertain to medical emergencies where maternal and infant health depend on the physician knowing what drugs, if any, a woman may have taken. But other criteria like the deviations from the monthly and weekly visits to the obstetrician, are rooted in the way the poor use the health care system. Poor women tend to delay prenatal care which risks the pregnancy and turns them into candidates for drug testing.

To evaluate bias in drug testing and reporting, a Florida study identified the drug using pregnant women in the community and then compared them to the group of women selected by public and private hospitals for drug testing (Chasnoff, 1990). The study first collected urine samples from black and white women receiving obstetrical care in private and public hospitals. It found no significant difference in the prevalence of positive results between private and public patients or between black and white women. It did, however, identify a significant difference between socio-economic status and race. Middle-income, white women tested positive for marijuana, while low-income black women tested positive for cocaine. The second phase of the study reviewed the characteristics of pregnant women that medical providers tested under the Florida child abuse statute. The women actually tested by medical providers came from poorer socio-economic backgrounds than the middle- and low-income women whose urine samples had tested positive for drugs. But the strongest bias revealed by the study was racial. The rate of reporting was ten times higher among black women than among white women. The racial discrepancy held true for black women receiving care in both public and private hospitals. The research team suggested that discrimination reflects (1) the reluctance of private physicians to risk alienating affluent patients, and (2) stereotypes about minority drug use held by doctors practicing in large urban hospitals.

Despite technical deficiencies and discrimination, drug tests are the vehicle by which medical providers refer drug-exposed infants to social service agencies. Under Florida's Child Abuse Statute, medical providers must report exposed infants to the Department of Health and Rehabilitative Services (Chasnoff, 1990). Community health nurses are then required by the Florida statute to determine the suitability of the home and whether the agency should continue supervision or recommend to family court that the child be placed in foster care. The foster care solution is well documented in New York City (Chavkin, 1989) where a positive drug screen, evidence of maternal drug use, and child neglect must be reported to Special Services for Children. The agency investigates, files charges in Family Court, and places neglected children in foster care. The number of children, shortage of foster homes, and delays in investigating have created the so-called boarder baby crisis, the approximately 300 babies under the age of two that are to be found on any given day boarding in New York City hospitals.

TREATMENT:
FROM LIMITED OPTIONS
TO ONE-STOP SHOPS

Both the child abuse and drug trafficking approaches rest on the assumption that current drug programs can accommodate the pregnant women referred for drug treatment by family or criminal courts. There is, however, widespread recognition that the assumption is false. Congressman George Miller, Chairman of the Select Committee on Children, Youth and Families, reports that "two-thirds of the hospitals have no place to refer substance-abusing pregnant women" (Kolbert et al., 1990:5). The need for drug treatment programs that include prenatal care is urgent.

Existing treatment programs discriminate against pregnant women. In a recent survey of 78 drug treatment programs in New York City, Dr. Wendy Chavkin found that 54 percent refused to treat pregnant women: 67 percent refused to treat pregnant women on Medicaid, and 87 percent had no services available for Medicaid patients who were both pregnant and addicted to crack (Chavkin,

1989). The bias against admitting pregnant women reflects the perception that obstetrical care adds unacceptable risks to drug rehabilitation (McNulty, 1988; Moss, 1990).[7]

In Michigan where the situation is similar only nine of the thirteen residential treatment programs available to women will "consider" pregnant women (McNulty, 1988). Long waiting lists, delayed examinations, and admission policies restricting treatment to women who are less than three months pregnant deter pregnant women attempting to get help. A Detroit study found that the average lag time for an initial prenatal appointment at Detroit hospitals was 4.2 weeks (Potti, 1990). The initial appointment does not ordinarily include an obstetrical examination which is scheduled about two weeks later, making the total waiting time, from first contact to initial examination anywhere from three to thirteen weeks (Potti, 1990).

Limited treatment facilities and restricted admissions cast doubt on official responses to the problem. Katha Pollit mentions that Jennifer Johnson had sought admission to a drug abuse clinic but was turned away, presumably because she was pregnant (Pollit, 1990). Punishing women who are not likely to get the treatment they seek, Paltrow argues, "raises serious questions about prosecutorial ethics" (Paltrow, 1990:11). Similarly, the lack of programs that admit pregnant women creates untenable choices. If a woman has a drug problem and a family to care for, she must choose between helping herself or caring for her family (McNulty, 1988). Typically, there is no choice. When women coming before the criminal or family court are ordered into drug rehabilitation, their children are placed in foster care.

Despite inadequate facilities, our survey of available literature has identified programs combining prenatal care and drug treatment. Born Free, associated with the San Diego Medical Center, is the country's first residential treatment program for pregnant addicts. It now has several homes for women and their children. The women are required to undergo detoxification either in the program or under another auspice before entering residential treatment (Abraham, 1988). Harlem Hospital Center, one of the first in the country to care exclusively for pregnant addicts, has had some success (French, 1989). In Detroit, the Hutzel Hospital takes virtually all high-risk pregnancies in the city, including pregnant addicts, and provides prenatal, delivery, and post-partum care. It encourages women to enter day or residential treatment in the Hutzel Recovery Center. Patients enter treatment on a voluntary basis, but patients facing court dates chose treatment in order to retain custody of their older children (Teltsch, 1990). Also, the Neil J. Houston House in the Roxbury section of Boston cares for pregnant addicts who have been convicted of crimes and who would have normally served at least five months in state prison. The program requires detoxification, covers delivery of the baby, and then requires participation in a one-year follow-up program (*New York Times*, 1989). Finally, the Family Center at Thomas Jefferson Medical College of Thomas Jefferson University, like Hutzel Hospital, has a self-referred, high-risk obstetrical clinic (Reagan, 1987). Other programs, including MABON, Hale House, and CARE, rely on court referrals for patients.

The programs for which we hold out the most hope are voluntary, involve family-centered treatment, and offer a variety of social services in addition to prenatal care and drug therapy. Pregnant drug users voluntarily seeking help with the pregnancy and for the drug problem have the greatest chance of recovery. Short of self-admissions, court referrals that offer women a choice between entering treatment or serving custodial sentences represent more difficult trade-offs. The element of coercion introduced by court orders reduces the likelihood of recovery, but the terms of the choice are important. Entering a treatment program that keeps the mother, her newborn, and older children together is better than remanding the mother to prison and forcing her to surrender the children to foster care. But little is gained if the treatment option looks like boot camp or participation entails loss of her children. Such punitive choices serve to drive women away from prenatal care and drug treatment almost as much as prison. On the other hand, the chance for maternal or family recovery disappears entirely when women have no control over what happens to them or their children.

Social therapies that keep families together fare better than those that treat family members in isolation. High on our list are the residential treatment and follow-up programs that admit the mother, the newborn, and older siblings. Such programs attend to the needs of the whole family, although the focus on the mother unfortunately overlooks the effect of the adult male drug user on the family. Nonetheless, the principle keeps children out of the already over-burdened and frequently dangerous foster care system.

And finally, programs that recognize that drug abuse is a medical problem with deeper social roots stand to contribute more than others. Most programs offer classes in prenatal and infant care, parenting, nutrition, and general health care as well as drug, alcohol, and AIDS education. Others add coping skills, day care, and job training. And still others combine all these services in "one-stop shopping centers." By most accounts, community-based one-stop shops are the vehicle for delivering the range of services required by a particular community (Abrams, 1988; French, 1989; Teltsch, 1990; *New York Times*, 1989; Reagan et al., 1987).

CONCLUSION

Two ill-conceived national policies have greatly exacerbated maternal drug use. Aimed at eliminating cocaine production in South America, the national drug policy directs less money to drug treatment facilities which are needed to accommodate all who seek rehabilitation, including pregnant women. Rehabilitation ranks third after domestic enforcement and international drug control efforts according to priorities set by President Bush. The health care system's financial difficulties, precipitated by a reduction of federal funds, makes health care the province of the insured. Hospitals and clinics which continue to serve the poor risk bankruptcy. Being poor and pregnant may still get you prenatal care, that being a public health priority; but being poor, pregnant, and drug-dependent puts you in jail, your children in foster care. Humane alternatives have neither been created nor defended in the decade-long attack on social services.

It is easy to oppose the prosecution of drug-using pregnant women. Medical and public health organizations condemn the prosecutions as discriminatory. Women's groups have cited violation of fundamental reproductive rights. Such prosecutions, some medical and health care professionals argue, are detrimental to the health and safety of women and their children. They undermine the trust in the confidentiality of the physician-patient relationship. They drive women at high risk of complications during pregnancy away from the health care system, creating a situation that is potentially harmful to women and their children.

While the prosecutions have received more attention, it is fair to say that the reporting laws have done more harm. Defining drug use as child abuse and requiring medical providers to report drug use admittedly allows more room for debate. There is something compelling in the fact that these laws are designed to protect newborns. But consider the following. Defining the use of controlled drugs as child abuse does not, as some think, solve the problem. It only shifts the burden from the criminal courts to the family court, breaks up families, and produces boarder babies, half of whom go into congregate or foster care. The boarder baby crisis makes a mockery of claims that the statutes protect children.

The drug use as child abuse formula ought to be opposed for several other reasons. Although this paper focused on controlled drugs, some states have included alcohol use in the definition of child abuse, raising the possibility that a range of otherwise legal conduct may fall within the meaning of child abuse. Additionally, reporting procedures under the child abuse statutes are discriminatory, they undermine patients' confidence in physicians and drive the women in need of help away from care facilities. Finally, drug testing is an unwarranted invasion of women's right to privacy. The decision to test rests on subjective standards, its application is discriminatory, and evaluation of results are plagued with technical problems.

The most telling criticism that can be made against the drug trafficking and child abuse approaches, however, is the lack of treatment programs for pregnant drug users. Without treatment, prosecutions are simply punitive stop gaps, and reporting laws force minority and poor women to surrender their children. Health care, drug treatment, and social services must be, as we have already argued, among the first priorities if the goal is to help these women and protect their children.

NOTES

1. Health providers determine drug use in three ways. The mother may tell the health provider she has used or is currently using drugs. The health provider may, in addition, screen the mother's urine or that of the newborn for drugs. Among the estimated 375,000 babies exposed to drugs (both licit and illicit drugs), some suffer withdrawal symptoms at birth.

2. Dr. Ira Chasnoff, head of the Perinatal Center for Chemical Dependency at Northwestern University Medical School, is founder of the National Association for Perinatal Addiction Research and Education, a group which advocates mandatory testing of pregnant women for drug use.

3. Of the 375,000 drug-exposed newborns, 100,000 are thought to have been exposed to cocaine. The U.S. Department of Health and Human Services uses the term addicted to refer to these infants, presumably on the basis of tremors produced when the umbilical cord is cut and the drug supply stops.

4. The prosecution of drug-using pregnant women has produced unlikely alliances. While Patricia Toth might be expected to take the prosecutors' side, she prefers treatment provided the pregnant drug user takes advantage of it. Otherwise, Toth argues that pregnant women do not have a license to use drugs nor immunity against prosecution as child abusers.

5. See Chasnoff. Studies have not conclusively established the extent of the harm posed by prenatal drug use. Ill effects are not always exhibited by the infant and the effects of poor nutrition and lack of obstetrical care are not emphasized by prosecutors.

6. Pollit discusses the lack of adequate medical care for poor minority women, substandard living conditions, spousal abuse, and poor diet as factors that have significant impact on pregnancy but which legislatures have refused to address.

7. According to a 1985 study on prenatal care in Orlando, Florida, "it's safer for a baby to be born to a drug abusing, anemic or diabetic mother who visits the doctor throughout her pregnancy than to be born to a normal mother who does not" (Paltrow, 1990:8).

REFERENCES

Abraham, Lauris 1988 "They Cure Their Habits to Save Their Babies: Unique Program Helps Women Stay Off Drugs." *American Medical News* January 8, p. 2, 50-51.

American Public Health Association n.d. "Legal Brief to *People of the State of Michigan v. Kimberly Hardy*."

Angel, Carol 1988 "Addicted Babies: Legal System's Response Unclear." *Los Angeles Daily Journal* February 29, p. 1, 24.

Chasnoff, Ira J. 1990 "The Prevalence of Illicit-Drug or Alcohol Use During Pregnancy and Discrepancies in Mandatory Reporting in Pinellas County, Florida." *New England Journal of Medicine* April: 1202-8.

Chasnoff, Ira J. 1988 "Newborn Infants with Drug Withdrawal Symptom." *Pediatrics in Review* March (9): 273-277.

Chasnoff, Ira J. 1987 "Perinatal Effects of Cocaine." *Contemporary OB/GYN* May: 163-176.

Chasnoff, Ira J., Kayreen Burns, William J. Burns, Sidney H. Schnoll 1986 "Prenatal Drug Exposure: Effects on Neonatal and Infant Growth and Development." *Neurobehavioral Toxicology and Teratology* 8: 357-362.

Chavkin, Wendy 1989 Testimony before the House Select Committee on Children, Youth, and Families. U.S. House of Representatives, April 27.

Churchville, Victoria 1988 "D.C. Judge Jails Women as Protection for Fetus." *Washington Post* July 23, pp. A1, A8.

Curriden, Mark 1990 "Holding Mom Accountable." *American Bar Association Journal* March: 50-53.

Drucker, Ernest 1989 "Notes From the Drug Wars." *The International Journal on Drug Policy* 1(4): 10-12.

French, Howard W. 1989 "For Pregnant Addicts: A Clinic of Hope." *New York Times* September 29, p. B1.

Goetz, Ellen, Hilary Fox, and Steve Bates, 1990 "Poor and Pregnant? Don't Go to South Carolina. . . . " ACLU Memorandum: Initial Report on RFP's (Reproductive Freedom Project) Carolina Investigation, February 1.

Kaltenbach, Karol and Loretta P. Finnegan, 1984 "Developmental Outcome of Children Born to Methadone Maintained Women: A Review of Longitudinal Studies." *Neurobehavioral Toxicology and Teratology* 6: 271-75.

Kolbert, Kathryn, Lynn Paltrow, Ellen Goetz, and Kary Moss, 1990 "Discriminatory Punishment of Pregnant Women." ACLU Memorandum, February 15.

Koren, Gideon, Karen Graham, Heather Shear, and Tom Einarson, 1989 "Bias Against the Null Hypothesis: The Reproductive Hazards of Cocaine." *The Lancet* December: 1440-42.

Kusserow, Richard P. 1990 "Crack Babies." U.S. Department of Health and Human Services, Office of the Inspector General, OEI-03-89-01540, June.

McNulty, Mollie 1988 "Pregnancy Police: The Health Policy and Legal Implications Punishing Pregnant Women for Harm to their Fetuses." *New York University Review of Law and Social Change* 16: 277-319.

Moss, Kary and Judy Crockett, 1990 Testimony on Children of Substance Abusers before the U.S. Senate Subcommittee on Children, Family, Drugs and Alcoholism, February 22.

New York Times 1989 "Trying to Free Children From Shackles of Crime." August 30, p. A9.

Paltrow, Lynn 1990 "When Becoming Pregnant is a Crime." *Criminal Justice Ethics* 9 (Winter/Spring): 41-47.

Paltrow, Lynn, Hilary Fox, and Ellen Goetz, 1990 "State by State Case Summary of Criminal Prosecutions Against Pregnant Women." ACLU Memorandum, April 20.

Pollit, Katha 1990 "Fetal Rights: A New Assault on Feminism." *The Nation* March 16: 409-18.

Potti, Lisa 1990 Testimony before the House Select Committee on Children, Youth, and Families. U.S. House of Representatives, April 23.

Reagan, D.D., S.M. Ehrlich, Loretta P. Finnegan, 1987 "Infants of Drug Addiction: At Risk For Abuse Neglect and Placement in Foster Care." *Neurotoxicology and Teratology* 9: 315-377.

Sherman, Rorie 1989 "Keeping Babies Free From Drugs." *The National Law Journal* October: 1, 28.

State of Oregon 1985 "Women, Drugs, and Babies." Unpublished survey conducted by the Division of Youth and Family Services.

Teltsch, Kathleen 1990 "A Drug Recovery Center that Welcomes the Pregnant Addict." *New York Times* March 20, p. A4.